To Annette
My other sister
the quiet one
Love Ya
Harvey

The Raping of
America

The Raping of *America*

Politics

Greed

Corruption

Crime and Deceit

Harvey Hawkins

Copyright © 2015 by Harvey Hawkins.

ISBN:	Softcover	978-1-5144-2420-9
	eBook	978-1-5144-2419-3

All rights reserved. No part of this book may be reproduced or transmitted in any form or by any means, electronic or mechanical, including photocopying, recording, or by any information storage and retrieval system, without permission in writing from the copyright owner.

Any people depicted in stock imagery provided by Thinkstock are models, and such images are being used for illustrative purposes only.
Certain stock imagery © Thinkstock.

Print information available on the last page.

Rev. date: 11/12/2015

To order additional copies of this book, contact:
Xlibris
1-888-795-4274
www.Xlibris.com
Orders@Xlibris.com
716535

Contents

Dedication ix
Prologue xi

Part 1
The Discovery 1
    The Mayflower 6

Part 2
The Building of a Nation 9
    Slavery in new America 11
    Trade, Farming and migration 13
    Problems with Britain and France 16
    New government is formed 17
    The Revolutionary War 1775-1783 18

Part 3
The Louisiana Purchase 22
    The Westward Movement 25
    The Indians 27
    The Sioux Indian Nation 30
    The Apache Indian Nation 31
    Geronimo 32
    The Cowboys, Outlaws and Lawmen 33
    The Outlaws 33
    The Lawmen 35

Part 4
Slavery, Civil Rights and the Plight of Black Americans 39
    What is Jim Crow? 43
    The struggle continues 48

Part 5
Black Achievement in America 52

Part 6
The Industrialization of America 74
    Cotton, the Agricultural Giant 75
    The Textile Industry in America 76
    The Agricultural Revolution 77
    Tools and Machinery 78
    Energy Sources 79
    Wood 79
    Coal 80
    Oil and Gas 82
    Electricity 83
    Thomas Alva Edison 84
    Metals for Industrial Use 84
    Refrigeration 85
    The washing machine 87
    The Automobile 87

Part 7
Growth and prosperity 90
    The Railroad and its Influence 92
    Business Developement 94
    Labor Union's 94
    Aviation 96
    Population explosion 98
    National Parks 99

Part 8
Environmental Disasters 102
    Clear cutting Forest Timber 102
    West Virginia and Eastern Kentucky Coal Sludge spill 104
    Three Mile Island Nuclear Meltdown 105
    The Monsanto Company Chemical Poisoning 106
    The Love Canal 107
    What is the Superfund? 108
    The Great Pacific Garbage Patch 109
    The Texas City Disaster 109
    What is the Federal Tort Claims Act? (FTCA) 110
    Picher, Oklahoma Lead Contamination 110

The Exxon Valdez oil spill of 1989 111
The British Petroleum (BP) oil spill in the
    Gulf of Mexico 112
What is the MMS? 115

Part 9
Education, Crime, and corruption 116
    Crime and Corruption 118
    Watergate 118
    Some of those accused of, or found guilty of, a crime 119
    What is a Ponzi scheme ? 124

Part 10
Politicians, a Broken trust 128
    The Poor People's Struggle for Economic Justice 133
    The Savings and Loan Crisis 134
    What is TARP? 137
    A Violated Trust 137
    Governments Wasteful Spending 138
    The Iran-Contra Scandal 139
    The Impeachment of President Bill Clinton 141

Part 11
America Raped, fleeced, and broken 144
    The Economy 149
    What is NAFTA? 150
    What is the WTO? 151
    Political Strife 156
    America in crisis 158

Part 12
The Presidents of The United States Of America 161
        GEORGE WASHINGTON, Number 1, 1789-1797 162
        JOHN ADAMS, Number 2, 1797-1801 163
        THOMAS JEFFERSON, Number 3, 1801-1809 164
        JAMES MADISON, Number 4, 1809-1817 165
        JAMES MONROE, Number 5, 1817-1825 166
        JOHN QUINCY ADAMS, Number 6, 1825-1829 168
        Andrew Jackson, Number, 7, 1829-1837 170
        Martin Van Buren, Number 8, 1837-1841 171
        William Henry Harrison, Number 8, 1841-1841 172

John Tyler Jr., Number 10, 1841-1845 173
James Knox Polk, Number 11, 1845-1849 174
Zachary Taylor, Number 12, 1849-1850 175
Millard Fillmore, Number 13, 1850-1853 177
Franklin Pierce, Number 14, 1853-1857 178
James Buchanan, Number 15, 1857-1861 179
Abraham Lincoln, Number 16, 1861-1865 180
Andrew Johnson, Number 17, 1865-1869 185
Ulysses S. Grant, Number 18, 1869-1877 188
Rutherford Birchard Hayes, Number 19, 1877-1881 191
James A. Garfield, Number 20, ... 193
Chester Alan Arthur, Number 21, 1881-1885 194
Stephen Grover Cleveland, Number 22, 1885-1889 196
Benjamin Harrison, Number 23, 1889-1893 198
Stephen Grover Cleveland, Number 24, 1893-1897 199
William McKinley Jr., Number 25, 1897-1901 201
Theodore Roosevelt, Number 26, 1901-1909 203
William Howard Taft, Number 27, 1909-1913 206
Woodrow Wilson, Number 28, 1913-1921 208
Warren G. Harding, Number 29, 1921-1923 210
John Calvin Coolidge, Jr. Number 30, 1923-1929 214
Herbert Hoover, Number 31, 1929-1933 217
Franklin D. Roosevelt, Number 32, 1933-1945 221
Harry S. Truman, Number 33, 1945-1953 227
Recognition of Isreal 230
Dwight D. Eisenhower, Number 34, 1953-1961 234
John Fitzgerald "Jack" Kennedy, Number 35, 1961-1963 236
Lyndon Baines Johnson, Number 36, 1963-1969 240
Richard Milhous Nixon, Number 37, 1969-1974, ... 244
The Watergate Scandal: Nixon's downfall 247
Gerald Rudolph Ford Jr., Number 38, 1974-1977 248
James Earl "Jimmy" Carter, Jr., Number 39, 1977-1981 250
Ronald Wilson Reagan, Number 40, 1981-1989 252
George Herbert Walker Bush, Number 41, 1989-1993 256
William Jefferson Clinton, Number 42, 1993-2001 258
George Walker Bush, Number 43, 2001-2008 261
Barack Hussein Obama, Number 44, 2008-12 incumbent 265

About the Author 269

Dedication

To the spirit of my parents Nathan and Jewel Hawkins, that will live in my heart forever, and to my grandsons Nathan Wesley, Matthew Curtis and Elijah Hawkins, for the thankfulness and great joy that they brought into my life. Thanks to my wife Mildred for her steadiness and dedication to the family unit.

Prologue

America is the greatest nation on earth. This country has a very colorful beginning. This story is one of adventure and exploration, of discovery and disappointment, of war and peace, success and failure, of riches, greed and corruption. This is the story of an industrial revolution and the improvement of man's existence in America over hundreds of years in the making. There were many lives lost during man's quest for a new beginning. They were driven by the desire to change, by the need to reach out beyond their present surroundings and capture the ever-elusive dream of untold wealth and unimaginable riches.

The path taken by the founders and builders of this great nation would lead them through many struggles and difficult adversities, from early contact with Native Americans, to the current events of today. We will take a trip through the building of a nation and the multitude of changes that occurred along the way. The hardships experienced while establishing the colonies, to the pillaging of the land and its resources. We will explore the documented history of the out and out, raping of America in several forms. This is a great story with many tragedies and many triumphs. We will bring to you the story of heroic men and women struggling to survive in a new and hostile land.

This writing will delve into the story of crime and greed throughout our history. A story of control, exploitation and slavery, and how the hundreds of years of bondage of an entire race of people resulted in a non-violent revolution and civil unrest. It is important to revisit America's shameful and total dominance of the only true Americans, the American Indian. The mistreatment of these people by white immigrant Americans, will leave a scar on the soul of this nation that can never heal in the hearts of mankind. They destroyed the will and broke the conscience of a people trying to survive in the face of great difficulties that they could not possibly overcome. We will examine the double cross by white America, the military and the United States Government, against the only true Americans. The relocation of a people that was free to move at will and live freely on the American plains and in the forest of the eastern and southern regions of this country. The Indian Nations stretched from the Eastern seaboard to the desert country of Arizona, and from the Dakota's to the Florida Everglades. There were Indians living in the northern ranges of the North American Continent, as well. Today, the land known as Canada was the home to many Indian tribes.

This story will take you from this country's Louisiana Purchase, to the westward migration. We will examine the western plains and the colorful story of the cowboys. The land beyond the mighty Mississippi River was unforgiving; in many parts of the great southwest, the land was harsh and dry. There were droughts, windstorms and severe hot or cold weather. Water was a rare and valuable commodity. Thousands would die in their effort to cross these territories.

During the hundreds of years following the westward movement, America would go through a metamorphosis that would change a land of un-scarred beauty, to one of questionable long-term promise to be and remain, America the beautiful. This is my perception of this wonderful land, as we know it, during and after its discovery.

The information gathered in this book came from many sources. It is with my deepest thanks and gratitude to the book, The Americans, The history of a people and a nation, by Winthrop D. Jordan, Miriam Greenblatt and John S. Bowes. The book, American Citizenship by Steck-Vaughn Company. The American History Channel on the cable network, The Associated Press, and other educational and informational venues on many cable channels.

Part 1

THE DISCOVERY

North America was an unexplored and relatively unknown continent, known only to the original inhabitants who probably crossed an existing land bridge from the land that is now known as Russia, to what is today known as Alaska. During the fifteenth, sixteenth and seventeenth centuries, Spain, France and England, were looking to expand the old world in their search for new territories and the riches that could possibly come from their incursions into the unknown lands beyond the eastern horizon.

This was a period in world history where man was driven by the urge to satisfy his curious nature. A curiosity that has driven man to every land mass, the world's oceans and the far reaches of outer space. Many Europeans believed that the world was flat. They believed that beyond the horizon were a drop off and the end of the world. During the 1400s, Queens and Kings, sailors and navigators began to nurse their curiosity and desire to seek new territories.

Christopher Columbus was a sailor with a love for sailing and an itch to launch an exploratory expedition into those mysterious waters that stretched eastward to the horizon. History says that Queen Isabella of Castille, assisted him in acquiring three ships for this expedition. He had an interest in finding out what lay beyond the eastern horizon; he wanted to find a way to the eastern shores of Asia. With the blessings of the Queen, Columbus selected and supplied three ships for this journey into the far horizon beyond the shores of Castille. He set sail with the Nina, the Pinta, and the Santa Maria.

After many months of sailing in search of this new opportunity, they were finally approaching land. During the fall of 1492, the lookout in the crows nest on the Pinta, spotted land. The crow's nest was located near the top of the sail mast. A sailor would man this post with eyes that searched the horizon for the sight of land. They made landfall in a chain of islands that would later be called The Bahamas. The island was called San Salvador. Columbus would set up trading post on the island of Cuba to trade with the native inhabitants. Columbus believed he was somewhere off the coast of Asia. He would establish several trading posts in this chain of islands so that he could begin trading with the island inhabitants. Columbus would return to England following this expedition without having found the riches that he sought. This was a disappointment to him, and Queen Isabella as well. The Santa Maria sank in the waters surrounding these islands. There are salvage operations today that are still trying to locate this ship. Columbus continued to sail on several expeditions, but never found the treasured gold, silver and jewels that he sought. He was unable to reward his backers with fine silks, spices and riches, that he believed he would find. Columbus died without realizing the greatness of what he had accomplished, but he kept a diary that detailed his journey.

I believe Columbus was a man with a vision that suggested that the world was larger than the average persons perception indicated. His love for sailing and exploring the unknown, was a passion that has driven many men since the beginning of time. He had no concrete proof that his endeavors would generate great wealth, but he was willing to take the risk that it would. Some men are driven by the desire to take chances; Columbus was one of those men.

There was a Portuguese navigator called Ferdinand Magellan; he set out on an expedition with five ships and a crew of about three hundred men. He set sail on a westward coarse that would take his expedition around the tip of South America through a strait that would later bare his name and give him a place in history, "The Strait of Magellan". His expedition faced many dangers; he was killed in the Philippine Islands leaving his men to finish the voyage. This was a very long, dangerous and difficult adventure. Sailing uncharted waters on small ships for many months was hazardous. Most of his crew and all but one of his ships, were lost to severe weather and illness. After three years and a great deal of nautical and medical difficulties, the only surviving ship returned home suffering great loses to the crew. The crew suffered with bouts of scurvy, dysentery and high fever from a shortage of fresh water and supplies. It was a miracle that they survived the trip.

The exploratory expeditions were to continue. During the year 1607, there were many adventurers from country's such as Spain, Holland, France and others who had already established colonies along the eastern coast of North America. The earlier explorers spread out from the Aztecs in Mexico, to the shores of Florida. An Italian explorer named Amerigo Vaspucci was fortunate enough to have America named in his honor. According to history, a publisher, after hearing of his exploits, decided to call the new land America in one of his publications, the name was now established.

The English were late entering this search for new territories. Queen Elizabeth the 1st gave Sir Walter Raleigh her permission to launch an expedition that would take him across the Atlantic in search of new lands. Her orders were to stay away from the current holdings of other countries. She wanted to avoid any possible conflict with countries that were currently there. Pensacola Florida was the place of the first settlement, more than 450 years ago, eleven ships sailed into Pensacola and started a colony.

In the year 1584, Raleigh made an attempt at establishing a colony on Roanoke Island, Virginia, but the venture failed. He would make another attempt in 1586. Raleigh would leave the new colony that he was trying to establish and return home. Upon his return to the colony, he was surprised to find that there were no survivors. There were neither trace of the inhabitants, nor any indication of their fate. Did they starve to death? Did Indians massacre them? This represented a set back and a disappointment in Sir Walter Raleigh's efforts to colonize an area along the eastern seaboard. This lose did not discourage him, or alter his efforts, as he would make another attempt to colonize. This time the English would find success in their efforts to establish successful colonies in this new land. The French would continue to struggle in their attempts to improve on their successes at colonizing America.

The English were looking to settle on the shores of the Virginia coast to establish a colony there. In the month of April, 1607, Captain Christopher Newport and his crew, set sail on a journey with three small ships, the Discovery, the Goodspeed and the Susan Constant.

After many weeks on the seas, the Captain was successful and made landfall. The crew disembarked and walked into a land that was exciting and new. The land was flat and heavily wooded. There were tall trees and fruit growing wild. The Captain decided to board the ships and sail up a river that was wide enough to accommodate the flotilla. Here, they would search for a spot to build a fort for safety.

If the English were to be successful in establishing new colonies in this strange and unknown land, they would have to prepare for any unsuspected dangers. If this were to be true, they would need a more strategic site location to defend themselves against possible enemies. If the new settlement should face no hostilities, a sound and secure shelter would still be necessary

The possibility of building a new colony here must have been inviting. The trip was funded by what was called the Virginia Company. Therefore, the colony would be named for its supporters. They called the settlement Jamestown. Having traveled up this river to this location, they decided to name the river the James. This chosen location turned out to be less than desirable, it was almost surrounded by water and the ground was flat and swampy. This left them susceptible to an array of different illnesses. He believed that there could be inhabitants, so the Captain wanted to find a place to build a fort. He was right. On their trip up river, they saw Indians called Algonquin's. The meeting was friendly and uneventful. If the Algonquin had the benefit of hindsight to know what the future would bring, they would reverse that first encounter and they would probably say, don't let them get off the boat.

The settlers gave no thought to laying out a plan to achieve some degree of successful habitation on these new shores. They were lazy and didn't put in the work that was required to sustain them in this new settlement. They came to this new world looking for freedom from the British rule. The Virginia Company was looking to establish colonies for permanent residence. However, the settlers had their own agenda. They gave no thought on how to survive in this strange land. Gold and silver became their attraction. The land needed to be cleared for any sustainable crops; preparations were needed for housing and other requirements. The presence of the three ships gave them false confidence.

During the month of June of the following summer, The Captain set sail back to England with two of the ships. There were 104 people left behind at the new settlement. They had not done the chores necessary to aid them in their effort to survive. Their situation started to fail them and became increasingly worse. During the first month after the ships departure, they started to become ill and die. In a few short weeks, more than twenty-five of them had succumbed to their failures to prepare.

Planning and organization are the most important mainstays in a situation such as this. Nobody took up the challenge and now they were paying for it. They soon ran out of food and were beginning to starve to death. As their numbers continued to dwindle, they had to face the fact that there were no place to seek help and support. They had become victims of their own lack of attention to the details of survival. This was a group of men without direction and leadership. They were wondering aimlessly through the final days of their lives, with no hope and no visible safety net.

As the remainder of the survivors clung to life, the Indians came to their rescue. They provided fresh meat, fish, bread and many other staples necessary to nourish them back to health. The settlers knew that this was truly a blessing and their debt to the Indians were tremendous, but time would erase that gratitude. The natives had given them a handout and a hand-up, when all seemed to be lost. There was a lesson learned from this life threatening experience, one that they would have to rectify immediately and the recognition that the need for leadership and planning was detrimental to their successful habitation.

John Smith decided to pick up the mantle so he set out to address this problem. He knew that in order for this settlement to have a chance to survive, there had to be some form of leadership and guidance. He started to learn all he could about the land that surrounded them. He knew that if they were to survive, he needed to know what was out there and what was available to them to assure their survival. He explored the area and met with the Algonquin Indians. He met their chief Powhatan and assured him that their intentions were peaceful and this would be a temporary stay, then they would leave his land.

Powhatan had a daughter named Pocahontas. John Smith and Pocahontas became friends. The stories of their relationship varies from the two of them being lovers, to just a solid friendship. One of the stories is that the Algonquins wanted to kill John Smith and Pocahontas was instrumental in saving his life.

This relationship between the English and the Indians were not always a peaceful one. The fact that the Indians had saved them from a certain death, had no bearing on the events that lie ahead. There were times when they had skirmishes and bodies were left on both sides. The fact that the Indians were instrumental in their survival, brought no weight to bare on their disagreements. Regardless of those up and down moments, John Smith and Pocahontas had a long friendship. Pocahontas would marry John Rolfe and would return to England with him. John Smith would leave the colony himself and return to England as well. He named the colony New England, in honor of their homeland.

By the time John Smith decided to return to England, several hundred new settlers and tons of additional supplies, had arrived at the settlement. The colony was growing in size and the requirements for survival were increasing at a rapid pace. During the following year, the settlers were beginning to suffer again from the lack of food and supplies. Their numbers had grown to more than four hundred and their needs had grown with them. They were about to face their most difficult days of struggle. During that winter of 1609-1610, the settlers were starving to death. By the time spring rolled around, some of them had resorted to eating rats. According to history books, their numbers had been reduced to about sixty survivors. John Smith called the colony "A miserable hell.

The Mayflower

In the early sixteen hundreds, many Englishmen were unhappy with the Church of England. They believed that the church, reverting back to the old days of Rome, had lost its identity. They wanted to separate from the Church of England and set up their own church. They called themselves, Separatist Puritans, referencing the idea that they wanted separation from the Church of England. They held secret meetings for fear of the King finding out about their plans. Failure to follow the state church was a violation of the King's orders. They were determined to make this change. A small group fled to Holland. The Dutch had exhibited more tolerance to different religious beliefs.

On August 6, 1620, The Mayflower, under the authority and leadership of Captain Christopher Jones, set sail from the port of Plymouth, England, under the British flag. A second ship, the Speedwell would sail with them. The Speedwell began to leak so badly that both ships returned to port.

They remained in port for several weeks; they decided to keep the Speedwell in port because the ship was unfit to sail. The 102 men, women and children from the Speedwell were added to the Mayflower passenger list. Captain Jones, along with thirty crewmembers, set sail in search of the new world. The Mayflower sailed alone carrying more passengers than the Captain had anticipated. In addition to that, they sailed without the comfort of a support ship. Their heading would take them to Virginia, but after 64 days at sea, they wound up on the shores of Cape Cod Bay and named it Plymouth. This was the New England that Captain John Smith had given name to.

New England was outside the authority of the Virginia Government. Before leaving the ship, forty-one men, along with William Penn and Governor John Carver, would hold conference; a decision was made to write an agreement on how they would be governed. They agreed that all would be treated equal and the laws would be binding on Puritans and non-Puritans alike. After the signing, the Mayflower moved into the harbor of New Plymouth. As a result of their preplanning, the Mayflower brought a sense of community and government, along with responsibility and brotherhood, that was necessary to survive. The Pilgrims endured an extremely harsh winter; their only shelter was the Mayflower. Captain Jones remained with them to provide that shelter until they could build their own. Without the Mayflower remaining through the winter, it is likely that the new inhabitants of this new world may have perished.

The Pilgrims knew they were being watched, but had not made contact with their observers. This gave them pause and a reason for caution. December had arrived and they began to realize that they would suffer a much more severe winter than they were use too in England. William Bradford called it a hideous and desolate wilderness. Many of the Pilgrims would succumb to the lack of housing and diseases. At the end of winter, only fifty-six would remain alive. The cold harsh winter and the environment took a toll on them that nearly ended this colony.

On April 5, 1621, the Mayflower sailed for England without any bounty from the new world. The ship carried only a belly full of rocks, leaving their human cargo behind. The observers that they had not yet encountered, were the Indians that taught the remaining settlers how to survive. They planted corn using small fish in each hole as fertilizer. Governor Carver succumbed to disease, and William Bradford became their second Governor. Edward Winslow did most of the negotiating on their behalf as they made peace with the Indians.

They continued to build shelter in preparation for the upcoming winter. The Indians taught them well, and they reaped a good harvest.

One day, the Indians arrived unannounced with ninety warriors, apprehension set in and the Pilgrims became nervous, but soon settled down. In an act of brotherhood, they had a festive celebration with their new allies. This became known as the first Thanksgiving; the celebration went on for three days. Both sides could visit each other in peace, but their lives were changed forever.

When the Pilgrims arrived to these shores, there were already a society that had been here for hundreds of years, therefore, the Pilgrims were immigrants to a land that were already inhabited.

The Virginia's, The Carolina's and New England, had settlers already, but as time passed, the move was westward from the east coast. The Pilgrims were a very hardy people and were willing to suffer life-threatening hardships to inhabit this new land. Having the ability to live and worship as they pleased and to implement their plans to direct their own lives, was worth the sacrifice. It is the dream of all men to be independent and self-sufficient. When there are laws and governmental rules and regulations that hamper his growth, or restrict his ability to be creative, he will ultimately find a way to end the control.

The Pilgrims sought their relief by boarding small ships and crossing vast bodies of water to achieve their goal. There were many dangers associated with this venture, but the lure of a new beginning in a new world was the greater attraction.

Part 2

THE BUILDING OF A NATION

The colonies had begun to expand. More English Puritans were arriving in New England; setting-up a holy community of their own in this new land was their priority. To do this successfully, a new and independent government would have to be established. John Winthrop, a lawyer, was one of the Puritans. A charter was required to settle in New England; he assisted them in that effort and they were able to obtain that charter. This charter would contain rules for a joint-stock enterprise; it also included land grants and a form of government. Leadership, laws and strict rules were necessary to create a greater possibility of a successful colonization. Now that Winthrop had this crude form of government called The Massachusetts Bay Company in place, he and the others sailed for New England taking with them the authority for an independent government.

In 1630, the movement of English people to New England had greatly increased in numbers. They would begin to pour onto the shores of New England in greater numbers than ever before. John Winthrop would have nearly a thousand to accompany him on his return. The new Puritans would have a greater ability to sustain themselves in this harsh land due to easier access to procurement of goods and services from England.

The Puritans endured many hardships, all in the name of worship. They wanted to be able to worship freely and with great determination and perseverance; they would earn the right to govern themselves. In order to have greater success in reducing the possibility of failure, the Massachusetts Bay Company's newly recruited Puritans were much better off than some of the previous settlers. In order to successfully steer the recruits to a greater standard of possible achievement, Winthrop was able to establish a supply line to accommodate the necessary needs for survival in this hard land. The ships kept coming bringing the supplies necessary to sustain them. They had to live by the rules and guidelines set by the MBC, or face banishment from the colony. The primary purpose for crossing oceans and finding and colonizing new territories by the British explorers, was to bring Britain into this search for newfound wealth from trade, discovery, or even seizure, if necessary.

As the population grew, settlers wanted to branch out and expand their personal holdings, but the land surrounding them were owned by the Indians. Therefore, the only way to do this was to buy it from the Indians, or take it by force. Buying this land was out of the question. The settlers began to attack the Indian encampments, and drove them from their lands in the Virginias.

In 1676, Nathaniel Bacon led a rebellion; he rebelled for several reasons, but the treatment of Indians was one of them. The main causes had to do with what's dear to all Americans, the right to vote, a voice in government and fair taxes. The differences between the hand-full of rich and the many poor posed a degree of unrest and concern in the settlement of Virginia.

There was a system set to monitor, or grant land to those who came to Virginia. It was called the Head Right System. Under this system, anyone who paid his way to Virginia would receive fifty acres of land and for every person that he brought with him; he would be granted another fifty acres. Therefore, if a settler could afford to buy servants, or own indentured slaves, he would get fifty acres for each of them. This gave the richer farmer an advantage. The more servants he had, the larger his potential for agricultural advancement. This gave him an advantage over poorer farmers.

When men begin to build communities that are intended to grow and prosper, the need for laws and rules is a certainty. In order to have a peaceful existence with minimal conflict, law and order must be established. There had to be a system put in place to govern and control the newly and ever developing colonies. The Puritans sought new lands so that they could free themselves from English rule. However, in order to establish new settlements with an ever-growing populace, government is a necessity.

The poorer settlers became more and more angry with the Virginia government. Bacon, being disturbed about the circumstances, decided to become a bridge for justice. Bacon led his armed farmers and ex-indentured servants to Jamestown to present his demands. The government made promises to Bacon but nothing happened. Bacon was determined to strike out at this unresponsive government. He and his militia not only considered the Head Right System unfair and unjust; it was also a government that overtaxed the people and tried to protect the Indians without giving them the protection that was necessary. His efforts were unsuccessful. Sometimes the greatest plans for those that fight for justice, often fail or go astray. The rich planters with all of their land and indentured servants to tend it, remained in control of political affairs. Even though Bacon went on the offensive and burned Jamestown, it did not help his cause. A great deal of unrest followed as a result of this rebellion; servants ran away, colonist died in the fighting and the first armed rebellion in this new nation's history, was unsuccessful.

Bacon did not live to resolve this conflict, he died of a fever and the rebellion fell apart. The wealthy planters were able to maintain control. They decided that a lesson had been learned here; therefore, they would turn to black slaves for labor. The new Americans had experienced a form of political rape, and justice had not been achieved.

Slavery in new America

All of the colonies practiced the right to own slaves; none of the English colonies were without them. The unanswered question is when did slavery of Africans have a beginning in the new world? Some of the English used captured Indians as slaves. The English soon learned that enslaving Indians was not an easy proposition. The captured Indians were determined not to succumb to this forced labor and proved to be difficult to control. They were captured during battle skirmishes, or, was captured and sold by Indians engaged in battle with enemy tribes. The Indians were in their homeland and without a great deal of planning or effort, could easily escape. They lived on this land all of their lives; therefore, they knew the terrain like the back of their hand. They knew all of the trails, the streams and the countryside, but most of all, they had relatives that would aid them in an attempt to flee their captors. The Puritans found this to be unworkable. The indentured slaves were theirs only for the purpose of labor and did not fully meet their needs. Many of them were armed and therefore, not trusted.

The colonials decided that it would be much more prudent to obtain and use African slaves. They would be much easier to control because they were cut off, and had no way of reaching their homeland. They would be far more conducive to the required needs of the landowners. The colonies decided to go forward with the use of Negro slaves. The African slaves began to arrive in greater numbers during the 1700's. West African slaves were brought to all of the colonies. Maryland and Virginia wrote slavery into law. There were slaves in Massachusetts, the Carolinas, Virginia, Pennsylvania; even New Netherland after it became New York. Land acquisition was spreading, farmland was increasing in size, therefore, the free labor that came with slave ownership was attractive and prudent for their profit margin.

Most of the slaves were taken from West Africa; the slave traders did not go inland to capture them, but purchased them from tribal leaders. Trying to transport slaves overland for long distances, could have posed grave danger to the traders. Slavery was already in existence, even though they were used differently from the way the new Americans used slaves. Many had been captured in battle. They were used as household slaves, as soldiers, some served as governors of regions. However, most became slaves in Africa because they had been captured in battle. No man became a slave in Africa because of his skin color. Those that were taken by slave traders were sold for profit.

They were loaded into the belly of ships like cordwood, shoulder to shoulder. Chained together and lying on their backs. The traders utilized every available inch of space. They would lay there in urine and excrement. Poor ventilation and disease took the lives of possibly millions during this period. The slaves that became too weak to continue this journey were thrown overboard to drown. The holding of slaves in the New America would continue for another 250 years. It would take a Civil War to end this disgrace on mankind, and put an end to man's inhumanity to man, in terms of slavery in America.

Blacks resisted the practice of slavery and the trading of slaves from its inception in early America. Beginning from the 1600s to its end in 1865. They resisted it on the ships from Africa. They resisted it in the fields and in the big houses. They resisted through organized rebellion by leaders like Nat Turner, and they resisted by simple defiance and instant acts of courage. They started uprisings and killed their masters, and were killed in return. It was slave against master; they continued to fight back and many gave their lives in the fight against inhumane treatment. They were beaten with a lash and tied and bound for long periods. They were hunted like animals and forced back to the master that they escaped from. Through great strength and determined, resolve and their refusal to succumb to evil, control and the hate surrounding them, slaves won in the arena of humanity and freedom. The struggle for equal rights and a level playing field in the game of life was still illusive and would require great determination to overcome.

Trade, Farming and migration

The Puritan migrants had to become resourceful in order to improve their living conditions. They also needed a way to gain the goods and services that they found difficult to provide for themselves. The migrants in the south ran an array of small family farms. They raised rice in the Carolinas. In other colonies there were corn, peas, tobacco and other crops. They used mules, oxen, and horses to clear the land. The whole family worked the farm; this was necessary for their survival.

In the northern areas, they bought their supplies from the ships that traveled the shipping lanes bringing goods from England. They began to manufacture some of these goods themselves. They sold such goods as nails, bottles, and cooking utensils. The British Empire's merchant ships would carry staples from the southern colonies to England. This new nations economy was not built on a monetary system, but on what they called barter. This was a form of trade exercised by the Puritans to obtain needed goods and services. If one migrant had eggs, the other may have had butter, they would then make the trade that satisfied both parties.

A system of taxation had been established; however, it was not popular, but it was necessary. The taxes were used to support the small number of orphans, or pay representatives to attend meetings. The origin of this form of taxation could come from the colonial government, towns, counties, or maybe small villages. No matter where the imposition was originated, they were still considered a nuisance. To give the farmers a since of control, they chose paid representatives. The representatives had to be voted for on a yearly bases and probably followed the dictates of the voters.

Farming was the primary method used for providing necessary food and materials made from animals, or produce grown or raised by the colonist. Therefore, only a small percentage of the population lived in cities. The business minds of that day, knew that cities would have to be established along the waterways for shipping purposes. The seaports would give them access to world trade and commerce. The English government allowed the establishment of colonies in the new world with the expressed idea of finding and growing produce, or products, that did not exist in England. They would have them ship the raw materials to England for reprocessing for sale in other countries and to the colonies as well. This would give England a new pathway to change.

England was determined to establish mercantilism; therefore, the feudalism system known to exist in Western Europe would end.

Feudalism: was the social, economic and political system of Western Europe in the middle Ages. Under this system, Vassals held land on condition of giving military and other services to the lord owning it, in return for protection and the use of the land. This was about to change for a new system called mercantilism.

Mercantilism: The economic system prevailing in Europe in the 1500's and 1600's that favored a balance of exports over imports, preferably in a nation's own ships and through its own trading stations or colonies, receiving in return, whenever possible, precious metals. National wealth was being measured by the amount of gold and silver possessed. A nation's agriculture, industry and trade, were regulated with that end in view, as defined in the book, The Americans The history of a people and a nation. Mercantilism became dominant as feudalism waned, and the focus of national power shifted from those who owned land to those who controlled money and trade.

Now that the principles of mercantilism were in effect, the English government had to consider the possibility of descent. Many questions had to be considered. Would the colonist do all of their trading with the English, or would they prefer to trade with other governments? Would they prefer to buy cloth from French manufacturers, or maybe sell their products to the Dutch or others, rather than the English? England decided that there would have to be a system of checks and balances; they wanted the mercantile system to work as designed and the English Government would be the prime receiver of the goods coming out of the colonies. This represented a monopoly by the

British and put them in control of all raw materials shipped from American shores. The English Government was sure that they had a right to establish supervision over the colonies and the colonies did not disagree.

The attempts to supervise the mercantile system began in earnest after the restoration of King George the II in 1660. The English Parliament passed a series of Navigation Acts to regulate the trade and shipping of the American colonies. The Navigation Acts of 1660, and 1663, set forth certain basic and strict regulations to safeguard the mercantile system.

When the colonies traded goods to any European country, they had to be shipped by way of England. This system created jobs for the English dockworkers and at the same time, the port duties filled the English treasury. This represented an economic boom for England. A small group of bureaucrats were responsible for colonial affairs; they were called the Lords of Trade. In 1664, they sent a royal commission to the colonies to remind them of their obligations and their duty to abide by the Navigation Act. King William got wind of violations of the Navigation Act from others who listened to men like Edward Randolph who knew more about colonial trading practices than anyone else.

New rules were established to firm up the Navigation Act. The crown appointed colonial Governors in eight of the colonies. The governors had important legal powers. They even had the power to veto laws. By the 1700s, most of the Indians had been defeated in their immediate areas and the colonies were enjoying the protection of one of the world's most powerful nations.

The country was growing at a tremendous rate, in order to facilitate continued growth, the colonies knew that they were in a difficult position with Spain in control of Florida, the territory south of the Georgia border. To insure the safety of the colonies, a military outpost was established to protect the Carolina's from Spain. This settlement would serve a dual purpose; it would secure the southern border and also serve as a place of refuge for people that had been imprisoned because they did not pay their debts. In those days, if a man did not pay his bills, he probably would end up in debtor's prison. To establish this new settlement, twenty men under the leadership of General James Oglethorpe in the year 1732, obtained a charter for a new colony south of the Savanna River. This new colony would be called Georgia; it would become the thirteenth colony. This new colony prevented any further encroachment from

Spain on the other established colonies north of Florida. By the time Georgia officially became a royal colony in 1752, the differences between this new colony and its closest neighbor South Carolina, was minimal. The farmers from South Carolina came in and started planting large tracts of land with rice and other similar products and using slaves to do it. The previous was spelled out in the book, "The Americans, The History of a people and a Nation".

Problems with Britain and France
The events leading up to the revolution and new government

The British Government and the colonies as well, believed that France posed a problem to both of them. Britain and France were fighting each other all over the world trying to broaden their empires, mostly at the expense of each other.

From 1689, to 1763, Great Britain and France were at war on four different occasions. Even though the fighting was mostly in Europe, all of the wars were causing great concern within the colonies. This conflict invaded the new America. The English settlers fought the French settlers and their Indian allies.

The French concentrated most of their biggest outpost and settlements in Canada, however, they did settle along the Mississippi River all the way to New Orleans. While the settlers from Britain drove the Indians from their surrounding lands, the French were trappers and made the Indians their allies. Because of this, they did not need to colonize vast amounts of Indian land. The French fur trappers considered the Indians hostile savages, as did the English colonist. The French were looking for wealth and had no desire to settle colonies in America, a land far removed from their homeland of France. As a result of this, by 1760, there were only about 60,000 French people in the entire land called Canada. The English colonist had grown to 1.5 million people. The Frenchmen married many Indian maidens and considered them a people with a particular culture that the French respected. This friendship with the Indians gave them an ally that would help to balance the numbers and improve the odds in a conflict. Whenever there were war between the French and the British, the French would call on their ally, the Indians and attack the English settlements.

In 1756, war broke out between Great Britain and France. The Europeans called it the Seven Years War, but in the new America, it was called the French and Indian War and had been going on since 1754.

This war officially began when Robert Dinwiddie arrived in Virginia as the new royal governor. In 1754, he sent out a group of Virginia militiamen under the command of a twenty two year old colonel named George Washington to the forks of the Ohio River. Colonel Washington and his small force of about 400 militiamen erected a small fort for security, and called it Fort Necessity. The French, considering this a threat that had to be eradicated, attacked with a force twice the size of Washington's, forcing Washington to surrender. After the British were defeated at Fort Duquesne, The British sent William Pitt to lead this war effort. George Washington would have the pleasure of joining him in the capture of Fort Duquesne, and renamed it Fort Pitt, that would later become Pittsburgh.

Britain believed that they needed to tightened control over the colonies following the fall of the French. They began to encroach upon them when they left more than 10,000 troops in the American colonies to publicly show their superior power. There were a great distrust of a standing army by the colonies. The British signed many new acts into law. The Quartering Act of 1765, required that wherever British troops were stationed, the colony had to provide them quarters. Denying a free people their rights of choice in the face of perceived military threat, will automatically breed confrontation. The British also demanded that they would provide traditional rations, including rum, beer, and cider. This was an imposition that the colonies believed unfair. The colonies were fed up with the continued control by the British and organized a resistance movement that would become the Revolutionary War. The records of the period indicate that Crispus Attucks (a black man), would be the first to die in what was called the Boston Massacre. The colonials had decided that upon successfully defeating the British, the colonies could go forth with building their own nation.

New government is formed

The leaders of this new country were trying to establish a system of government that would develop and approve laws that would govern the populace with justice and equity for all. They would find this task very difficult. This did not include the only true native Americans, or the slaves that was forced into servitude. Both were exempt from the process, slaves were bought and sold, whipped and worked, the same as horses and cattle. The slaves had no rights as human beings. They were absent from fairness and void of protection from American laws.

Building the government would be a work in progress, but only for those that they chose to be included in that process.

In those days, the new Americans were still part of the British Empire. Most of them were still loyal to the King of England. That was before the British Government tried to meddle in their everyday lives. The British had tax agents collect stamp taxes on newspapers, pamphlets and legal papers. During this period, the citizens of Boston were forced to give lodging to British Red Coats. The people began to call the King a tyrant. Therefore, instead of paying the new stamp tax of 1765, the colonist sent threatening letters to the King's tax collectors. They drove the tax collectors from their homes, stripped them naked and tarred and feathered them.

The Revolutionary War 1775-1783

The revolutionary war was a war between the kingdom of Great Britain and the thirteen British colonies in North America. The colonies believed that the British authority had stepped beyond the boundaries of fair play. They believed that the tyranny that they had endured, and the lack of representation from the British, was the catalyst that forced them to reject the legitimacy of the Parliament of Great Britain. They would no longer allow the British to have the authority to govern them without representation. The dissention was growing and the colonies were prepared to challenge the British government by force.

On March 23, 1775, in Richmond Virginia, a meeting of the House of Burgesses was held, they were undecided whether to mobilize for military action against the encroaching British military force. Patrick Henry, the Governor of Virginia, spoke to the house and ended his speech with the words, "Is life so dear, or peace so sweet, as to be purchased at the price of chains and slavery? Forbid it, Almighty God! I know not what course others may take; but as for me, give me liberty or give me death."

The desire for independence from Great Britain was greater than the fear of the powerful military forces that the British could launch against them. The revolutionaries gained control of each of the thirteen colonial governments, then set up the Second Continental Congress and formed a Continental Army. A petition to the King to intervene with the parliament for them resulted in the Congress being declared traitors, and the states in rebellion. The Americans responded in 1776, by formerly declaring their independence as a new nation, the United States of America; claiming sovereignty and rejection on the basis of tyranny and the lack of allegiance by the British Empire.

Seeking to coordinate military efforts, the Continental Congress established a regular army in June 1775, and appointed George Washington as Commander-in-Chief. At the beginning, his army had 20,000 men, two thirds in the Continental Army, and the others in various state militias. At the end of the American Revolution in 1783, both the Continental Navy and Continental Marines, would be disbanded. About 250,000 men were serving in this cause. However, during the resistance, General Lord Cornwallis chased Washington's army through New Jersey and across the Delaware River. With the winter weather becoming more severe each day, the British entered winter quarters. George Washington was in command of an army that was suffering in its own right. They were under clothed for the severe weather, with insufficient supplies and ragtag footgear. George Washington understood the adverse situation that faced his troops, but he knew that their dedication to the cause would overshadow these problems. Washington decided to take the offensive and cross the Delaware on Christmas night. His troops captured nearly 1,000 Hessians at the battle of Trenton on December 26, 1776.

Sometime late in 1776, General George Washington, the head of the Continental Army and the Commander in Chief before there was a President of the United States, would ask Betsy Ross to sew the first flag for the United States of America. He gave her a design with a six pointed star, she showed him how she could cut a five pointed star with a single snip of the scissors. The flag would have thirteen stripes representing the thirteen colonies, and there would be a star for each colony, or state. The committee of three, George Washington, Robert Morris and George Ross, entrusted Betsy Ross with making our first flag. On June 14, 1777, the Continental Congress, seeking to promote national pride and unity, adopted the national flag. "Be it resolved: that the flag of the United States be thirteen stripes, alternate red and white; that the union be thirteen stars, white in a blue field, representing a new constellation."

Although France had been providing weapons, ammunition and supplies to the rebels beginning in 1776, the continentals capture of a British army in 1777, led France to formerly enter the war on the side of the United States. This entry evened military strength with Britain, Spain and the Dutch Republic. The Dutch were French allies, so they went to war with Britain as well. Though the war lasted until

1783, a pivotal event was the surrender of General Lord Cornwallis and his entire army of 7000 men on October 19, 1781 at Yorktown.

During the year 1776, when the revolutionary war started, a group of Americans meeting in Philadelphia decided that they had had enough; they would no longer tolerate the tyranny of the British and their superior forces. They decided that they would fight and perhaps die, rather than submit. A young Virginian named Thomas Jefferson was given the job of writing a "Declaration of Independence," for America. Jefferson listed many Acts of King George the III, to try to prove that the King was a tyrant. Fifty-six delegates from the 13 American Colonies signed the Declaration of Independence. Each signer realized that he could "be hanged by the neck until dead", for this act of treason against the British Empire, but that never happened.

While building this new government, there would be a need for a new constitution that would established the way the country would be governed. Three areas of government would finally be put into place, the Executive branch, the Legislative branch and the Judicial branch. The American Indians and the slaves would be absent from fairness and void from the protection of the newly established and ever developing governmental system. Women were not completely equal and were not mentioned in the new constitution, or the Bill of Rights that specifically stated that all "men" are created equal.

The ships were arriving from England on a regular basis, carrying goods, materials, and more settlers. There were a great need for expansion and growth. The new colony of Georgia restricted land ownership to 500 acres, but farming tobacco, cotton and many other farm products required larger tracts of land. With the Indians no longer being a threat to the land surrounding the colonies, the attention of the colonist turned to growth and expansion.

The British Empire had been rejected and suffered defeat in the revolutionary war; the new America was free to continue to build, grow and prosper at will. This new land called America was vast and presented many opportunities to flourish, expand and to explore unbelievable beauty in its mountains, valleys, and plains.

George Washington would become the first President of the United States and would be the first President to serve more than two terms in office.

America's defeat of the British Empire and break from British rule, set it on a path of self-determination and self-sufficiency. They began to give their attention to the continued building and expansion of a great nation.

The builders of this country, the fathers of its government and the architects of its design, would establish plans that would give this new government integrity. The Declaration of Independence and the Constitution of the United States, was the plan that would govern us all. Nothing seemed to be left to chance. The constitution established individual rights such as the freedom to worship, freedom of the press, freedom of speech and many other guidelines of common sense and reasonable behavior. The problem with any laws, or guidelines that subject the population to those that have another agenda in mind, is that some men will always challenge a specific set of rules. Sometimes that agenda has devious intent and criminal connotations. America, with all of its greatness, would find that this would surface decade after decade. There would be crooked politicians and businessmen, as well as, legislation by our leaders that would cause the people of this great nation a good deal of harm. These things, as we travel through time, will show and describe the intended and unintended consequences of laws, treaties and other ideas that caused a great nation to suffer, "The Raping of America".

Part 3

THE LOUISIANA PURCHASE

By the early 1800's, most of the Native Americans east of the Mississippi River had already been wiped out, or, posed no real threat to the settlers. The greedy and double-crossing Pilgrims systematically destroyed that culture. The only true Americans were raped of their homes, their land and their true identity as a free people. Even though they no longer represented a true hendurance to the expansion needed by the new settlers.

The new Americans were becoming more and more concerned about their ability to engage themselves in a westward movement. Their concern was predicated on the fact that the French owned the land west of the Mississippi River. To the east lay the Atlantic Ocean. To the south was Florida, owned by the Spanish. To the north was Canada; therefore, the only open country was across the Mississippi River.

In 1803, President Thomas Jefferson was in office when he heard that the French wanted to sell the Louisiana territory. This territory included The Port of New Orleans and millions of acres stretching west from the Mississippi River to the Rocky Mountains. If Jefferson failed to make the purchase, the United States would have no control of the Mississippi River. This presented an opportunity that Jefferson just could not ignore. The President recognized the fact that if the French closed the river to trade, United States farmers in the west could face great difficulty trying to ship their crops to market. He was determined to act on this purchase because failure to do so, could mean that western settlements faced the possibility of suffering great loses of income.

President Jefferson decided to go forth with the purchase. The Louisiana Purchase was the acquisition by the United States of America, of 828,800 square miles of the French territory called Louisiana. In 1803, the United States paid 60 million Francs ($11,250,000), plus cancellation of debts worth 18 million Francs ($3,750,000), at a total cost of 15 million dollars for the Louisiana Territory. The purchase encompassed all or part of 14 current U.S. states and two Canadian Provinces. The land purchased represented about 23% of the territory of the United States today. This land included the city of New Orleans and moving north and west to the Mississippi River, including Arkansas, Missouri, Iowa, Oklahoma, Kansas, Nebraska, the part of Minnesota that were west of the Mississippi River, most of North and South Dakota, northeastern New Mexico, portions of Montana, Wyoming, and Colorado east of the Continental Divide, and Louisiana west of the Mississippi River. The purchase was critical in the Presidency of Thomas Jefferson. Many Americans didn't believe he had the authority to make the purchase because of it being possibly unconstitutional. Although he felt the U.S. Constitution did not contain any provisions for acquiring territory, Jefferson decided to purchase because he was not going to allow France and Spain to have the power to block American trade access to the Port of New Orleans. This purchase was edged on the west by the Rocky Mountains.

Having acquired this vast tract of land, President Jefferson knew that this land would have to be explored and mapped, so he called upon two men to lead an expedition. This would be the first overland expedition undertaken by the United States to the Pacific Ocean and back. This effort would require men of true determination and will. He chose a team lead by Meriwether Lewis and William Clark and assisted by the Indian Maiden Sacajawia and Toussant Charboneau. The expeditions goal was to gain an accurate sense of the resources being exchanged in the Louisiana Purchase. The expedition laid much of the groundwork for the westward expansion of the United States. The United States did not know exactly what it was buying, and France did not know exactly what it was selling. The purchase was made in the blind without benefit of exploration prior to closing the deal. Several weeks following the purchase, President Thomas Jefferson, a man that had always pondered the idea of western expansion, had Congress appropriate $2,500 to fund the expedition. Jefferson wrote a letter to the Congress--- The Missouri and Indians inhabiting it, are not as well known, or rendered desirable by their connection with the Mississippi and consequently, with use of an intelligence officer with ten or twelve chosen men, might explore the whole line, even to the western ocean. This represented an enormous challenge to any explorers.

Jefferson had long thought about such an expedition, but was concerned about the danger. The expedition to the Pacific Northwest was intended to study the Indian tribes, botany, geology, western terrain and wildlife in the region. This expedition would also elevate the potential interference of British, and French Canadian hunters and trappers who were already well established in the area. The expedition was known as The Corp of Discovery. Louis and Clark left Pittsburgh on August 13, 1803, with a party of eleven hands, seven soldiers, a pilot, and three young men on trial, who agreed to go throughout the voyage.

They began the journey on May 14, 1804, with a party of 33. They met with Lewis in Saint Charles, Missouri and followed the Missouri River westward. This was a small party for such a huge mission through unknown territory.

Sacajawia was a Shoshone Indian who was married to Tousant; she would serve as translater and guide. There were still a need for caution and worry. They would meet many different Indian tribes along the way. Some were friendly, but some were suspicious and not so trusting. Lewis and Clark took along many items that were to be used as trade material for the Indians that they did encounter. Most of it were trinkets, like beads, cloth and cook ware.

The expedition continued to follow the Missouri to its headwaters and over the Continental Divide by horseback. They had many large canoes to travel the waterways, but there were so many water falls in the rivers and streams that they encountered, they had to abandon the canoes, for they were too heavy to carry around some of the falls. On December 3, 1805, the Pacific was in view. On September 23, 1806, the Corp had reached St Louis and completed its journey. The gateway to the west was now open.

The Westward Movement

The expedition was successful and a complete report had been given to the president. Americans began to ponder this great opportunity to expand westward across the Great Plains. This land spread from the great lakes region to the badlands of Oklahoma, to the Black Hills of the Dakota's, to the Desert Southwest, and the Rocky Mountain ranges, then on to the Pacific Coast. People were anxious to venture into the unknown for land, riches and opportunity, but danger would be a constant companion.

This land was teeming with game of all sorts. There were deer and antelope, buffalo and small game. Rivers that ran clear with an abundance of fish and other water species.

The pioneers had many things to consider before embarking on such a journey. One of the most important aspects of such a long and dangerous journey was the starting time. The weather ahead of them would be a factor in their ability to successfully complete this most difficult journey. The water supply along the way, or the ability to find adequate feed for the livestock, was a major consideration. A wagon master, a man that knew the trail and would make all of the decisions concerning how, when and where to travel, would escort them. He would decide on when to cross-rivers and when to camp for the night.

The travel would be long and tedious; the distance traveled per day could range from no miles to 15 to 20 miles depending on the weather and other factors. Rain would have a devastating impact on progress and could reduce that travel time to as little as one mile a day. River crossings could be very dangerous and difficult. If they were shallow, the oxen, mules, or horses, could pull them across, but if they were deep, they had to be floated across. Breakdowns presented a problem as well. A broken axle, or wheel, could cause a major problem for that traveler.

The pioneers that settled in the frontier of North America were farmers, doctors, shopkeepers, blacksmiths, lawyers and so on. They came from all over the United States to start new lives. Those that wanted a new start went to Texas, Oregon and other areas of the frontier for the inexpensive, or free land. They were called homesteaders; some were prospectors looking for gold.

The Oregon Trail was the longest overland trail in North America. England still had a hold, or a say, in the northwest. In the 1840's, they made an agreement with America; they agreed that Oregon would belong to the first country to settle the most people in that area. The

United States encouraged people to move to Oregon by offering land for homesteading. In 1843, the great migration to Oregon began. The trail started in Independence, Missouri, and went past Chimney Rock, Nebraska, on across the southwest tip of Wyoming and into southern parts of Idaho. The trail ended in the northwest corner of Oregon, it took approximately six months to travel the 2,000 mile route.

Before the gold rush of 1849, California was sparsely populated as Americans rushed to find riches. Thousands left their homes and headed to the California gold fields. Remember that this was not an easy journey, but they believed that the risk was worth the reward. Many would die along the way, from drowning, disease, Indians and accidents. The trip had to be made before winter set in. The Rocky Mountains stood in their way, but had to be crossed before the snow started to fall.

They all crossed at the same point. They stopped at Fort Bridger along the way. Beyond the mountains lay the desert and the overland trail. The southern route went from Missouri to the Santa Fe Trail. They would travel four abreast for protection from Indian attacks. Beyond Santa Fe, the desert began. This is where many wagon train travelers were attacked and massacred by Indians. From there, they would follow the Platte River.

The Donner Party was a wagon train that took a chance and started too late in the year of 1846. Wagon master Hastings encouraged the people to follow him. They had to chop their way through immigration canyon. They knew the season was late; therefore, they had to move fast. When they reached the meadow, snow began to fall. They were trapped in the mountains as the winter snows grew in depth. They ran out of food for themselves and feed for their animals. As starvation began to set in, they ate the animals, and when they were gone, they turned on the Indians and began to eat human flesh. This was a wagon train that was doomed from the start. They even ate their own dead. The wagon master should not have taken the chance on crossing so late in the year, as a result of that decision, many were doomed to death.

More than 400,000 settlers made the trip west, this was a great migration. Water was a rare find and much of it had alkali that would kill humans and animals. They traveled along the Platte River for hundreds of miles. The land was a sea of grass that was alive with game. The Indians were friendly and wanted to trade until they realized that their game was disappearing. The wagon train would travel from landmark, to landmark, such as Chimney Rock, or Independence Rock. The Great Plains lie ahead. After about six months of very dangerous and difficult travel, they would reach their destination of Oregon, or California.

California was won during the Mexican American War and became the thirty-first state of the union. Gold was discovered in that state and the rush for gold and the possibility of becoming rich began. Gold mining camps were built to accommodate the miners. Most were abandoned when the gold ran out. Most mines were not successful, but others would open businesses to supply the miners and were able to grow into western towns. There are ghost towns scattered all over the abandoned gold fields of the west.

The Indians

The Native American population stood in the way of white advancement, therefore, the whites decided that they had to be eradicated, or, confined them to reservations. There were many different tribes ranging from coast to coast and border to border and beyond into Canada and Mexico. The Native Americans own the distinction of saving the pilgrims from starvation during their first winter on the eastern shores of this great land. For all the support that the Indians gave them, they were doublecrossed at every turn. Broken treaties, lies, deceit and murder. This is the story of a proud people who were never given the chance to live in American society like other immigrants that came to this land. The only true Americans, put away like dogs in a kinnel.

As this country progressed towards expanding its borders and growing its territory, the true owners of America stood as a barrier to this wanted and needed advancement. The population was growing by leaps and bounds, and the Indian lands were hampering that advancement. By the early 1800's, most of the Indians in the eastern area of America had been defeated, driven out, or placed in some form of reserve. The most appalling story that I became privy too was the plight of the Cherokee Indian Nation. If there ever was a rape of mass proportions and sanctioned by a government, this was it. The raping of the only true Americans.

As I traveled north on I-75, an interstate highway in the USA, I stopped at a rest area for relief. While there, I read a monument to the Cherokee Indian Nation and the "Trail of Tears." During the remainder of my journey northward, I couldn't get it off my mind.

This was a people that complied with the ideas of the white man in terms of progress and conforming to his ways, yet, their lives were destroyed so that white men could gain land for their own use.

By the early 1800's, the state of Georgia had made every effort to drive the American Indians from their lands and into the frontier. To justify their dastardly deeds, they used the Treaty of Indian Springs. This gave the state of Georgia the vehicle needed to justify blight on American history, and one that nobody cares about. The Creek Indians were already gone from Georgia. The Cherokee was a different story with a different set of circumstances. The Cherokee Nation remained in occupation of their land until gold was discovered in northern Georgia; they stood in the way of recovering the yellow iron called gold and the riches that came with it. People were far less important than gold, especially Indians.

During this period in American history, Andrew Jackson was President of the United States. Jackson was an Indian fighter and had no concern for them. All of the killings, land theft and enslavement of these people fit his mode of thinking and under his Presidential leadership, became federal policy.

The Cherokee Indians were living their lives in a similar fashion as the Europeans that invaded their lands. They had a system of government and laws for their people. They had the ability to construct roads and build churches and a school system to educate their children in their ways, language and the direction of the Cherokee Nation. They were even cattle ranchers and many of them were dirt farmers. The Cherokee certainly had the ability to survive and prosper in the world of these new Americans and they could do it in a peaceful manner. That didn't matter. In 1830, the United States Congress passed "The Indian Removal Act". Many Americans were not walking in lockstep with Congress and was against it. Davy Crockett was a trailblazer and pathfinder; he was an Indian fighter as well. He was now in the United States Congress and was opposed to this act. President Jackson signed the act into law without delay. Crockett felt so strongly about his opposition to this act, that he would either leave the Congress or was voted out. His position was "I would sooner be honestly damned, than hypocritically immortalized". Even though the Cherokee fought the act in the Supreme Court twice and had established themselves as an independent nation, they were still ruled against.

Following the dictates of the act, the Cherokee would have to sign a treaty called "The Treaty of Echota". The leaders of the Cherokee signed it and that gave President Jackson the legal vehicle to move against the Cherokee Nation. What followed would be the greatest wrong perpetrated on the rights of the native Americans in their own land. This was rape on the grandest scale of rotten and dishonest authority.

In 1838, President Jackson initiated orders to begin a death march that would make the Bataan death march of World War II perpetrated on American soldiers by the Emperor of Japan, look like a church social in comparison.

Lewis Cass was appointed Michigan's first territorial Governor in 1813. He helped lead the settlement of the state and kept peace with Britain after the war of 1812. Cass later served as a U.S. Senator and ran unsuccessfully for president. He also served as Secretary of War under President Andrew Jackson. Cass enforced The Indian Removal Act, that forced 16,000 Cherokee Indians to march from Georgia to Oklahoma. More than 7000 Cherokee men women and children died on the trail to Oaklahoma where they were forced to go against their will. A march of more than a thousand miles without adequate food, shelter and supplies to sustain them along the way. Later he championed causes that landed him on the wrong side of history. Such as, The Doctrine of Popular Sovereignty, to allow territories to decide whether to keep slaves and the Fugitive Slave Law that required U.S. citizens to return runaway slaves to their owners.

This was a sad state of affairs for a new country with a constitution that guaranteed individual right to life, liberty and the pursuit of happiness. One that said all men were created equal and were promised by the framers of this great document, with the support of the United States Government, to carry out the promise. You will not find in this document the words "unless you are an American Indian" Therefore, the enforcers of the framers intent, failed to carry out their vision on how this new government should treat all people within its borders. The Trail of Tears was a trail of injustice and a great wrong perpetrated on a race of people for the gains of the white men in America. The shame and stench of this atrocity will live forever in the annals and nostrils of American history, but will America be judged by this dirty deed? No! The first Thanksgiving was in its rearview mirror and long forgotten. The red skinned true Americans didn't matter. And that's a shame!

The Sioux Indian Nation

By 1889, the Sioux Indian Nation was searching for any method available that would turn their struggle around. They turned to a new religion called "The Ghost Dance". The dance represented a combination of the old times and the new Christian teachings. They believed that if they pulled the old and new together, things would go back to the days before the white man came. The whites believed that this would lead to unrest and a possible uprising. White settlers became fearful; the cries from the whites became the catalyst for the worst experience in Indian/White relations. The Sioux wore the short shirts that they believed could stop bullets. The governments mistake was putting an Indian agent at the Pineridge Reservation that had no knowledge of Indians. Daniel Royer, the agent, sent out a panic call of a possible uprising. The war department took action to avoid another Indian outbreak.

The military was dispatched to the Pine Ridge, and Rose Bud Reservations in the Dakota's in November 1890, believing that there would be an Indian war. There had not been a war for many years. The press added to the fear by fabricating this emergency; many Indians became fearful and fled the reservation. Sitting Bull finally let his people join the dance after counsel and accepted the new religion. Nelson Miles was the commanding general, he arrested the Indians that he believed dangerous and ordered the arrest of Sitting Bull. When they told Sitting Bull he would be moved, he told them to get his horse, then he decided he didn't want to go. His supporters heard that they were going to arrest Sitting Bull; they made an effort to stop it. Bullets went everywhere; in the end, 8 lay dead including the great chief. His gray horse became a symbol for the Indians. Many fled south to Chief Big Foot for support. The order had gone out to take Chief Big Foot and his people and deliver them to the railroad in Nebraska. From there, they would be shipped to Oklahoma. Bigfoot's band was marched south by the army and led to Wounded Knee under the command of Colonel Forsyth. Forsyth was to carry out the orders of General Miles. Bigfoot put up a white flag over his tepee, indicating peace. They were told to give up their arms, they gave up about thirty weapons, but the soldiers believed there were more. Black Coyote got up with a rifle in his hand and said it was his and nobody would take it. Suddenly, a shot was fired and the massacre began. The Indians were being shot down like pigs in a barrel, so they broke out, men, women and children. The Sioux and soldiers alike were shot down. When it was over, 25 soldiers had been killed, but that was nothing compared to the Indians that lay dead; over 200 men, women and children were killed. While many Indians lay wounded, the bodies were recovered at two dollars a body. The media had its Indian war that never existed. The Indian Bureau had thrown up its hands and this was the result. Wounded Knee was the final confrontation, and the end of 100 years of fighting.

The government and the American people had finally gotten retribution for the massacre of George Armstrong Custer and 276 men of the Seventh Cavalry at the little Big Horn on the Rosebud. There is no notoriety given to the atrocities attributed to Custer. Ask anyone about Custer's involvement in the battle of Washita River, and they will probably look astounded from a lack of knowledge. Custer and his troop attacked a sleeping Indian village while the warriors were away. They killed 100 women, children and old men. This was a mass murder carried out by the United States Cavalry on American Indians with little publicity, but when the Indians win, its pull out the guns boys, full speed ahead.

There was a great warrior from the Lakota Sioux Nation; his name was Red Cloud. The United States Cavalry considered him one of the most fierce and competitive opponents that they ever faced. He was an excellent guerilla fighter who waged a massacre that rarely gets any notoriety. Red Cloud controlled the Powder River country for twelve years. His greatest achievement against the U.S. Cavalry was called the Fetterman Massacre. The military attachment was told not to chase a small war party of Indians but did and was led into an ambush by Crazy Horse. They slaughtered the entire detachment. This victory for the Sioux Indians is mostly unknown.

The Apache Indian Nation

Throughout American history, the question has risen, who was the greatest Indian Chief to face the United States Army in battle? What Chief gave them the most difficulty in their search and destroy missions against them? The Apache was called the greatest light Cavalry in the world. They had the ability to disappear in the desert country of Arizona and New Mexico without a trace. It is believed that Cochise was a master warrior and technition in guerilla warfare when it came to combating the Cavalry, or the Mexican Forces.

Cochise and the Chiricahua Apache Indians, were not at war with the United States. He left them to themselves. His raids against the

Mexicans were constant, but the American settlers were left alone. His war against the soldiers began when he went into their camp to defend his people from charges that they abducted a white American boy. Cochise entered the soldier's camp under a flag of truce, the commander of the soldiers apparently saw this as arrogance and ordered the entire party seized. Cochise and the accompanying chiefs, would not admit to this act. One from his party was killed. Cochise managed to escape by cutting his way out of the compound where he was held, though wounded more than three times. The Federal Troops hanged his friends and brother. Cochise began hostilities against the Americans as a method of revenge for the hangings. This act by the military officer in charge, started a war with Cochise that would last for eleven years. The sound of his name and his ability to shut down the free travel of settlers, created fear in white men. Cochise gave his friendship to a white American named Thomas Jeffords. There are many stories attributed to that friendship, but the one that sticks the most is that Cochise hated a liar. Some of the Apaches that were by his side were Mangus Coloradas, and Geronimo. Cochise died June 8, 1874, his son Taza became chief of the Chiricahuas.

Geronimo

The name of this great warrior who refused to surrender to the American forces and fought them for several more years, is the most popular name in Indian folklore. Geronimo was famous for his raids and fighting ability against a formidable opponent. He was elusive, and was able to avoid capture by both the Americans and the Mexicans. The Mexican government put a bounty on Indian scalps; this sent Geronimo into a raiding frenzy that brutalized his targets and left no place safe from his reach.

General Miles dispatched Captain Lawton, the commander of B Troop at Fort Huachuca, Arizona, to lead this country's efforts to bring Geronimo and his band into captivity. Geronimo and his band of 36 men women and children, facing hunger and exhaustion, returned to the United States from Mexico and surrendered. Geronimo was sent as a prisoner to Florida. He was later transferred to Fort Sill, Oklahoma, where he died in 1909.

The Cowboys, Outlaws and Lawmen

The old west has a colorful past. There are many stories of cowboys, Indians, outlaws and the lawmen that brought them to justice. Being a cowboy was far from being a glorified profession. He lived in a bunkhouse with many wranglers and the living conditions were far from pristine. They worked long hours and during cattle drives, their time belonged to the cattle that they were driving. There were long hot days under the summer sun, and cold days in winter. They had to contend with rustlers, Indians and an extremely hostile terrain.

Their days were long and their lives were short, there were many dangers associated with moving livestock hundreds of miles to a buyer, crossing streams, mountains and even desert like stretches of wild country. Being a cowboy was a hard, tough and lonely life. He was a symbol of the American west. The man himself had to be tough and dependable to handle herds of cattle in such adverse conditions for 20 or 30 dollars a month. The period of the cattle drives only lasted for about fifteen years. They were men of adventure, they were hundreds of miles from any town, therefore, they administered justice frontier style. After the turn of the century, the cowboy became a folk hero and movies glorified him.

The Outlaws

The west was basically a lawless frontier, in most cases, men had to protect themselves from harm. Most men carried guns as a necessity in what was mostly a lawless period in the development of the old west. Some men were gun-toting criminals. Some of these men were notorious and their exploits live today in American history. There were many; we will visit a few.

Billy the Kid, alias William H. Bonney, or Henry McCarty, was a teenage outlaw in the American southwest. Western folklore would have us believe that he killed 21 men in his short lifespan. In fact, he only killed 4 men that can be directly attributed to his lone gun. He killed his first man when he was 12 years old. Frank "Wendy" Cahill, was a bully who often harassed the Kid. Cahill attacked Billy and the Kid killed him during an argument.

Later on he relocated to New Mexico. His mother died and his stepfather would not be responsible for his upbringing. He found work on a ranch owned by an Englishman named John Tunstall.

While herding horses to Lincoln, a man named Dolan, along with Sheriff Brady's men, ambushed them, Tunstall was killed. Dick Brewer was appointed constable to bring in the murderers. The Kid and others were deputized; they called themselves the Regulators. They arrested Bill Morton and Frank Baker, but they believed the sheriff would release them so they killed them. They also ambushed the sheriff and his deputy and killed them. He was offered a pardon for his cooporation and spent 3 months in jail without receiving it, so he walked away. After being tried and convicted for murder, and scheduled to hang on May 13, 1881, the Kid escaped from the courthouse jail in Lincoln by killing both guards. He then fled the town of Lincoln. On July 14, 1881, in Fort Sumner, New Mexico, the Kid is shot dead by Sheriff Pat Garrett as Garrett waited in ambush under cover of darkness in a bedroom. He was 19 or 20 years old.

He singlehandedly killed 4 men and was involved in 5 shootings that led to the deaths of 5 others.

John Wesley Hardin was called Texas most notorious and dangerous gunfighter of all times. It has been said that he was so mean that he once shot a man for snoring. In spite of his pension for killing, he was a star like figure to the ladies of that time period. He also earned the respect of other gunfighters, such as Ben Thompson, Bill Hickok, and Bill Langley. It is said by his own admission that he killed more than 40 men. He killed his first man named Mage, a black man, when he was only fifteen years old. His father encouraged him to go into hiding until the passage of time cooled the memory of what he had done. During the years that he was on the run, he killed more blacks, soldiers and police officers. Most of his victims were white and Mexican and they were killed for personal reasons.

In a town Called Comanche, Texas, on May 26, 1874, Hardin was celebrating his 21st birthday when he shot and killed deputy sheriff Charley Webb. The town's people wanted Hardin's blood and someone got a rope. Hardin was able to escape. Several years passed and Hardin continued to kill but was later caught by the Texas Rangers and tried for 2nd degree murder. He was convicted and served 16 years in the Huntsville Prison in Texas. He was paroled and pardoned by Governor Jim Hogg. He met his death at the hands of constable John Selman who shot Hardin in the back of the head in El Paso, Texas on August 19, 1895.

Jesse and Frank James were the most famous of all the outlaws of that era. Jesse was born September 5, 1847, in Missouri. He fought in the civil war but later joined up with William Quantrell and his raiders. In 1863, they raided Lawrence, Kansas and murdered 178 men, women, and children. He also rode with Bloody Bill Anderson's gang. In June 1865, Lee surrendered to Grant and the war was over. On Febuary 13, 1866, the James Gang robbed the Clay County Savings Bank. This was his first alleged robbery, but there was no evidence.

The authorities could never prove what robberies the James gang was guilty of. His allies were the Younger and the Dalton brothers. They were charged with all bank robberies no matter who committed them. Jesse was called the Robin Hood of the west, even though there is no proof that he gave to anyone.

Jesse and his gang planned a raid and bank robbery on a bank in Northfield, Minnesota. He heard that the bank would be loaded with money. The robbery was a failure when all of the men in the town laid an ambush for the gang. Some of the Daltons and Younger brothers were wounded, or killed; Frank and Jesse escaped unharmed. The James gang was destroyed.

Bob and Charlie Ford, his own gang members, murdered Jesse James as he straightens a picture hanging on the wall of his home. Bob Ford shot him in the back of the head. A killer, who wanted the fame of killing Jesse James's killer, would later kill Bob Ford. Charlie Ford committed suicide in 1884. Frank James was tried repeatedly, but was never found guilty of any crime.

Ben Thompson was said to have killed 10 men before leaving Texas. At age 42, he was shot to death watching a song and dance act.

Clay Allison was a cold-blooded killer, and an alcoholic. In 1876, at age 37, Allison was on his way to kill a neighbor when he was hit by a wagon and killed when the wagon wheel ran over his neck. Allison had already killed 15 men. There were many men who lived by the gun in those lawless days of the old west; the men mentioned here are just a few.

The Lawmen

Law and order is necessary in any society. As settlers moved into these territories, the only law that they knew was the law of the gun. However, settlements meant new growth and with this growth came the need for law and order. A society cannot sustain itself without rules, regulations, laws and people to enforce them. There were many stories about the courageous men that took on this challenge. Many died as a result of this undertaking. Some of them became notorious and legends of this great period in the expansion of the west.

Pat Garrett was known for killing Billy the Kid, even though he did it in ambush while lerking in a friend's bedroom in the dark.

Wild Bill Hickok (James Butler Hickok), was a lawman that was as tough as any. He ran for sheriff in several towns, but was elected in Abilene, Kansas; Wild Bill was involved in a dispute with a man named Davis Tutt over a watch that he lost to him in a poker game. Hickok told Tutt not to wear the watch in public. He said he would shoot him if he did. The following morning, when they walked out onto the street, Hickok asked if he was wearing the watch, and Tutt said that he was. A gunfight ensued and Davis Tutt was killed from a distance of 75 yards. Hickok was tried for the killing, but was acquitted. This would be the first ever-recorded quick draw in a gunfight. Quick draw gunfights did not exist. They were created in movie westerns for suspense and drama.

On August 2, 1876, while playing poker in Deadwood at the Number Ten Saloon, Hickok was sitting with his back to the door, a rule he had never broken before. He asked another player if he would exchange seats with him, but he refused. A buffalo hunter named John (Broken Nose Jack) McCall; walked in unnoticed. McCall walked to within a few feet of Bill and drew a pistol and shouted, "take that" before firing, Hickok was hit in the back of the head, killing him instantly. McCall would later be tried twice but eventually hanged for the murder. Hickok was holding a pair of aces and a pair of eights, both black. They would forever be called the dead man's hand.

Wyatt Earp was a tough and deadly lawman. His methods for maintaining law and order would earn him a place in history and western folklore. Ned Buntline gave him a pistol with an extra long barrell; he would hit law brakers over the head with it; rendering them subdued. In 1874, Wyatt was marshall in Wichita, Kansas, but moved on to Dodge City to work with **Bat Masterson** as a law enforcement officer. He left Wichita in 1879, and went to Tombstone, Arizona with Johnny Bean. He took with him Doc Holiday, a gun fighter and gambler and his brother Virgil Earp. His brother Morgan Earp would join him at a later date.

On October 26, 1881, a town drunk told Wyatt Earp the Clanton's and the McLaury's were waiting for them at the OK Corral. The Earp's and Doc Holiday met them there and as Virgil Earp yelded out "throw up your hands", Wyatt and Billy Clanton went for their guns first, and the shooting began. The shootout lasted maybe 30 seconds Tom and Frank McLaury, along with Billy Clanton, lay dead. Doc Holiday was wounded in the back. The only man left standing was Wyatt Earp. Later, Virgil Earp would be ambushed and crippled; Morgan Earp would be shot dead. Wyatt would find the killers and shot one so many times, it was hard to pick up his body. Wyatt Earp would die in California in 1929, never suffering a gunshot wound. (Tombstone Epitaph).

Elfego Baca was a self appointed lawman that had no qualms about shooting a man. He survived a gunfight where more than 4,000 rounds were fired into a cabin that he was in and he was not hit. The shooters did not know that the cabin had a recessed floor and he was below ground level. They called him the man that could not die. He later became a U.S. Marshall, and a politician.

This is a small profile on just a few of the lawmen that played a part in taming the old west, or maybe I should say, the new west. Staying alive in the towns and mining camps of the day, as a law enforcement officer, was a treacherous undertaking. Many lawmen had short lives, but we owe a debt of gratitude to them and the sacrifices they made in the name of law and order.

As the encroachment of civilization moved farther west towards the Pacific Ocean, the lawlessness of the old west disappeared from the streets of the western towns. The Pony Express and stagecoaches moved the mail and passengers into those areas. The railroad opened the way to an easier access to the vast plains of the American west. They provided a supply line for needed goods and services that was necessary for the expansion of this great Nation.

The Native Americans were left in the wake of this westward movement. People looked upon them as bloodthirsty savages. They were really a proud people forced into a fight for survival in a land that was taken from them by force.

The Native Americans produced some really great men. The Yutes and the Navaho were master builders, and successful farmers; they disappeared from the old west. The Native American did exactly what we as Americans would do today; fight to save our land, and our culture. America destroyed their culture, their pride and their way of life. Then locked them away like animals. With a little more compassion and a lot less greed, the Native Americans could have been delt with a little more humanely and the mass rape of a people and a culture, could possibly have been avoided.

The white men of that era and the people in authority, were not willing to tolerate the native Americans. They were looked upon as dangerous and hostile inhabitants of a land that white men wanted to control and own. They stood in the way of white progress and had to be eradicated. As a result of this mass murder and human round up, a whole people lost everything; they were driven from their homes and land and housed on reservations that would make a dog run for cover. America's shame will live forever.

The original owners of this vast land, a people with a nomadic way of life, a people with the hand that fed and sustained the original colonist, were put upon, killed, imprisoned and reservationalized. They were robbed of their way of life, and raped of their freedom in a land, regardless of its size, that had no room for them. The conscience of America!!! This is a sad commentary on a so-called civilized society and a perfect example of, The Raping of America.

Part 4

SLAVERY, CIVIL RIGHTS AND THE PLIGHT OF BLACK AMERICANS

You have already learned how slavery was introduced to this new Nation and the many years of inhumane treatment to human beings that were far from home and lost in a foreign and hostile land. Their story would go on for centuries and is yet to conclude.

For more than two hundred and fifty years, blacks were held in servitude and slavery to white Americans. They did not own this distinction alone. Clearly, there were others that suffered at the hands of whites who believed that they were superior. The American Indian and the Chinese, should be included. None suffered as harshly and with more disdain and outright hatred, than the African American. He was forced to live like dogs and work like mules so that his master could live in luxury and with great status. The slaves built the plantations that were carved out of the wilderness with the sweat of their brow and the skin off their backs. Time would necessitate a change in the plight of a suffering people. Black people came to this country on a path not of their own choosing. They came under the gun and the threat of death if they failed to yield to the powers of the slave owners.

In 1862, President Abraham Lincoln signed the Emancipation Proclamation. One of the oldest American Ideals is that any of our children can grow up to become what ever they want to become.

Prior to the start of the civil war, there was a case before the United States Supreme Court who's ruling in Dred Scott vs. Sanford, declared that Congress had no authority to prohibit slavery in federal territories. They thought this might settle the slavery question, but it only inflamed passions in both the north and the south.

On the battlefield at Antiedam, 23,000 men were killed, wounded, or captured in one day. This happened on September 17, 1862. Historians consider Antiedam, also known as Sharpsburg, a turning point in the Civil War because Confederate General Robert E. Lee's retreat from the battlefield gave President Abraham Lincoln the political strength to issue the Emancipation Proclamation five days later.

Abe Lincoln's life was the embodiment of this idea. His father, Thomas Lincoln, was a poor illiterate frontiersman. As a child, young Abe lost his mother and a sister to the riggers of pioneer life. He had no more than eighteen months of formal education. He lived in a log cabin in Kentucky, and worked extremely hard to educate himself. Much of his reading was done by candlelight, or next to the old fireplace. He was a man blessed with good character, leadership skills and political talent. He passed the "Homestead Act", to give Americans a chance at land ownership. Lincoln made himself into a world figure. His story has inspired many who followed him. Men like former President Bill Clinton and our current first black President Barack H. Obama. All three men overcame significant personal challenges in their early lives. Many historians believe that Lincoln was the greatest President of all, up to now.

Former President Franklin D. Roosevelt, who led the nation through the great depression of the nineteen thirties and won World War II posthumously with the help of our allies, was in my opinion, just as great a president as President Lincoln. However, it is said that he had a devious nature. Abe was honest and led the country through a four-year Civil War without lying or cheating. His kindness was even extended to his enemies. Near the wars end in 1865, he held no malice or vindictiveness towards anyone, while welcoming the Southern States back into the Union.

Fredrick Douglas pressed President Lincoln to realize and to recognize that the struggle that this country faced, and the terrible position of the blacks within it, must not be just to reunite the Union, but also to abolish slavery. Many scholars of that day began to focus on what appeared to be Lincoln's shockingly retrograde views on black social equality and the limitations of his Emancipation Proclamation. With the passage of time, and the setting aside of some of Lincoln's words and actions, many emphasized his growth and his political dexterity solidifying public opinion to give African Americans legal equality. I wonder, what impact would he have had on American society had he survived that fatal night at the Ford Theatre when he was assassinated by John Wilkes Booth.

The slaves were one group of Americans that did not share in the prosperity of this new Nation. The Civil War was one way to change their situation. The war was the biggest rape on this new nation that modern man will ever encounter. It pitted the north against the south, brother against brother, father against son, citizen against citizen, and as a result of this everlasting national tragedy, over 600,000 Americans would die as this country ran red with the blood of its children.

Several thousand slaves served in the armed forces on both sides. This service gave them an avenue to freedom. The question of slavery had already been examined by a number of states, and many took steps to abolish it. In the areas of the new country north of Pennsylvania, there were a small number of slaves; this made it easy to bring slavery to a gradual end. In the state of Massachusetts, the courts found that slavery violated the constitution of that state, which said that all men are born free and equal. Time and circumstances would force other states to change.

In other areas of the north, states passed gradual emancipation laws. The laws did not solve the problem of present day slaves, and did not abolish the total problem right away. They provided that slaves born from that day forward would be free at age 21 or 28, the laws named July 4th as the day when they would go into effect. In the southern states the principles were the same. However, there were a vast number of slaves to deal with. In Virginia and Maryland, there were considerable discussion on the abolishment of slavery. The idea of freeing slaves represented a problem to most whites, because there were many things to consider. First of all, they did not want blacks free, where would they go? What would happen to their plantations without free labor? The blacks were considered less than human, therefore, how could they look upon them as equal citizens? Some of the slave owners took it upon themselves to free some, or all of their slaves.

In Georgia and the Carolinas, the consideration was for profit and not for freeing slaves. It was far too profitable to maintain the status quo, than to start anew without free labor. The slaves in these states far out numbered the whites that controlled them. White Americans lived up to their revolutionary principles where it was convenient, but failed or refuse to do so when the idea or order met with great difficulty.

John Hancock, the author of the Declaration of Independence, continued to own slaves for his entire life. So John Hancock did not abide by his own decree, giving the appearance that he was exempt from his own Declaration of Independence.

The reality that slavery had just been abolished, brought fear into the lives of many slaves. What were they going to do, where would they go? The former slave owners offered them the opportunity to remain on the plantations and continue to work for them. Many would venture off looking for a taste of the real freedom that was just granted by President Lincoln's decree, but there were dangers lurking in the darkness and on the roadways. There were masked riders that would catch them and force them back to the plantations under the threat of death. Some men were paid a bounty for doing this.

On December 24, 1865, in the state of Tennessee, an organization called the Ku Klux Klan was formed and turned out to be this country's deadliest terrorist organization. The Klan was supposedly found as a purely social group. There was a time when millions of Americans belonged to the Klan. They preached the purity of the white race. It would rise up to battle issues that they believed threatened the white race. People joined for a since of belonging, a kinship if you will. They could have a common bond and a perception of inclusion. The Klan claims to be a defender of white women and the white race only. They hold their rituals in the shadows of darkness. After the civil war, much of the south lay in ruins. In Pulaski, Tennessee, on June 9, 1866, it was decided that all public appearances would be made in disguise. As the Klan grew, hooded night rides began, and all blacks were fair game for beatings, lynching, or burnings.

The 1867 Reconstruction Act, gave blacks the right to vote; soon after, a meeting was held by the Klan. The Klan had expanded to all southern states; following their meeting they began to terrorize blacks with threatening letters promising floggings, lynching and burning of their homes and churches. They were able to terrorize with virtual impunity. Several southern governors passed laws to disband the Klan, also called the invisible empire. On Thanksgiving

Eve, on top of Stone Mountain, Georgia, the Klan was reborn by William Simmons. The movie "The birth of a nation" depicted blacks as criminals and animals and the Klan as heroic; this changed the thinking of Americans that blacks needed to be controlled. It continues to this day.

Before this newfound freedom of 1865, Harriet Tubman struggled for many years using the underground railroad to free her enslaved brothers and sisters from the horrors of this disgusting and devastating cruelty to man. There were many whites that assisted the runaways by risking their own lives to aid them in their search for freedom. For decades to follow, black men would find themselves trapped in a never-ending cycle of sharecropping for the white landowners. He would be allowed to work the land for farming, and he would share his crops with the landowner. The sharecropper would never find a way to improve on his monetary condition because the landowner supplied him with housing, clothing, grain and feed in order to operate. When the crops came in, the landowner would say, well boy, you almost made it, but you were short. Maybe next year you will do better.

The injustices we suffered as a people, would continue in some form until today. There would be incidents of lynching and murder, bombings and burnings, Jim Crow and segregation, throughout the south. There would be many events that would begin to open the eyes of the American people to the tragedy and disgrace of the treatment of black Americans.

What is Jim Crow?

"Jim Crow laws were state and local laws enacted between 1876 and 1975 in southern states. They mandated racial segregation in all public facilities, with a supposedly separate but equal status for Black Americans." In reality, this led to treatment and accommodations that were usually inferior to those provided for Whites. This was Americans systematizing a number of economic, educational and social disadvantages. The segregation of public schools, public places, public transportation, separate restrooms, water fountains and separate restaurants for blacks and whites. The United States military restricted the civil rights and civil liberties of African Americans as well. President Harry Truman ended segregation in the military in 1951. The separation of educational facilities were overturned by

Brown vs. The board of education, The Civil rights Act of 1964 and the Voting Rights Act of 1965, gave Black Americans more freedom".

After suffering many years of the denial of human justice by white authority; in 1955, the Emmett Till murder by whites for whistling or winking at a white woman in the state of Mississippi, began to turn the tide. A teenage child murdered by white men in the most racist state in the union. White men that were allowed to go free. His face beaten beyond recognition, his eye gouged out of his head, barbed wire around his neck, a 75-pound cotton gin fan put around his neck and his body dumped into a river. His mother Mamie Till had the courage and the strength to have an open casket so that the world could see what these mad men had done to her son. This brutal senseless murder brought attention to the racist attitude of the south. This put an open eye on the civil rights movement in America. This murder and the sight of the body being unrecognizable as a human being, struck a nerve in the American conscience. The plight of blacks in America began to gain sympathy. In 1955, The two culprits were acquitted after one-hour of trail. People did not forget it, especially in black America.

During the same year, in December 1955, a black seemtress with the name of Rosa Parks decided that she was too tired to give up her seat to a white man on a Montgomery, Alabama bus, so she refused. Mrs. Parks was arrested and charged with violating a city ordinance. This act of defiance was the catalist that started the "Montgomery Bus Boycott". The leaders of the black clergy enlisted the aid of the Reverend Doctor Martin Luther King Jr. to lead the fight against the tyranny of a racist government and its policies. The boycott lasted 382-days and broke the financial backs of the white businesses in Montgomery. The U.S. Supreme Court ruled the segregation laws unconstitutional, so the blacks of Montgomery won the right to sit in the seat of their choice.

The fight continued with many non-violent marches and protest staged by Dr. King and the Reverand Ralph Abernathy, along with many from the clergy all over this country. This included white men and women. Dr King Jr. lead the second civil war, a war of non-violence, it reminds us of our strength as black people in this nation. There were labor leaders, businessmen, actors, farmers, students, educators and just the average human being, fighting for the right for blacks to live in this country with the freedoms enjoyed by others and guaranteed by the constitution.

In 1964, at a college in New York City, Andrew Goodman joined James Forman and Michael Schwerner; they came together and went to Meridian, Mississippi to join the movement. There they met James Cheney, a Mississippian, and John Lewis, who were civil rights leader in Mississippi. They made contact with the group, but the Klan's Imperial Wizard, Sam Bowers, targeted Schwerner. On June 21, 1964, one day after Schwerner joined up, the deputy sheriff of Nesheba County arrested them. Deputy police Officer Price released them at night, and proceeded to stop them on the road. He was accompanied by two carloads of Klansmen. He put them in the hands of the Klan. They were each shot at pointblank range. The last words of Schwerner were "Sir, I know just how you feel". President Johnson sent in one hundred and fifty FBI and Navy divers to search for the missing men. Their bodies were recovered and the men involved in the killings were tried and found not guilty. They were later charged with violating their civil rights and were found guilty. This forced Congress to get behind the voting rights bill. The war for civil rights would now turn to the state of Alabama with its vicious racist and police dogs.

There would be continued struggle in this effort until President Lyndon Baines Johnson signed into law The Civil Rights Act of 1964 and the Voting Rights Act of 1965, the supreme court justices were ridiculed for their ruling. The events that finally initiated the culmination of the wrongs of the civil rights movement, took place with the televised coverage of Police Chief "Bull" Connor and his police dogs and water hoses as they attacked non-violent marchers, knocking them to the ground and being severely beaten by police with batons. This was an embarrasment to America as this scene gained coverage on the world stage. Public opinion is a mighty tool when used to the advantage of the oppressed. The world was tired of the killings and beatings of people merely seeking basic human rights. They were sick of the attacks on the freedom riders, or the blacks beaten at food counters.

They saw the results of the bombing of the 16th street Baptist Church in Birmingham, Alabama and the death of the four little innocent black girls killed while in Sunday school. Over three decades, 60 black owned homes and churches were bombed. The church served as a staging area for the movement. Four men were involved in setting the bomb to go off at service time. The church received a call that only said, "three minutes". At 10 a.m. came the shattering sound of an explosion, four girls dead, twenty wounded.

The bombers were arrested but were only charged with possession of explosives. J. Edgar Hoover, the head of the F.B.I., hated Dr King and turned his back even though he had evidence and knew who the bombers were. In 1976, the Alabama Attorney General reopened the case against Robert "Dynamite Bob" Chambliss, the bombers niece testified against him and he was convicted and died in prison.

In 1964 in Mississippi, a movement to register blacks to vote would lead to the death of Vernon Dahmer, President of the local N.A.A.C.P. Dahmer owned a large farm and was able to fund his own actions. On July 9,1966, he was on the radio urging citizens to visit his store to exercise their right to vote. Billy R. Pitts, a Klansman, said Sam Bowers ordered the attack on Dahmer's home and business. Two carloads of Klansmen, under the cover of darkness, threw gasoline bombs into Dahmer's house. Vernon fired back while his wife and children got out of the house by escaping through the back door. Vernon escaped before the house was engulfed in flames, but his lungs had been fatally damaged from smoke. Twelve hours later he was dead. President Johnson ordered an F.B.I. Investigation and the killers were identified. Bowers four henchmen were convicted, but he was not. In 1998, thirty-two years after Damer's murder, Sam Bowers was convicted for Dahmer's murder and got life in prison.

America saw the continued burning of black churches, and the murder of Medger Evers in ambush under the cover of darkness by Byron De La Beckwith. His gun was found at the scene with a fingerprint on it. He was tried in 1964, but was not convicted. He was tried twice in two and a half decades and still escaped conviction. In 1989, after reviewing the case, District Attorney Ed Peters reopened the case and after the third trail and his bragging for years to get the credit, Beckwith was convicted and given life in prison, 31 years after the murder.

The assault on the marchers at the Edmund Pettis Bridge in Selma Alabama was shameful. A state trooper murdered Jimmy Lee Jackson before going onto the bridge. The fifteenth amendment prohibited discrimination in voting. However, on February 18, 1965, at a demonstration in Alabama, Jackson saw his father being beaten, so he intervened and was shot in the stomach. The authorities refused to treat him so he died. King used his death as a rallying cry when he told the crowd that Jackson's death must not be in vain. Dr King said it was time to redeem the soul of America. They would march the 50 miles from Selma to Montgomery, Alabama.

On March 7, 1965, the attempted march took place. The Reverend James Reeb, a white minister, watched the events as they unfolded on television and immediately went to Selma. On March 9, 1965, he attempted a march again and was met by state troopers, they prayed and turned back. The Reverend Reeb met and had lunch with three activist; they were attacked. Reeb was hit in the head and suffered a blood clot and massive concussion, three days later he died. President Johnson went on TV and spoke to the nation and said, "we shall overcome". On hearing those words from the President, King shed a tear. Three men were picked up for this act, but were not convicted. The march was known as Bloody Sunday. Horses trampled the marchers and they were tear-gassed by state troopers that clubbed John Lewis. The nation expressed sympathy for the marchers; change was in the making.

Viola Luizzo, a Michigan housewife, was the only white woman murdered in the civil rights movement. She was from Detroit but grew up in the Jim Crow south. She watched the same footage that Reeb saw. She went to Selma for the next march across the Edmund Pettis Bridge. The march was successful and she was in Montgomery three days later. She and Leroy Moten, a black man, were driving from Montgomery when the Klan followed them for more than twenty miles on highway 80. They pulled along side of her and fired a shot striking her a fatal wound to the head; she was killed instantly. Moten played dead and survived the attack with non-lethal injuries. Days after her murder, President Johnson announced on TV that the murderers were arrested. An FBI informant, Gary Rowe was in the car. Why didn't he stop it? Johnson ordered Congress to conduct a thorough investigation on the Klan. The three were found not guilty of her murder. The Federal grand jury found them guilty for violating her civil rights, and they were sentenced to ten years. On July 9, 1965, Congress passed the voting rights act.

Even though they were met with violent act, after violent act, they never waivered from their intended goal of achieving freedom. They sang the song "ain't going to let nobody turn me around" and they continued walking in spite of the threat of death. They were killed for it, they were jailed for it, they were beaten and lynched for it, but they kept on walking and kept on talking until they reached the "Promised Land".

The assassination of Dr Martin Luther King Jr. in Memphis, Tennessee on April 4,1968, at the Lorraine Motel by James Earl Ray, was the most devastating event in the movement. A people already beaten and abused, slandered and murdered, their spirit still strong, would go forth unbroken, still in search of the dream.

The struggle continues

As blacks continued their migration from the south to the rust belt of the northern cities in search of meaningful employment, the oppression was still prevalent. Many found living quarters in the housing projects of those cities. This was a place that had high-rise buildings to house poor people. Places like the Brewster Projects in Detroit, Michigan, or Cabrini Green in Chicago, Illinois. Poor blacks were simply warehoused in a living hell of roach and rat infested, crime ridden, drug dens of death and fear. A gathering of lost and unmotivated tenants, trapped in a whirlwind of poverty, of broken dreams and opportunity denied. They were victims of government assistance and the authorities willingness to look the other way. American citizens lost to the possibility of improving America because of the lack of equal educational opportunity and the never-ending cycle of welfare, or government assistance.

Dr King said, "It was time to live in a nation that is as good as its promise." After four hundred years of toil and strife, black America began to question the authenticity of America's democracy, its devotion to change and its promise to uphold the rights of mankind. When would there be a transformation of American politics and devotion to its moral values. The time was now for America to end the racial divide and bring this country together. There must be a dawning of a new day.

Disease, poverty, drugs, hunger and illiteracy, were killing them now. Blacks were no longer killed by the rope and slavery, beatings and rape at the hands of slave owners and the Klan. Even though their struggle had improved, it was not nearly over. The oppression was redesigned; it had been modernized to fit the times and given the appearance of greater opportunity. The killer now was child neglect, drugs, black on black crime, menial jobs, fatherless homes, low expectations, all depriving a race of people of their right to the true American dream. Black people were lost in a storm of oblivion. They had been raped of their culture, denied their dignity, ravaged and raped of intelligent educational opportunity. They were denied the basic human rights of life, liberty and the pursuit of happiness. Blacks had suffered one hundred years of Jim Crow laws in the south.

Lets take a look at the so-called improvements in American society for black people in today's America.

On August 27, 2008, Barack H. Obama, a black American won the nomination of the Democratic Party for the office of President of the United States of America. On this day, this nation rose up and witnessed a political and human rights metamorphysis. A change that will live forever in the annals of American history. Free from the racism and human degradation of a race of people. Free from the violation of the intent of the Constitution of the United States of America with the mandate and appreciation of the promise that all men, white men, black men, Protestants and Catholic, Jews and Gentiles are created equal.

Weathering the plight of a people that struggled to survive through the hundreds of years of human bundage and slavery, through the abuses of power perpetrated on them by local, state, and the federal government. Remembering the handfull of black students in 1956, trying to enter Little Rock High school under armed military protection ordered by President Dwight Esenhower. Remembering the non-violent marches of Dr. Martin Luther King Jr., or the freedom riders, the lunch counter sit-ins, or the police dogs and water hoses of police chief Bull Connor, or Rosa Park's determination. When Dr. King asked President Johnson for this act. He said, "Make me do it." The Civil Rights Act and the Voting Rights Act by President L.B. Johnson came as a result of the march on the Edmund Pettis Bridge. This was a disgrace and a tragedy on the soul of America, "That made him do it" The Alabama State Troopers on horse back with tear gas and nightsticks exposed an open wound. Public opinion brought pressure on the Johnson administration; he succumbed to the criticism and sent 2,000 Federal troops to protect the marchers on their second attempt to march to Montgomery, some sixty miles away. The whole world witnessed that atrocity and act of aggression on the black people of America. They saw the beating of Congressman to be, John Lewis. In order to right a wrong, an apology was made in 2009 to Lewis by Erwin Wilson the perpetrator and former KKK member. Mr. Wilson immediately began to receive threatening phone calls.

We have been truly blessed to receive a degree of relief, and as a poet once said, we have put out our hands and touched the face of God. As a result of that contact, he blessed us with Barack Obama, "Thank God almighty, we are free at last". Or, are we?

We are no different than any other man. For hundreds of years we struggled for equal rights. We wanted to be recognized as human beings with love for our families, and the fact that we suffer pain and heartaches, disappointment and failure, the same as the white man. We strive for a better life, we search for meaningful employment, we embrace the comfort of religion, and wrap our selves in God's love and grace the same as any other man.

We were not stopped when an assassin succumbed to the notion and the words of a writer who said, "Behold, here commeth the dreamer, let us slay him and see what becomes of his dream". That dream was delayed, but was mostly realized in November 2008. Racism is not dead, but merely suppressed. Joe Louis, possibly the greatest heavyweight fighter of all time once said about this nation during World War II, "We will win, because we're on God's side." That applies to the black race. Only a black man understands what it is like to be black in America. With Obama being an advocate for change, maybe our tomorrows can be better than our yesterdays.

In the words of another writer, "we have miles to go before we sleep." The suffering that blacks must face in America, and learn to live with, has many faces. Crime is a part of their daily reality. Often disregarded and ignored by white America because of citizen apathy. For the black family in America, crime is a deterant to progress, but government is a wall of hinderance when they accept the status quo of the black Americans plight. Blacks are not the only poor people in this great nation. There are far more poor whites than blacks. This is because blacks represent only about thirteen percent of the American population. When those numbers are adjusted for that fact, blacks are the greatest number of poor American residents.

The shameful fact is that poor people get five free meals in school, (once a day, five days per week). While they get twenty-one free meals in jail (three meals a day, seven days a week). Black women are incarcerated at twice the rate of white women. Black unemployment is twice that of whites. Unarmed black men are killed by police at a far greater rate than unarmed white men. The poor are likely the most uneducated and therefore, need more assistance to survive. Many work two jobs in order to survive, and still need food stamps to sustain their families. In the eyes of society, they are failures, even though they work everyday for the minimum wage set by this government. The school systems are poor in black America. Before "Brown vs. The board of education in 1954," black schools in the south-received hand me downs from white schools. When they were through with their books, or athletic equipment, the black schools received the books and equipment; that practice continued until 1976.

Many schools in the south did not provide a quality education for the diminished, the devastated and the downtrodden in white owned and controlled America. Schoolbooks were used and passed down from white schools to black schools, not to mention that some black schools only went to the seventh grade. They were certainly separate, but not nearly equal by any means. Many of the books were damaged with book covers missing, or pages that were written on. Ocassionally, there would be a page missing. This in turn took a page out of the educational book of life in the black community. Thank God for Thurgood Marshall and the Supreme Court Case that he successfully pitched, desegregating schools in America.

The African American race will continue to survive and find ways to prosper in America. The playing field may not be level, but the size of our determination supercedes the playing field and the altered rulebook. We have learned to expect adversity; we know that the rules of the game will change when it's our turn at bat. But the long ball is hit with strength, technical training and personal achievement. We will find the fences in this game and control our destiny. We have lifted many barriers that restricted the boundaries of democracy, but the journey is not as long as it has been, nor as short as it will be. We shall overcome this raping of America.

Part 5

BLACK ACHIEVEMENT IN AMERICA

America is called the greatest nation on earth, the melting pot of society, the land of liberty, the home of the brave. In its five hundred plus year history, 1492 to 2015, this idea has not fully applied to America's black population. America advanced far beyond other nations because of its people. Their burning desires to create, to invent and to climb the heights of successful achievement. To build a free society and to worship at will within that society. She has welcomed almost all comers to her shores. There is a statue called Liberty that stands in New York Harbor, in her raised right hand she holds a tourch that lights the way to freedom. At her base is the words, "Give me your tired, your hungry, your huddled masses longing to breath free," It should have read, unless they are black or Mexican.

This idea did not apply to blacks in any form and even today, many are restricted from entry. The Haitian people have the most difficulty of any people on earth trying to gain entry into this country. They have sailed rickety boats or other floatation devices across treacherous waters trying to find a better way of life. Thousands have died in the attempt. The law says that they must put their feet on the dry land of this country in order to be given a chance to stay.

The Coast Guard inevitably seeks them out and returns them to their homeland.

During the 1980's, The President of this country, Ronald Reagan, opened its borders to the Cubans. There were flotillas from Cuba and there were Americans that went to Cuba by boat and aided them in their quest to leave their homeland for America. They were welcomed with open arms by the American Government.

Immigrants are most likely to be pulled by the attraction of the opportunity to fashion a better life in a new and free land. The Refugee is not pulled in, but is pushed out. If given a choice, he would remain in his homeland. Some writer once said that "political exile is the last step of a process of profound political disaffection".

Sometimes change in a country's doctrine, or its political leaders, will precipitate a need to leave. As with Castro, who proclaimed himself a Marxist-Leninist and said he would die that way. As a result of this, and the United States support for, along with the failure of the Cuban exiles in the "Invasion of the Bay of Pigs", the United States instituted punitive policies against Cuba. They started a trade embargo and cut the sugar quotas. Nevertheless, the Cubans in the flotilla were welcome to this country.

We are going to take a look at black Americans that achieved greatness dispite the handicap of their skin color. How great would Black Americans have been had it not been for slavery and the concerted rape of a race of people by a land filled with white immigrants? Examine the following list of black achievers. The following are a mere pittance of the actual number.

Crispus Attucks (1723-1770) Was one of five men killed in Boston, Massachusetts. It has been said that he was the first to die in the American Revolutionary War and is the only massacre victim whose name is commonly remembered. The early abolitionist movement lauded him as an example of a Black American who played a historic roll in the history of the United States.

In the fall of 1768, British soldiers were sent to Boston to control growing colonial unrest. Town's people hurled rocks and sticks at the soldiers. Some accounts say Attucks attacked the soldiers throwing one to the grown, others say he was merely leaning on a stick when a soldier was struck with a thrown piece of wood. The soldiers opened fire killing five Americans and leaving six mortally wounded. Attucks was said to be the first to die with two bullets in the chest, they later erected a monument to honor him.

Bishop Richard Allen (1760-1831) It could be said that Richard Allen is one of the most formidable people, black or white, born in this nation. Born into slavery he created one of the largest and most prestigious religious denominations in America. The African Methodist Episcopal Church.

Sojourner Truth (1797-1883) During her lifetime she became an abolitionist, a suffragist and a spiritualist. She was the second youngest child born into a family of thirteen children in Ulster County, New York; her birth name was Isabel Baum. She was taken from her parents and sold in 1808 to cruel slave owners. In 1827, she escaped and took refuge with white sympathizers believing that she was a "Pilgrim of God". She believed that she was predetermined to travel and spread the truth. She traveled through many states speaking to thousands of people.

Nat Turner (1800-1831) Revolts by slaves during this period numbered in the hundreds, but there were three that posed critical safety concerns for the white population. All three were betrayed before their plans got off the ground. Only Nat Turner was effective. He and sixty armed men killed fifty-eight whites in forty-eight hours. Some called him a fanatic, he was self educated and believed that slavery was an abomination of the spirit and should be excised from existence. He and his men were cornered and more than one hundred were killed. Sixteen were hanged. Nat Turner's upheaval and unrest was instrumental in shaking the foundation of slavery. He was found guilty and hanged.

Frederick Douglass (1817-1895) was born in Maryland in 1817; his plantation owner was cruel and often beat Douglas. He was later sent to new owners, Hugh and Sophia Auld in Baltimore. Sophia began to teach him how to read. Hugh became angry and stopped it. This motivated Douglass to teach himself. In 1838 he escaped to New York with his future bride Anna Murray. In 1845 he published his autobiography, "The Narrative of the Life of Frederick Douglass". He was a great orator and public speaker.

Douglass backed Lincoln for president and encouraged Blacks to join the Union Army. He served as an adviser to President Lincoln and encouraged him to emancipate the slaves in this country. In 1877, Douglass was appointed to the post of United States Marshal for the District of Columbia.

Harriet Ross Tubman (1823-1913) was born a slave. She lived a life of mistreatment and oppression. She married John Tubman a freed man. After the marriage, fires of freedom burned within her. Her husband refused to escape with her so she left on her own.

For the next ten years she was a conductor on the Underground Railroad. Her trips south to free her fellow slaves totaled 19 and she brought over 300 captives to the north and freedom. They placed a 40,000-dollar reward on her head, but she continued and never lost a slave. She was an active abolitionist and an advocate for women's rights. She died in 1913.

Granville T. Woods (1856-1910) and Elijah McCoy, McCoy developed a system where by trains could operate smoothly. It was an automatic oiler that would provide continuous lubrication. That did nothing to stop the many wrecks that were occurring because of unscheduled trains. There was no way to communicate with each other. Then came the genius of **Granville T. Woods**. In 1887, Woods invented the induction telegraphy system. This allowed each engineer to communicate instantly with other moving trains, creating safety. White's hailed Woods as the best electrical engineer in the world. In 1884, he invented the steam boiler-boiler furnace, he continued in 1888 with a method to supply current to a car from an overhead wire, sending the current down from a small grooved wheel called a "troller". This became the trolley car, and in 1891, he invented the electric railway system. Then came the chicken incubator that could incubate thousands of eggs at one time. Then he invented the "third rail" now used by subway systems around the world. Then he invented an improved telephone transmitter that he sold to Bell Telephone Company.

Elijah McCoy and Woods held fifty patents during the period from 1871 to 1900. African Americans held more than 400 patents. Thomas Edison and Lucius Phelps laid claim, in court, to having invented the induction telegraph even though Woods invention preceded theirs by many years. He spent his money fighting it in court and left no legacy for his children.

Booker T. Washington (1856-1915) was born in 1856 on the Burroughs Tobacco Farms, his mother a slave and his father a white man from a neighboring farm. In 1865, after the Emancipation Proclamation was read to joyful slaves, they moved to Malden, West Virginia to join his stepfather. He worked in a mine and was taken in by a wealthy towns-woman who encouraged his longing to learn. At 16, he walked most of 500 miles back to Virginia to enroll in a new school for black students called Hampton Institute. Later, he was the principle and guiding force behind Tuskegee Institute in Alabama, which he founded in 1881. He became recognized as the Nation's foremost black educator. He is best remembered for helping Black Americans rise up from the economic slavery that held them down long after they were legally free citizens. He died at age 59.

George Washington Carver (1860-1943) was born in Diamond Grove, Missouri. He was an inventor and botanist and was best known as America's great peanut inventor, at a time when inventing was a rarity for African Americans. The son of a slave, he attended Iowa State University earning a BA in 1894, and a Masters in 1896. He joined the faculty of Booker T. Washington's Tuskegee Institute. He created more than 325 products from peanuts. He worked with sweet potatoes, soybeans, pecans, and other crops, and is credited with changing the face of agriculture in the American south. He was also an accomplished artist who displayed paintings at the 1893 Chicago World's Fair.

Bill Pickett (1861-1932) worked for Zack Miller, the owner of the very large 101 Ranch in Oklahoma. Miller said that he was the greatest cowhand that ever lived. Pickett's mother was a Choctaw Indian; his father was a Black man. Pickett invented Bulldogging. While riding horseback, he would chase a steer down and leap from his horse and grab it's horns and twist the steer to the ground. He joined a Wild West show and toured the United States and much of the world even though Black cowboys were not allowed to compete. He died in 1932, after being kicked in the head by a horse that he was training. There is a statue of Bill Pickett in front of the Fort Worth Cowtown Coliseum and in 1971, he was inducted into the Cowboy Hall of Fame in Oklahoma City.

James Weldon Johnson (1871-1938) was born in Jacksonville, Florida in 1871. He received his education in Jacksonville, Atlanta, and Columbia Universities. He studied law and became the first Black admitted to the bar in the state of Florida. In 1900, He wrote the lyrics to "Lift Every Voice and Sing" (The Black National Anthem) with his younger brother providing the music. He died of an automobile accident in Maine in 1938. He was a great poet as well. His poem "The Creation" is a wonderful piece of work.

Mary McLeod Bethune (1876-1955) was born in 1876, into a family of fourteen children. Her father was a sharecropper and raised rice and cotton in Marysville, South Carolina. Mary was an excellent scholar and received a scholarship to Scotia Seminary in Concord, North Carolina. She later received another scholarship to attend Moody Bible Institute in Chicago, Illinois. She was appointed to teach at Haines Normal and Industrial Institute, in Augusta, Georgia. The Founder, Lucy Craft Laney, inspired her to start a school of her own for poor African-American girls. On October 4, 1904, she opened the Daytona Educational and Industrial Training School in Daytona, Florida for girls. The school eventually merged with the all-boys Cookman Institute becoming Bethune-Cookman College.

Garrett A. Morgan (1877-1963) After witnessing a two-car collision on a main intersection where two people were badly injured, he invented the three-color traffic signal, which became the traffic light in use today. In 1912, he and his brother Frank invented the gas mask, a hooded head cover with an inlet opening to allow air to reach the victim. After demonstrating its value in dramatic rescues, orders started to pour in from all over the country, especially from coal mining companies. A newspaper showed the picture of the inventors as being African-American and all orders stopped. He had to hire a white man to pose as the inventor in order to continue sales, cutting into his profits.

Ethel Waters (1896-1977) was an actress, blues singer and a dancer. The song "His Eye Is on the Sparrow" gave her visibility, but her launching of Stormy Weather in the Cotton Club in 1933 gave her notoriety. She made her first recording for Black Swan Records in 1921. Her major hits were "Down Home Blues" and "Oh Daddy".

Paul Robeson (1898-1976) Attended Rutgers University where he was elected to Phi Beta Kappa in his junior year, and valedictorian in his senior year. He earned a law degree from Columbia University. He went to work for a New York law firm where his career was short lived because a white stenographer refused to take dictation from a "Nigger". He left the position and went into the theater. He was also featured in films such as Show Boat, and Shakespear's Othello. He traveled to Russia and identified with the plight of the Russian descendants of Serfs as much as he identified with the plight of his own people. He also became receptive to communist ideology. When he returned to the United States, he was blackballed. The lavish career he enjoyed was gone forever.

Marian Anderson (1900-1993) was considered one of the greatest contralto singers in the history of music. She began singing in church and joined the Philadelphia Choral Society and sang at many churches. In order to become an acclaimed opera singer, she decided to study abroad. She traveled back and forth between Europe and the United States. She gained critical acclaim from a concert in Berlin and gave a renowned performance at the Metropolitan Opera

House in New York in 1955. White's refused to allow her to sing at Constitution Hall in 1939, so she was forced to perform in front of the Lincoln Memorial. As time passed, Anderson's farewell tour began at Constitution Hall and ended with a concert at Carnegie Hall on Easter Sunday, 1965.

Adam Clayton Powell, Jr (1908-1972) was born into a middle-class family that afforded him a life with the ability to develop his intellect. He studied at both Colgate and Columbia Universities, leaving with an M.A. in religious studies. Five years later, his father handed over the pulpit of Abyssinian Baptist Church. He was a great orator and his preaching inspired his congregation. He mixed religion and politics and encouraged his followers to protest up and down the streets of Harlem. In 1941, he ran for New York City Council. He won the election and became the first African American to do so.

In 1944, he became the first black congressman from the Eastern seaboard since the days of reconstruction. He fought for school integration and an anti-lynching bill, he was an advocate for civil rights and the war against poverty. He opened many doors for blacks while serving in congress

In 1967, irate congressmen leveled a trumped-up charge of misuse of funds against him stripping him of his seniority and power and refusing to seat him. The Supreme Court not only vindicated Powell of those charges, but charged racism as the cause of the charges, but a white media had damaged his reputation. He regained his seat in 1969

Thurgood Marshall (1908-1993) was born in Baltimore, Maryland. His father was a Pullman Porter and his mother was a schoolteacher. He attended both Lincoln and Howard Universities law schools and graduated from both. Most of his clients were poor people and he became known as "The Little Man's Lawyer." He was the first African American to serve on the Supreme Court of the United States. He was a lawyer that was best remembered for his high success rate in arguing before the Supreme Court, and for his victory in "Brown vs. The Board of Education."

President Lyndon B. Johnson nominated him to the Supreme Court in 1967. His father instilled in him an appreciation for the Constitution of the United States and the rule of law. When he attempted to apply to the University of Maryland law school, the Dean told him he would not be accepted because of the schools segregation policy. Later, as a civil rights litigator, he successfully sued the school for this policy in the case of "Murray vs. Pearson".

He sought admission and was accepted at Howard University School of Law. He set-up his own law business and began working for the NAACP (The National Association for the Advancement of Colored People) in Baltimore. He served on the Supreme Court for 25 years; he died of heart failure at the age of 84.

Benjamin Oliver Davis Jr. (1912-2002) was born in Washington, D. C. His father, Benjamin O. Davis Sr., was the first black man to be promoted to the rank of brigadier general in the United States Army. In 1936, he became the first black man to graduate from the United States Military Academy in nearly fifty years. He faced total rejection from his peers at the academy. No cadet spoke to him, nor did his roommate. He ate his meals alone and had no friends for the intire four years of his tenure at the academy. Even though the odds were stacked against him, he graduated thirty-fifth in his class of two hundred seventy-six cadets.

He applied for and was turned down for pilots training due to a racist rule that no black officers were allowed in the United States Air Corps. He was assigned to Fort Benning, Georgia, commanding a black service company. In 1940, blacks fought their way into the segregated air corps. He was sent to Tuskegee for pilot training. The 99th squadron became an active training unit and Captain Davis graduated in the first class of pilots on March 7, 1942. In 1943, Davis led the 99th to fly its first mission. While fighting racism, they left a great legacy of competence and excellence not matched by any other group of pilots in history.

In 1949, President Harry Truman officially integrated the military and Davis attended the Air War College in Montgomery, Alabama. In 1950, he was promoted to chief of the Air Defense Branch of Air Force Operations.

In 1959, he became the first black officer to be promoted to major general. In 1965, he was promoted to lieutenant general and became Air Force Chief of Staff in South Korea. In 1970, he retired and served as an assistant secretary of the Department of Transportation from 1971 to 1975

Jesse Owens (1913-1980) was born in Oakville, Alabama. He was seven of eleven children born to sharecroppers. His family later moved to Cleveland, Ohio. Jesse almost died from recurring pneumonia; his mother nursed him back to health. Jesse was very thin and frail; Charles Riley, his athletic coach in junior high school, encouraged him to run to build up his strength. Jesse was working so he could not run after school. The coach asked him to come to school an hour early so that he could run before the start of the school day. The coach brought him breakfast to help him build up his frail body.

Jesse ran track in high school, and was elected student council president. Jesse married his wife Minnie Ruth Solomon. Jesse's great athletic ability allowed him to score more than half of his teams points, so they began calling him a "one man team". He received many scholarship offers; in the beginning, he turned them down because he believed that he should not live better than family. He attended Ohio State University where on May 25, 1935, in the big ten championships, he broke five world records and tied a sixth in a forty-five minute period. He tied the record for the 100-yard dash with a time of 9.4 seconds. He surpassed the long jump record by 8 1/4 inches, he beat the 220-yard dash record by 4-tenths of a second while simultaneously breaking the 200 meters record. He ran the 220-yard low hurdles in 22.6 seconds breaking the record for the shorter 200 meters simultaneously.

During the 1936 Olympics in Germany, he won the 100-meters in 10.3 seconds, the long jump by leaping 26 feet 5 inches, and the 200-meter dash in 20.7 seconds, and leading the 4 x 100 meter relay team that broke the world record in 39.8 seconds. This made him the first person ever to win four gold medals in the Olympics. Hitler was in the stands watching the Olympic games and was furious to see a black man destroy his so-called white superior race of athletes.

In 1955, President Eisenhower named him the "Ambassador of Sports" and he toured around the world for the State Department. He retired in 1971.

Joseph Louis Barrow (1914-1981) was born in Chambers County, Alabama. His family moved to Detroit, Michigan in 1926 after the death of his father. Joe's educational level was poor because of the educational system for blacks in the south. He was set back one grade and as a result of this, Joe lost any desire to attend. During the depression he started to box as a way to earn money. Louis's amateur career was successful, so Joe moved up to the heavyweight division. Trying to get a shot at the title proved to be very difficult. No black fighter since Jack Johnson was the heavyweight champion, nor was permitted to fight for the title. To inhance his problems, Louis had an entirely black entourage and management cadre. Mike Jacobs, a white fight promoter began a partnership with Louis's mangers to set the stage. Louis promised to not follow in the big show off footsteps of Jack Johnson and he was ready to fight.

Louis won his first fight on July 4th, 1934. Then defeated a huge former champion, Primo Carnera in 1935. From this huge defeat, Joe earned the nickname, "The Brown Bomber." In 1936, he lost to the German Max Schmeling in the 12th round. The loss set up a rematch that had racial and political overtones. Adolph Hitler's war machine was taking over Europe, and Nazism was becoming a threat to America and the rest of the world. Schmeling represented Nazism and Louis was the symbol of democracy and black pride. Louis knocked out Schmeling in the first round with such force Schmeling was hospitalized. In 1937, Louis became champion.

Louis went on to defend his title twenty-five times. The next 8 champions to follow him did not accomplish this feat. He held the title for 11 years, eight months, and seven days. Longer than anyone else in boxing. His record was 63 wins and 3 losses with 49 knockouts.

He was hounded by the United States government for back taxes. He gave a lot to this country. He even donated an entire fight purse to this government during its war effort in World War II. He was old and broke and was driven into degrading undertakings for a man of such stature. Frank Sinatra aided him when he was down and out. He died in 1981 of a heart attack

John H. Johnson (1918-2005) rose from humble beginnings to fame and fortune by servicing the African-American community with news about Black life, achievement and entertainment.

He was born in Arkansas City, Arkansas. A town where there were no public high school for African-Americans. His mother moved the family to Chicago in 1933 during the great African-American migration for better opportunities following the accidental death of his father. Johnson went to work for Supreme Liberty Life Insurance firm. One of his duties was to collect news and information about African-Americans and prepare a weekly digest for pace. He believed that a Negro newspaper could be sold and marketed. In 1942, Johnson made a loan and published the first issue of Negro Digest, a magazine patterned after Readers's digest. It featured articles about the social inequalities in the United States and gave a voice to the concerns of African-Americans. Within a few months the circulation reached 50,000 a month in sales.

In 1945, Johnson went on to launch his second publication, Ebony that focused on the diverse achievements and successes of African-Americans. Six years later he created Jet, a pocket sized weekly publication that highlighted news of African-Americans in the social limelight, political arena, entertainment, business and the sports world. He went on to add new magazine ventures, book publishing, Fashion Fair cosmetics, several radio stations and majority ownership in Supreme Liberty Life Insurance. By 1990, Johnson's personal wealth was estimated at $150 million.

Katherine G. Johnson (1918-) At the beginning of the space age there was a black woman helping to steer the coarse. She joined NASA's Langley Research Center in Hampton, Virginia, in 1953. Dr. Johnson is considered one of the early pioneers in the space movement. Dr. Johnson graduated summa cum laude in 1937 from West Virginia State College. She began her career as a high school teacher in Virginia. Her job at the Langley Research Center was that of a pool mathematician. She was transferred to the NASA flight research program where she made significant contributions to the growth and development of the space program.

Her work consisted of complex algebraic equations and calculating interplanetary trajectories. Lives hung in the balance of her accuracy. As a member of NASA's historic 1961 team, Dr Johnson's calculations placed Alan Shepard, America's first astronaut in space, right on target. Subsequently, she charted the course for astronauts John Glenn in 1962 and Neil Armstrong's first moonwalk in 1969.

She is credited with developing the first emergency navigation systems where she mapped exactly what stars the astronauts should see at specific points in their missions. Her work continued with developing techniques for locating underground minerals for the Earth Resources Satellite Program. For the Apollo missions, she analyzed data gathered from tracking stations around the world and developed better navigational procedures.

She received the Group Achievment Award, NASA's Lunar Spacecraft and Operations Division, and other NASA Awards conferred in 1970, 1980, and 1985.

Erwin Lawrence (1919-1944) was a captain and commander of the 99th Fighter Squadron. He died a hero's death as he attacked a German airfield. He was one of sixty-six Tuskegee Airmen to give their last full measure of devotion to their race and country. He was one of 300 Black GI's who graduated from the fighter Pilots training at Tuskegee Army Airbase in Tuskegee, Alabama, forming what became known as the Tuskegee Airmen.

Captain Lawrence and his fellow pilots shipped out to Italy in April 1943, with no combat experience and began the most impressive air battle record of any group in history. Their mission was to escort allied bombers through treacherous European airspace, preventing

German fighters from attacking the Allied bombers in hair-raising dogfights. The Tuskegee airmen gave protection all the way into the bombing territory instead of staying back out of flak range as the white fighter pilots did. The other bomber pilots began to reject the white fighter pilots and request the black pilots to escort them on their bombing runs.

By the end of the war, the black pilots had destroyed more than 950 vehicles on the ground and 400 enemy aircraft. They set a record by having 13 kills in one day. They also sunk a German destroyer. They achieved greatness even though they were vilified, and called derogatory names by some whites and not spoken to by others.

The fact that they were in a totally segregated unit made them targets of discrimination for supplies, guns and planes. They received the oldest and most broken down equipment. They were only accepted as shepherds and not as fellow human beings. They accomplished a record unmatched by any other group in aviation history.

Jackie Robinson (1919-1972) His mother moved from the Deep South to Los Angeles with her four kids. They were the first black family in the neighborhood. They became victims of many racial incidents, including a cross burning.

Jackie had a love for sports and participated in four different sports with great skills. While attending U.C.L.A., Jackie left to join the army in 1944. During that year, he was court martialed for refusing to sit in the army transports colored section. He won the court marshall and received an honorable discharge.

Before the forties ended, Branch Rickie would take a chance on Jackie and sign him to a Brooklyn Dodger baseball contract. Jackie had the right temperment to withstand the racial incidents that would come his way from his white teammates and the fans. As expected, the first black man to play major league baseball in modern times would need a great deal of discipline. He would have to exercise a tremendous amount of personal restraint to remain on the roster. Jackie was up to that task.

He won the Sporting News Rookie of the Year Award and led the Dodgers to a league pennant. He earned "The Most Valuable Player Award" in 1949. Six years later the Dodgers won a World Series Championship. He retired from baseball in 1956 and was inducted twenty-five years later into the Baseball Hall of Fame.

James Baldwin (1924-1987) James Baldwin was born in New York City. He was raised in the black district of Harlem. He became a novelist, essayist and playwright. He wrote about racial injustices in the

United States, and explored the personal lives of African-Americans in the mid-twentieth century. He became a major interpreter of the struggles of American Blacks. Baldwin felt that he had to leave the United States and its institutional racism in order to develop his talents, he moved to Paris, France, where he spent most of his life. He was made commander of the Legion of Honor, France's highest civilian award.

Baldwin's first novel, Go Tell it on the Mountain (1953), largely autobiographical, detailed his early childhood, religious encounters and his family's life in the south. His essays, Notes of a Native Son (1956), described the lives of African-Americans. Baldwin's writings became more militant and were directed at the mistreatment of blacks at the height of the civil rights struggle. These novels established Balwin as a major literary voice. He was a major supporter of the civil rights movement with Dr. Martin Luther King Jr., Medgar Evers, and others. He supported it with his money, presence and literary works. He never forgot where he came from and did all he could to reduce the hatred of Whites towards his people. His works were numerous.

Malcolm X (1925-1965) He was born Malcolm Little in Omaha, Nebraska on May 19, 1925. His father was brutally murdered by the Ku Klux Klan when Malcolm was a boy. He moved to Boston, Massachusetts when he was sixteen, the east coast area fascinated him. Before his twenty-first birthday, he was convicted of burglary and sentenced to six years in the state prison at Charlestown, Massachusetts.

While in prison, Malcolm became an avid reader and read every book he could get his hands on, he even read the dictionary from cover to cover. This newfound knowledge changed his life, but his most important lesson was discovering the Nation of Islam. Elijah Muhammad was impressed with him and appointed him to assistant minister of the Detroit Mosque. Malcolm was later dispatched to Philadelphia. In 1956, Malcolm was appointed minister of New York's Mosque, the largest in the country. His words cut deep into ones soul and he commanded attention whenever he preached. He demanded justice for his people "by any means necessary." By 1963, Minister Malcolm's demand for black dignity could be heard around the world. After making Hajj in 1964, he traveled to Africa and established ties with black leaders across the continent. When he returned to America, he abandoned the Nation of Islam and formed the Organization of African Unity. He embraced Pan-Africanism in the tradition of Marcus Garvey and Dubois. He also made many enemies. By the end of 1964, his home was firebombed and he was receiving death threats daily. He told his biographer, Alex Haley, he didn't expect to live to see his book in print. Malcolm X was assassinated on February 21, 1965 as he prepared to address an audience at the Audobon Ballroom. His wife and their four daughters were seated in the front row.

Martin Luther King Jr. (1929-1968) Martin Luther King Jr. was born in Atlanta, Georgia on January 15, 1929. His mother Alberta Williams king was a schoolteacher. His father was pastor of Ebenezer Baptist Church.

King was an extremely bright student and entered Morehouse College at age fifteen, graduating in 1948. He then entered Crozer Theological Seminary in Chester, Pennsylvania, and was chosen valedictorian of his class in 1951. He received his Ph.D. from Boston University.

In December 1955, a black woman name Rosa Parks decided that she was not going to stand up or go to the back of the bus so that a white man could sit down. She was arrested for violating a city ordinance. The black community was going to fight. Dr King Jr. was chosen to head the Montgomery Improvement Association in Montgomery, Alabama. Dr King mobilized the black community into a non-violent 382-day boycott of the bus lines. White businesses suffered as well. Dr. King overcame continual arrest, brutal physical abuse, and even the bombing of his home. The U.S. Supreme Court declared the bus segregation laws unconstitutional, and blacks were then able to ride the buses on equal footing.

King became a national hero; he organized the Southern Christian Leadership Conference in 1957. Its purpose was to assist other communities in protest campaigns and in voter registration.

Dr. King led a successful campaign in 1963 in Birmingham, Alabama, for fair hiring practices in that city. The brutalities suffered by the people were most severe. Facing Police Chief Bull Conner with his vicious dogs and his water hoses. 1963 was the year of Dr. king's historic march on Washington with King as the keynote speaker. It was there that he delivered his "I Have a Dream" speech. A speech that is consider as the most eloquent ever delivered in this country. The following year he received the coveted Nobel Peace Prize.

1964 was also the year of the Selma-to-Montgomery Freedom March for voter registration. This was the crossing of the infamous Edmond Pettis Bridge. President Lyndon B. Johnson Signed the Civil Rights Act into law in the same year. It was the struggles of Dr. king and his followers that precipitated that action. In 1965, President Johnson followed by signing the Voting Rights Act into law.

Dr. King then took his crusade to the northern states and into the rift-making, controversial field of the Vietnam War. He even declared that the United States was "...the greatest purveyor of violence in the world." His aim was to build a coalition between the growing peace movement and the civil rights crusade.

Then King reached into the War on Poverty to aid the poor of this nation, which took him to Memphis, Tennessee. On April 4, 1968, while standing on the balcony of the Loraine Motel in Memphis, an assassin named James Earl Ray fired a bullet and took the life of Dr. Martin Luther King, Jr.

Lorraine Hansberry (1930-1965) Came from a family that valued education highly. Her grandfather was a professor at Alcorn A & M College in Mississippi and her uncle, William Leo Hansberry, developed the first African studies curriculum at Howard University in 1923. She attended Chicago's Art Institute, the University of Wisconsin and completed her studies in Guadalajara, Mexico.

While in New York's Greenwich Village, she was disenchanted with what she called "a whole body of material about Negro's cardboard characters." She resolved to write plays that were sensitive and responsive for African-Americans. She wrote her first play, A Raisin In The Sun, to dramitize the rights of all Americans to have an equal opportunity for decent housing. A Raisin In The Sun opened on Broadway in March 1959, and was a resounding success. Hansberry became the first African-American, and the youngest American, to receive the New York Drama Critics Circle Award for the 1958-1959 seasons. A Raisin In The Sun became the first play by an African-American writer to be produced on Broadway in twenty-five years. It was made into a movie, which signaled a wider interest in stories with relevant themes for African-Americans.

Lorraine Hansberry died of cancer at age thirty-four after having written only three plays, A Raisin In The Sun, The Sign In Sydney Brusteins Window, that opened to mixed reviews and Les Blanc, which unfolded the theme of Africans battling the effects of colonialism. She never lived to see this play open.

Colin L. Powell (1937-) is a retired U.S. Army General and former Chairman of the Joint Chiefs of Staff appointed by President George H. W. Bush. At age 52, he became the highest ranking military officer with the Department of Defense. He served two tours of duty in

Vietnam and had a prominent roll in the military operation, Desert Storm, during the 1991 Persian Gulf War fought in Iraq.

He was born in New York City and is the son of Jamaican immigrant parents. General Powell attended City College of New York and achieved an MBA degree from George Washington University. While attending CCNY, he joined the ROTC and in 1958, graduated with a rank of Second Lieutenant. While in the military; he received many awards including the Distinguished Service Medal, the Purple Heart and the Legion of Merit award. As a civilian, Colin Powell has received two Presidential Medals of Freedom, the President's Citizens Medal and the Congressional Gold Medal. He is also the recipient of honors from many foreign countries including Canada, France, Germany, Senegal, Greece, and Jamaica. He received an honorary Knight Commamder of the Bath, conferred by H.M. Queen Elizabeth II.

He continues to serve his country in many capacities. Colin Powell's book, My American Journey, chronicles his rise to the highest ranks in government from life in the roughest sections of New York City.

George R. Caruthers (1939-) When the peoples of this world view the sharp pictures of the Planetary system and their features, we are not aware that the pictures were taken by a camera and supporting devices created by an African-American, Dr. George Carruthers. Since 1982, he has held the enviable position of Senior Astrophysicist Head, Ultraviolet Measurements Group of the U.S. Naval Research Laboratory.

Carruthers father was a civil engineer; his involvement in that arena stimulated his thoughts in the scientific field. After finishing near the top of his high school class, he went on to attend the University of Illinois where he received his Bachelor's Degree in Aeronautical Engineering and his Master's Degree in Nuclear Engineering a year later. Two years after that, he was awarded a Ph. D. in Aeronautical and Astronautical Engineering with minors in Physics and Astronomy. His principal areas of study in his graduate work were high temperature gas dynamics and the recombination of atomic nitrogen.

Dr. Carruthers began his career at the Naval Research Laboratory in 1964. The Laboratory was seeking someone with post-doctoral aeronautical and astronautically engineering experience. Because there are so few people in the world that have reached that level, color was of small consequence and he was accepted. His experience has been in far-ultraviolet astronomy and optical geophysics. He has engaged in studies performed from rockets Apollo-16, Skylab, the Space Shuttles, and unmanned satellites. He has also developed electronic imaging devices. Among scientific results obtained from rocket experiments was the first detection of interstellar molecular hydrogen in 1970.

Dr. Carruthers was principal investigator for the Far Ultraviolet Cameras experiment launched on space studies mission 1991. He is principal investigator for the Far UV Imaging Spectrograph flown on the shuttle (1995) as the USAF/National Aeronautics and Space Administration (NASA) payload. He is the principal investigator for the Global Imaging Monitor of the Ionosphere planned for flight on an unmanned satellite (ARGOS), in 1998. He holds memberships in many organizations and has received many awards.

Muhammad Ali (1942-) was born Cassius Marcellius Clay in Louisville, Kentucky. His bicycle was stolen while he attended a show at the Columbia gym. While reporting the theft, he noticed the boxers working out in the gym. As he watched and listened, he began to think that if he learned to box, he could beat-up the thief for stealing his bike.

His parents gave him permission to follow through with his newfound interest. Ali was determined and worked very hard to advance his skills. In his first fight, he won with a split decision. In 1959 and 1960, he was a golden gloves winner, and in 1960, he became a member of the United States Olympic Team and won a gold medal in the light heavyweight division.

He was befriended by Malcolm X and in 1964, following his shocking defeat of Sonny Listen for the heavyweight championship of the world; he announced to the world that he was a member of the Nation of Islam and that his name was no longer Cassius Clay, but Muhammad Ali.

In 1966, Ali made it clear that he had nothing against the Vietnamese people; he didn't believe in the war and spoke his mind. In 1967 after being previously classified by the United States Military as 4-F, meaning that he was not qualified for military service, the government changed his status to 1-A, now he was qualified. Ali refused to retract his statements about the war in Vietnam and went on to sign a contract with Herbert Muhammad as his boxing manager. He was notified to report to the draft board for induction into the military services of this country. Ali reported as instructed but refused to take the one step forward that is customary and stood his ground based on his religious and moral beliefs. He was stripped of his title and refused a license to fight in this country. His passport was confiscated so that he could not leave the country. Ali received a five-year sentence for refusing induction into the armed forces of the United States of America. In 1970, the United States Supreme Court overturned his conviction and Ali returned to the ring still speaking his mind.

Possibly the greatest fights in the history of boxing was the trilogy with Joe Frazier. Ali winning two out of the three. He regained the heavyweight crown by defeating George Foreman in a fight held in Africa called "The Rumble in the Jungle."

His greatest fights were waged in the public arena as he fought for the rights of oppressed people here and around the world. He gave us a since of pride and strength that gave us hope and a belief that we could be anything that we wanted to be. He is truly "The Greatest of all Time."

Carol Moseley-Braun (1947-) Is a native of Chicago, IL and the daughter of a police officer. In defiance of the segregation laws or practices of her day, she refused to drink from a water fountain marked "colored only" at the age of nine. She defied the Jim Crow laws and practices and would go to white only restaurants, refusing to leave until she was served in the same manner as the white patrons.

She attended the University of Illinois and studied law at the University of Chicago. She received the U.S. Attorney General's Special Achievement Award for her outstanding work in her first position as a U.S. prosecutor. She was the first African-American to hold an executive office as Recorder of Deeds for the Cook County Government. She became the first woman and African-American assistant majority leader while serving as an Illinois State Representative. History was in the making.

In 1992, she defeated Republican Richard Williamson, to become the first African-American woman elected to the United States Senate. Only three other African-Americans had ever become United States Senators. She was the first woman to be appointed to the Finance Committee and held membership on the Housing and Urban Affairs, the Judiciary, the Export Expansion and Agricultural Development, and the Small Business Committees.

Senator Moseley-Braun co-sponsored the Community Development Financial Institutions Act, which facilitates access to capital for neglected neighborhoods. She also sponsored legislation which authorized the National Park Service to commemorate thirty-eight historic sites along the Illinois Underground Railroad. During the signing of the bill, Senator Moseley-Braun stated, "The Underground Railroad bridged the divides of race, religion, sectional differences, and nationality. It also spanned state lines and international borders and joined the American ideals of liberty and freedom expressed in the Declaration of Independence and the Constitution, to the extraordinary actions of ordinary men and women working in common purpose to free a people."

Benjamin S. Carson (1951-) Dr. Benjamin Carson made history and worldwide news when he guided a team of seventy surgeons and successfully separated the Binder twins who were joined at the back of the head. This feat made history because prior to this attempt, brain surgeons formerly believed that the separation of conjoined twins could not be done. Following the success of the seperation, Dr. Carson has achieved fame for operating on brain disorders that are considered untreatable.

Dr. Carson delved into the realm of the impossible when he revived a procedure called the "Carson Twist." This procedure had been abandon because of the percentage of deaths related to it. It is called "hemispherectomy." Since the re-institution of this procedure, he has performed twenty hemispherectomies, nineteen survived and eighteen are practically seizure free.

Carson discovered his love of science while being punished by his mother for poor grades in school. He and his brother were forced to read two library books per week and submit book reports. Their grades began to soar. He won a scholarship to Yale, and the university of Michigan Medical School. He then served a residency at Baltimore's Johns Hopkins Hospital, the first black to do so. At age thirty-three he was named director of pediatric neurosurgery at Johns Hopkins, he was the youngest in the country.

Dr. Carson grew up the hard way, on the poorest streets of Boston and Detroit in a fatherless home while over coming a terrible temper. He developed one of the greatest medical minds in the history of health care.

Mae Jemison (1956-) Mae Jemison is a native of Decatur Alabama. The family relocated to Chicago, IL. seeking better educational opportunities and a better life. While still a very small child, she became interested in anthropology and archaeology. In school, she would spend hours in the library studying extinct animals and the theory of evolution, science fiction, and astronomy. In high school, much of her studies was in biology, physics and chemistry. Mae was a consistant honor student and upon graduation, she entered Stanford University on a National Achievment Scholarship and earned a degree in chemical engineering. She earned a second bachelors degree in Afro-American studies.

After graduating from Standford, Mae entered Cornell University's medical school. She graduated in 1981 and completed her internship at Los Angeles County Medical Center. From 1983 to 1985, she was the area Peace Corps medical officer for Sierra Leone and Liberia in West Africa.

In 1987, she joined NASA's program. She was one of fifteen candidates chosen from a pool of approximately two thousand qualified applicants. She became a mission specialist. In 1992, she was assigned to experiment with new compounds and metals as well as study the effects of gravity on the human body.

In 1988, Mae Jemison received the Essence Science and Technology Award. In 1989, she became Gamma Sigma Gamma's Woman of the year. Mae Jemison was the first African-American woman astronaut. She is also a member of the American Medical Association, the American Chemical Society, and an honorary member of the Alpha Kappa Alpha Sorority.

In 2005, there were 104 astronauts, eighteen of whom were women, five were African-American women. Mae Jemison was the first African-American woman astronaut to travel in outer space. Great pride is instilled in her people by her accomplishments

There were many African-Americans in our history that achieved greatness. The ones listed above are just a few of many. The people of African decent around the globe seem to suffer the greatest amount of pain of any people on earth. As I reflect on the tragedy that unfolded in the Island nation of Haiti, it is evident that tragedy of one kind or another seeks us out. The earthquake of 2010, that flattened the country of Haiti, and killed two hundred thousand of its people was devastating. The look in the eyes of the children, the fear on their faces, and the reality that they will never adjust to their plight, was heartbreaking. The sights seen through the media will profoundly change you. America, the pillow of world society, reaching out to rescue brothers and sisters and children in trouble; Americans of all colors and faiths yielding to the cries of distress and tragedy.

These are some of the reasons why it seems as though black people always suffer the greatest amount of pain of any people on earth. When you look back; what do you see? Four hundred years of slavery that will never be surpassed. Aparthied in South Africa.

Ethnic cleansing and murder in Rowanda. Starvation and murder in the Sudan. The Tsunami of 2005 killed thousands of people of color. Hurricane Katrina in the ninth ward of New Orleans in 2006 did the same. Haiti was hit by back-to-back hurricanes in 2009 and then the great hurricane that devastated the country.

We have always suffered the greatest tragedies, felt the greatest pain, suffered the most oppression, lifted the heaviest weight, and endured the greatest poverty.

God blessed the black people of America with Dr. Martin Luther King Jr. He became the final liberator of minorities in America. He launched a non-violent movement that would change a nation. Dr. King Jr. was a special personality. He said that it was time to live in a nation that was as good as it's promise. He was a man chosen by God to deliver black people, poor people, and other minorities from the terrible dredges of racism and segregation. They had been raped of their culture, denied their dignity, ravaged and raped of equal educational opportunity and the basic human rights of life, liberty, and the pursuit of happiness.

We had a desperate need for a leader that could withstand abuses both physical and mental. A man that could fold his arms and do it non-violently. Had he used violent tactics, the streets of this country would have run red with blood, and world opinion would have been against us. So he followed the example of Mahatma Ghandi. The magical thing is that he was able to convince hundreds of thousands of Black Americans to follow his non-violent philosophy.

He was our leader; he was our bridge over troubled waters, he was an unyielding, unwavering, undeniable dedicated force for the emancipation of the poor and down trodden. He was our umbrella in stormy weather. He was a victor not a victim in his quest for the prize of freedom. He kept his eyes on the prize.

Whether he was in the mist of violent racist, or hostile police officers, or in the glory of God's embrace, he was a dedicated ambassador who withstood beatings, jail, a stabbing, and continuous racial slurs. He watched his people being murdered, their homes and churches being burned, but he kept singing the song "Ain't gonna let nobody turn me around, I'm gonna keep on walking, keep on talking, headed for the promised land".

With the assassination of Dr. King Jr., one of the greatest men this country has ever known was wiped from the face of the earth. His memory, his work, and his impact on the soul of a nation will live forever, while Black Americans reap the rewards of respectful citizenship. Our gratitude goes out to Dr. King, he gave a feeling of pride to a people that suffered and endured so much, yet, never gave up on America.

One of my personal moments of great pride was the moment in the 1996 Olympic games when Muhammad Ali lit the Olympic torch to begin the games. My pride as an American and my love for this great athlete, who had the guts and fortitude to take on the United States government by refusing induction into the United States Armed Forces, and won, was a moment in time that will live forever in my memory. My heart was with him when he walked out onto the platform that night, there was a slight smile on his face, pride in his eyes, and gratification in his demeanor. As he accepted the torch from the Olympic runner, his hand shook uncontrollably, his body trembled from the shaking, his soul was exposed and the pride came shinning through for the world to see. I silently prayed as he shuffled to the ignition sight. I prayed that he would be able to complete this mission without assistance, he did. I looked on intently with great pride and respect; I could feel his pride and emotions as tears welled up in my eyes. That was one of the greatest moments of all time for me, a moment of reflection back to the early 1960's when he discarded the slave name, Cassius Clay, and faced the wrath and hate of white America. An Olympic Gold Metal winner himself, who threw his metal into the river at Louisville, Kentucky in protest of the way his people were treated. An act that inflamed political passion as white America turned their backs on him, and some black Americans were confused with his motives. We cheered when he won the Olympic Gold Metal; we were disheartened when he discarded it. This was a moment of camaraderie, because the whole world loves Ali. This was a moment of citizenship recognized and accepted by the greatest fighter of all times. America had finally found commonality in the differences that separated them and Muhammad Ali, the great Ambassador for America lit the torch for his country, and my heart went out to him. On that night, the raping of America got a reprieve, and the African American community yielded to the man who brought pride to our country and gained respect from the people that he represented. White America offered a salute to a great American that galvanized his place in history. The raping of America became minuscule in this great and memorable moment.

Part 6

THE INDUSTRIALIZATION OF AMERICA

The American Industrial Revolution began as soon as the Pilgrims boarded ships for the new world. Among the passengers were men of current day skills. As noted before, there were carpenters, blacksmiths, furniture makers, and others, with more advanced skills to follow in their footsteps. There were also criminals. Some men were forced to board ship as a way to rid the country of undesirables.

As the colonies began to grow and expand, the need for woodwork, housing, ironworks, cabinetry, and many other necessities began to surface. This need created an atmosphere that would expand into a great American Industrial might that would eventually become the envy of the world.

This revolution began in small towns and villages scattered throughout young America. Cotton was a big growth industry for farmers, therefore, many cotton mills and textile manufacturing facilities sprung up everywhere. There were mills to grind corn and wheat into meal and flour for consumers. Many were near water so that the force of the water would turn the wheel that ground the grain. The mill would have one man to service its operation. He was called the wright of the mill. He was a jack of all trades and performed many functions. As the industry developed, and more modern methods were used, he became a millwright and a skilled tradesman.

The growth of technology and the development of its advances, in terms of labor, economics, trade, procurement, and product growth, were attributable to the small farms and business entities of early Americans. The farmers had a great need for products made from iron. They needed plough shares, wagon wheels, horseshoes, and many other products that were supplied by the blacksmith. The blacksmith was able to forge wrought iron products such as weathervanes, nails, hinges, weapons, and many other needed materials.

Cotton, the Agricultural Giant

The farmers along the Eastern Seaboard realized that cotton was a growth product that could fuel an economic explosion. With the use of slave labor to grow and harvest this white gold, they were faced with the difficulty of providing a clean product for market. The cotton would have to be free of seeds in order to be marketable and profitable. The European countries would import unlimited amounts for their textile mills. The removal of the seeds was so labor intensive, that cotton couldn't gain a foothold as a marketable product with great economic returns from foreign export.

Hundreds of field slaves would move into a cotton field with long sacks on their backs. There they picked cotton from sun-up to sundown in steaming hot fields in waist high cotton. Where the cotton bowls and leaves would cut their fingers leaving them swollen and raw, while their backs ached with pain from the long hours of continuous bending. The women were old and broken before their time. They were hardened and calloused, over weight from their diets, broken in body, in spirit, and dreams.

Eli Whitney was an inventor that saw the need for a method of removing the seeds from cotton that was less labor intensive. He invented the cotton gin, a simple mechanized method of removing the seeds and reducing the need for high labor intensity. The cotton gin made short staple cotton into a profitable crop. Prior to this invention, the seeds were removed by hand, making it nearly impossible to make cotton a profitable business enterprise. It took many slaves hours of work to remove seeds from a small amount of cotton. Whitney received a patent on his cotton gin on March 14, 1794.

Cotton became an agricultural product that was expected to supply the European Nations. Profits soared with the ability to export clean cotton to new markets. Cotton production grew to millions of tons of production by the 20th century. During the 20th century, the cotton picker was invented and reduced the labor-intensive method of picking by hand to a mechanized operation eliminating the need for people power. Cotton would be called "King Cotton."

With these new methods of harvesting cotton, textile mills began to spring up throughout the south. With these mills, the owners were able to produce fabrics, cloth, yarn, rope, and clothing, filling a need here that had been greatly filled by European countries.

The Textile Industry in America

Samuel Slater has been called both the "Father of American Industry" and the founder of the "American Industrial Revolution." Slater was a businessman and an inventor with ideas and a plan to develop them. Anyone could see that the textile industry was going to provide huge profits in the American economy. Slater was a British citizen with skills in textile development, and wanted to lend his skills to this endeavor.

Ben Franklin and the Pennsylvania Society for the Encouragement of Manufacturers and Useful Arts, decided it would be beneficial to those with skills in the field of textile to apply their skills in the development of this growing enterprise. It would be highly profitable for anyone having those skills, and is willing to apply them to improving textile production in America; the rewards would be unlimited.

Samuel Slater of England, decided to migrate to America and take advantage of this offer. This would be a great opportunity to fulfill two desires, coming to America, and to apply a needed skill. Slater was employed in the textile mills of Britain and had considerable knowledge of the business. British law prohibited this kind of immigration. Britain had many textile mills and needed every skillful expert available. Slater arrived on American shores in New York City in 1789, in defiance of British law. He sought employment in the city of Pawtucket offering his services as a textile expert. He was given the opportunity to demonstrate his abilities by running the spindles that were recently purchased by the business owners. Samuel Slater informed the owners that the machines were worthless. Slater brought with him a knowledge and expertise in the textile industry that made him attractive to the owners and as a result, was made a partner.

By December 1790, Slater's production of spindled spinning machines, along with drawing and sowing machines, would increase the profitability of the industry. He took a water wheel from an old mill for use in supplying the power. All of his machines worked perfectly. Using the machines that Slater invented, the spinning industry took birth in America. As the years passed, cotton mills exploded onto the American business scene. With the ability to process cotton efficiently and less costly, cotton would become the king of agriculture in the southern states. Slave labor was no longer the engine that drove the new textile industry, machinery was. Now that the cotton gin could supply clean cotton, the door was open to tremendous growth and profits. Farmers would have a cash crop that would withstand storage. The businessmen would have machinery that would generate a sellable product that could be turned into clothes, house wares, bedding, and many other products that were less labor intensive and long on profits. Many textile mills began to migrate to the southern states where they could cut their operating cost by being closer to the raw materials, and acquiring cheaper labor cost. The textile mills were operated by steam engines and required coal to drive those engines. The southern move would precipitate ease in delivery and create a more cost-effective business endeavor.

The Agricultural Revolution

Between the eighteenth and nineteenth centuries, tools used in the farming business basically remained the same. When the Pilgrims settled in this country and began to establish farming methods, they eventually used a plow, a horse or mule and a rake of some sort. The same methods were being used in the nineteenth century. Technological advances were few then, but as the end of the nineteenth century was approaching, there were vast improvements in agricultural technology and farm production began to explode.

Plows were vastly improved; the size of the moldboard was increased for breaking new and unplowed ground. Many southern farmers call this plow a "middle buster." It usually required two horses to pull this plow through unbroken ground. The smaller plow was used to layout smaller furrows where the seed was planted. The newly designed plows allowed the farmer the opportunity to increase his productivity. Family farms spread throughout America and became the support system for families.

Farming would continue to improve as better machinery was invented and better farming methods were discovered. As the country continued to grow and the need for goods increased, businessmen began to find a greater need for products produced by farmers. Cotton was only one of many products that would be used to develop and meet newer consumer demands. Tobacco was grown as a cash crop and enjoyed a market in America and abroad. The shipping channels made available to supply European countries with goods, also provided an avenue to connect America with the old world.

Tools and Machinery

The inventors of the day, saw a need for new ways of increasing the production of goods and thereby increasing profitability. Machine shops were being established as a means to accommodate the increasing demand for new tools and easier methods to increase production of many products. Tools could be forged, shaped and designed in these machine shops.

John Stevens and his sons made a major contribution to transportation in America and abroad. The development of ways to use steam power to improve new means of transportation, would change mobility on land and on water. His ideas were rejected when he attempted to introduce a steam railroad to a country that was not ready for a mechanical idea that exceeded its concept of advancement in that arena. John Stevens III, went to the Congress and fought for the right to patent his idea. He was the inventor behind the effort to encourage the Congress to pass the Patent Act of 1790. This gave him recognition as the father of American Patent Law.

His sons continued their mechanical experiments in the machine shops operated by their father following his death. The four sons understood the idea and the necessity of continued development and growth. They worked together as successful businessmen and continued to invent products that improved transportation in the old and new world.

From 1815, to 1840, Robert Stevens was the primary builder of steamboats in this country. This was certainly a great accomplishment for any inventor; however, his contributions to improving railroad transportation in this country served a lasting need. Robert Stevens designed the solid metal T-Rail, now used around the world. Stevens was the president of the Camden and Amboy Railroad and first introduced all of his ideas on this railroad. He introduced the cowcatcher, the vestibule car, (caboose) the current method of attaching rails to cross ties, and many other improvements were created, or invented by Stevens.

The Stevens family is credited with devising methods for businessmen that allowed them to become more profitable and generate growth. The improvements on the railroad may have been the greatest attribute to mass transit in this country. The railroad provided a more efficient method of travel for millions of passengers traveling throughout this country. The railroad carried people, goods, cattle, mail, logs and food products, across all kinds of terrain at a much faster pace than horses and wagons. The rail cars provided a cleaner more comfortable ride for passengers.

Energy Sources

During the period of the colonization of the new America, survival was paramount to all else. The difficulties associated with the survival of the pilgrims that risked everything to achieve this monumental change in their quest for freedom and a new start, was the freezing months of winter that they had to endure. The basic method of providing life saving heat to ward off the severe cold and related elements of winter, was firewood. This was a basic fuel that was easily accessable. Wood served its purpose, but as time advanced, and the need for a different energy source was evident, coal became an energy source that generated greater heat and more flexibility.

Wood

Man has used wood as a fuel source since the days of the caveman. History would suggest that it is reasonable to believe that the use of wood to generate heat could encompass pre-historic man in its development as a fuel source.

As man developed the technology for an expanded use of wood as a fuel, the campfire would be moved from a hole in the ground to caves and tents. It was necessary to vent the smoke from the living quarters, so a hole in the top of the tent, or a hole in the cave would serve that purpose. Man learned to gain greater use from wood as he improved upon his living arrangements.

Wood has been used to warm mankind and to provide him with a method of cooking meat far longer than man's decision to record history. Many of the old world countries had access to forests that provided a source of wood on a constant basis. They learned to manage these wooded areas to provide maximum benefit for this heating and building source. The wood was harvested from old stumps and downed trees as they recognized the need for forest management.

The development of chimneys and fireplaces in early home building provided a safer way to exhaust the smoke from the structure. During the industrial revolution, the metal stove represented a great technological advancement. As man began to improve on his manufacturing expertise in metals, the stove became one of histories most important discoveries. They were mostly made from cast iron, but were not limited to one material.

The stoves were lined with firebrick to prevent the burning away of the metal over a period of time; the same as is done today in coke ovens and large boilers that generate extreme heat. The development of boilers as a heating source improved living conditions as the heated steam warmed radiators throughout the house

Benjamin Franklin was credited with developing the Franklin stove. The stove had an open front and a heat exchanger in the back. The heat exchanger never gained acceptability and was deleted in later versions. The "Franklin" stove is still being produced today bearing no resemblance to the original product.

As time and technology progressed, wood would be used as a primary heating source all over the world. It would be sold in cords, pellets, sawdust, and other by-products related to wood harvesting and subsequent businesses. Much of the harvesting served two purposes, it provided a source of fuel and it cleared deadwood from the forest floor. This would reduce the threat of forest fires. The wood used for this purpose is unsuitable for construction. Wood is one energy source that is renewable as long as the forests are well managed.

Coal

Coal is a burnable fossil fuel that is made-up of plant and animal remains that died and decomposed forming a peat in the wet and swampy areas of this planet. This process continued and repeated itself over millions of years. This organic matter, being under constant pressure for millions of years, became carbon deposits and coal was formed. Coal became the natural resource that fired the industrial revolution in America.

There are coalmines all over the planet, but the United States has the largest coal reserves in the world. These reserves could provide coal for the next 200 to 300 years. Coal mining is a dirty and dangerous business. Underground mining is a process whereby tunnels are dug deep underground along the base of a mountain or hillside. Tunnels can run in many different directions. There are shafts drilled or dug into the mines to supply a source of air. There are many hazardous conditions that miners are confronted with while working in the mine. The possibility of cave-ins and explosions from methane gas is always a constant threat.

When coal is discovered close to the surface or on a hillside, surface mining is used to recover it. The topsoil and subsoil is removed from the sight and placed on the side. The excavators move in and began to remove the coal. When the coal has been removed from the sight, the miners replace the subsoil and topsoil in an effort to return the land to its original condition. This reclamation process should preserve the land and in some cases, improves it. However, the citizens that reside within the boundaries of the coal mining community could have a different point of view. They believe that the reclamation of the land that has been strip-mined leaves them with a landscape that is far different from the natural land and elements found before. The new land is less attractive, and is subject to poor water quality. The communities believe that there is a definite destructive impact on both the land and the health conditions of its people.

With all of the negative ramifications generated by the use of this product, coal was still used to create energy for factories and to power machines, homes and power plants. Many homes and buildings were equipped with boiler-operated furnaces that produced steam for heating purposes and without coal as an energy source; the industrial world could be far different from the one we know. The use of steam to heat the radiators that heated those homes, businesses, factories, and other places where coal was more efficient as a heating and energy source, may have been necessary. Coal became the primary source of fuel and was used for many many years until forced air heat found its use in homes and buildings heated by gas fired furnaces. Coal was then used primarily to generate heat for producing electricity in power plants and other places that produced goods and services. Homes in the Midwest and other areas of the country were built with basements that had coal shuts for filling the coal binns. Coal arrived to the distributor on trains and was transported to homes and businesses by trucks.

Coal was a relatively cheap source of energy, but is not clean. It produced a smokey environment and unhealthy atmosphere. Coal was used to produce coke, a by-product that burned at a much higher temperature. This was necessary for the production of steel. The greatest use was, and still is, for the production of electricity. Coal releases carbons into the atmosphere that damages the ozone layer and assist in global warming; therefore, companies are searching for ways to produce clean coal and reduce the emissions to a safer level. It has been estimated that there are more than 800 million tons of coal in the United States, still unmined.

Oil and Gas

The use of oil and gas as an energy source is believed to have begun with the American Indians. There is evidence that they used the "burning springs" along two rivers located in West Virginia, the Kanawha, and the Big Sandy. Oil had no use to the early Americans and was ignored for many years. In the process of drilling for salt, oil was sometimes hit and had to be diverted elsewhere. Often times it was diverted to nearby streams, puluting them beyond the safe use for man or animal.

When the saltminers of the day finally realized the value of, and the potential for the use of oil and gas as a commercial product; the salt miners of the Great Kanawha Valley pioneered its use for oil in lamps, in factories, workshops, and homes, in areas where the need for home lighting was in great demand. Some of the old oil lamps of early America were just round black kettles with a wick that burned with a black smoke. The Rathbone brothers advanced this industry in a town where several thousand adventurers sprung up. Natural gas provided the town with a much more brilliant light and was cleaner to burn.

Kerosene would be developed and would be used in kerosene lamps all over America. There were many difficulties encountered in trying to claim this oil. Drilling posed a problem as it does today. The ability to drill through rock and certain soils would take technological advances not yet invented.

John D. Rockefeller would incorporate Standard Oil in Ohio. He would develop a firm called Rockefeller, Andrew & Flagler, that would go on to destroy most of his competition In Cleveland, Ohio and most of the northeastern United States.

By using unsavory and unethical and what some believed to be, illegal business practices, Standard Oil controlled 88% of the refined oil flows in this country. The state of Ohio successfully sued Standard, compelling that the trust be desolved in 1892.

In 1904, Standard controlled 91% of production and 85% of final sales, mostly kerosene, of which 55% were exported around the world. In 1909, the U S Department of Justice sued Standard under federal anti-trust law, the Sherman Antitrust Act of 1890, for sustaining a monopoly and restraining interstate commerce. Standard was ordered broken up; the monopoly was broken. Did Standard Oil take advantage of an opportunity?

Following the court action, and the invention of the automobile as a primary means of transportation for the American citizenry, many companies would spring up across America providing oil, gasoline, and kerosene to American consumers. There would be gasoline stations bearing the name of Standard Oil; they would disappear from the scene during the second half of the 20th century.

Electricity

It has been said that the greatest discovery of mankind was the wheel. Without the wheel, the world would not have been developed as we know it, and man most likely would still be living in caves. The technological advancements associated with the wheel are without comparison.

I believe that Electricity has to be the second most important discovery to impact the world and man's ability to advance to untold heights. This find has been credited to the Greeks. The discovery that simply rubbing together a piece of fur and amber could generate a form of electric shock, and would cause an attraction between the two materials, was a phenomenal find.

As the years passed and men continued to delve into this new discovery, the difference between positive and negative current were realized. It was also determined that different materials would serve as conductors, or insulators of electricity.

Benjamin Franklin has been called the father of electricity when in 1752; Franklin performed an experiment by flying a kite in a thunderstorm. When lightning struck the line that was attached to the kite, Franklin discovered that lightning and electricity were related. Franklin was also an inventor; he went on to invent the lightning rod, but it was an Italian physicist named Volta that earned the right to claim the discovery of electricity.

Thomas Alva Edison

Edison was an American inventor, scientist and businessman who developed devices such as the phonograph, the motion picture camera and the light bulb. The light bulb was and still is, a fascinating idea and subsequent realization. This great invention has illuminated the entire modern world. Edison was the originator of electric power generation. In 1882, Edison generated and distributed power from his Edison Illuminating Company to several homes in New York City. Edison's power distribution system provided 110 volts of direct current.

Nickola Tesla was the inventor of the more easily transmitted AC (alternating current) system. With this system, power could be stepped up to much higher voltages and stepped down upon reaching its destination for distribution. Alternating current is used today in homes, businesses, appliances, streetlights, factories and many other applications. The direct current that Edison invented is used in any device that is battery operated. Electricity is truly the second greatest invention ever, in my opinion.

Metals for Industrial Use

Iron was the metal that was used heavily in most of the products forged by American businesses. The iron was heated with charcoal, but they found that coke gave them a hotter fire, so the switch was made. Iron is a metal that is easy to work, or shape, because of it's makeup.

Steel is a metal that is much harder than iron; therefore, it can be used to provide support for heavy projects. Steel is an alloy consisting of iron and varying amounts of carbon. This gives it greater hardness and elasticity than iron; therefore, it is better used for tools, girders and machine products.

Zinc is a hard bluish-white metallic chemical element that comes from ore. It is used for coating iron and creating galvanized products that are resistant to rust.

Copper is a reddish-brown metallic chemical element that resists rust as well and can easily be shaped into thin sheets or fine wire. It is an excellent conductor of heat and electricity. Products made from copper are roofs, pennies, cooking utensils, large boilers, more so in the early years than now and many other products. Due to its high electrical conductivity, copper finds its greatest utilization in the electrical industry.

With the mining of the ore that produced these metals, America's industrial revolution was in full swing. There were many men of vision and foresight that had a burning desire to create and launch a business entity in this prosperous land. All of the basic needs for invention had been met. The discovery and the advancement of the metals that would be needed to support this new growth, was in place. In today's terms, the use of those materials may have been crude at best. With the advancement of new uses and the need for more sophisticated applications, the industry broadened. The building industry found a great need in the manufacture of tools, machinery and girders for constructing bridges and buildings. The development of an industrial society was on the turn.

The Stevens brothers had provided the engine that would drive a nation and the industrial revolution, the steam engine. The railroad would be the vehicle for change from the old frontier to the new industrialized and mechanized world of change and progress. The shipping lanes would go through a metamorphosis resulting in ships and boats being powered by steam engines, leaving sails and ores for the history books.

Refrigeration

From the beginning of time, man in his prehistoric state of development needed a way of preserving the meat that he brought to the cave from the hunt. Having to hunt and kill for food using crude and primitive weapons would dictate the necessity of avoiding waste. Having to bring down large animals with spears and clubs in an attack that required teamwork to feed a tribe of many, needed no waste. Therefore, the primitive man discovered that the deeper the cave the better the preservation of the food they kept.

Through the years as man began to develop his mind, the thinkers began to exercise there curiosity to find ways and means of making life easier and survival less of a challenge. Man began to use salt, sugar, or smoke, to preserve meat. Meat would be hung up in a smoke house or some other device and smoked for several days from a fire beneath the floor. Some meat was rubbed down in salt, or sugar, to preserve it. During the 1600's, France found a way to control temperatures and make ice. As this technology advanced to other parts of the world, ice became the primary method for keeping things cold. In 1779, ice was first shipped commercially from New York City to Charleston, South Carolina. The load had greatly reduced in volume by the time the trip concluded. Two New Englanders, Fredrick Tudor, and Nathaniel Wyeth, recognized that something had to be done to preserve ice over longer periods of time. He used different insulating products and materials in his search for a better and longer lasting way of reducing the melting of ice and sustaining it during delivery.

This change would revolutionize the ice industry, and provide a way for homes and businesses to provide and receive cold products to support their needs. These men built icehouses and found that cutting uniform blocks of ice for an easier way of delivery would transform the ice industry and reduce waste.

Homes in America would benefit greatly from this new cooling method by using iceboxes. The icebox would have a door for placing perishables inside. There was a small compartment used for holding a block of ice. On the bottom of the icebox was a slide in pan for catching the water from the slowly melting ice. This pan would have to be emptied as the ice would melt. The family home was now enjoying the latest product available to cool and preserved food.

There were several inventor's that developed different methods for cooling, but in 1859, an inventor named Ferdinand Carre of France, developed what is vapor compression refrigeration that is still used in today's market. In 1867, J.B. Sutherland of Detroit, Michigan, patented an insulated railroad car. The first refrigerated car to carry fruit was built in 1867 by Parker Earle of Illinois, who shipped strawberries on the Illinois Central Railroad. In 1949, Fred Jones patented a refrigeration system that was developed for the trucking industry. The unit was a roof-mounted device.

Air conditioning became a boon to businesses increasing their production by cooling their factories and the product used in the manufacture of goods. The ability to cool the air by removing the moisture became useful in textile mills, oil refineries, paper manufactures, drugs, soap, glue, celluloid, furs and woolen goods stored for protection; yet, hospitals, cars, hotels, restaurants and nearly every area of daily life would benefit. This was and still is a great technology.

The washing machine

There have always been many methods used for washing and cleaning clothes. Going back hundreds of years, homemakers would use what today seems like primative methods to accomplish this task. Clothes were washed along the banks of a stream where soap, or some other cleaning agent, was applied and they were beaten against a rock to agitate them clean. This method was commonplace for thousands of years.

As time passed, farmers would make there own soap from animal fat and a chemical called lye. The soap, in its liquid form, was poured into a large sheet pan to cool and cure then cut into bars. The southern farmer called it lye soap. The white clothes were put into a large black cast iron pot with a fire burning underneath. The hot boiling water and soap mixture, would clean the clothes. The rub board was used for the other clothing. The need for new and advanced technology in this area was evident.

Obviously, there was a technological need for developing a better method for getting clothing clean. The newly invented washing machine was hand operated. The dirty wash water would have to be changed and the rinse water was removed from the clothes with a hand wringer. Electricity would change the way clothes were cleaned forever.

The Automobile

The invention of the automobile would usher in a new industrial age of personal mobility. Americans and the world would have advanced from horse-drawn carriages to gasoline-powered motor cars. The beginning of the automobile industry happened much earlier than most people realize. In 1769, the steam-powered automobile with the capability of transporting people was introduced. In 1806, the first cars powered by internal combustion engines running on gas fuel appeared on the scene. This led to the introduction in 1885, of the modern gasoline, or petroleum-fueled internal combustion engine.

Cars powered by electricity briefly appeared at the turn of the 20th century, but largely disappeared until the turn of the 21st century when interest in automobiles with low emissions became the outcry of the automobile consumer. Electricity driven vehicles such as trolley and street cars, were used for mass transit. They basically disappeared from the streets of most of America during the 1960's, and 1970's.

The trolley cars ran on rails and made scheduled stops to pick-up passengers. The rails usually ran down the middle of main streets with platforms to service the system. The street cars looked the same as the current day buses, it ran on tires and was serviced with power from a cable on it's roof that was attached to the power lines that ran along the city streets. They can still be found in cities like San Francisco, California. The history of the automobile industry can not be fixed to a pacific era.

The advancement in its production must be determined by the method of perpulsion during those times. Most of the inventor's of the automobile technology were of German decent, but it was a great American manufacturer named Henry Ford that advanced the mass production concept of the assembly line. Instead of building cars by a team of workers on a platform and then moving the car from station to station, he saw the benefit of a continuous line of cars traveling pass the workers as they applied their parts to the automobile. The building of mass produced automobiles using this method would spread throughout the industry.

New car manufacturing companies would spring-up all over the land. Detroit, Michigan, would become the mecca for this new and most promising industry.

Henry Ford was the first to pay his workers five dollars a day for their services. He was also very controlling. Using a group of men led by a man named Bennett, Ford would invade the privacy and the homes of his workers, demanding that they met certain requirements to maintain employment with his company. He would examine the cleanliness of their homes, their children and their surroundings. This was an uncalled for invasion of his workers rights and would eventually lead to the organizing of his workers with the United Automobile Workers Union (UAW).

There were car companies that would be successful, but many would fail. Desota, Studebaker, Hudson, Packard, American Motors and many others would not survive this highly competitive industry. General Motors, Ford Motor Company and Chrysler Corporation, today called (FCAC) Italian owned, would become the big three of automobile manufacturing in America.

The automobile industry has been and still is, a lucrative business that helped to put America and the rest of the world on wheels. Credit must be given to the Duryea brothers because they were the businessmen that started auto manufacturing in the United States of America. In 1893, the Duryea brothers started the Duryea Motor

Wagon Company. Ranson E. Olds started the Olds Motor Vehicle Company that would later become Oldsmobile. This company would dominate this era of automobile manufacturing. Within a year, Cadillac, an offshoot from the Henry Ford Company, was producing cars in the thousands.

American manufacturing was primed to become the greatest producer of tools, machinery, appliances, automobiles, farm products and consumer goods in general, on the planet. This nation had risen up to it's potential as a leader in nation building. The original Pilgrims would be delighted to see where their adventure had taken the world as a whole.

With all of the accomplishments, the inventions, the land grabbing from the true Americans, the wars and suffering of a new nation in its infancy, America had become the greatest nation on earth. The one thing that Americans could not overcome was greed. This led to crime, corruption and the Raping of America.

The politicians would lead this country into unfair trade agreements for favor from the businessmen that pursued them for their vote on issues concerning their interest.

Now that we have built a new nation, we will look at how it started to come apart and the reasons behind this disgraceful discourse and shameful, "Raping of America".

Part 7

GROWTH AND PROSPERITY

"Oh beautiful for spacious skies for amber waves of grain, for purple mountains majesty above the fruited plains, America, America, God shed his grace on the, and crown thy good with brotherhood from sea to shinning sea." The writer of this song saw the beauty in this great new land and put it to song. A land that had everything, including the promise of freedom, riches and adventure. The glorious fruits of progressive achievement were at the fingertips of every American and the immigrants that sought its shores. America was not only a new country, but to many, a new world and a new way of life.

America had so much to offer. From the lower southern area was Florida, the southern half of a large watershed. The system begins with what are now Orlando and the Kissimmee River. This river discharges into the vast but shallow Lake Okeechobee, with it's Everglades and the abundance of wild animals and its wild species of plants and water foul. There are wetlands, marshes and canals, engineered by nature and an eco system that was perfectly balanced.

Traveling north through Georgia is Stone Mountain, a huge presence made of solid rock. Then view the beautiful shores of Savanna, Georgia, with its breath taking scenery that is mystifying. See the foothills of the Appalachian Mountain chain that snakes its way north through the state of Tennessee. Here you can find Lookout Mountain, where one can stand on a clear day and see seven states. The tallest point within the system is Mount Mitchell in North Carolina, standing 6,684 feet.

America shares her beauty as we travel north through Virginia with its beautiful and heavily wooded mountains and valleys. The beauty continues as we travel to the Catskills of New York. America continues to mystify the traveler as we move to Pennsylvania and the great Allegany. This country, with its vast beauty, also has the world's greatest supply of fresh water, the five great lakes. These lakes hold about 22% of the world's fresh surface water. They are Lake Michigan, Lake Superior, Lake Ontario, Lake Erie, and Lake Huron.

Then there is the mighty Mississippi River. The Mississippi is the largest river system in the United States and in North America. The river originates at Lake Itasca, Minnesota and flows slowly southward meandering through snake like turns and terminating 95 river miles below New Orleans, Louisiana. There it flows to the Gulf of Mexico; along with its major tributary, the Missouri River. The river drains all or parts of 31 U.S. states stretching from the Rocky Mountains in the West, to the Appalachian Mountains in the East. That also includes the Canadian-U.S. border on the North, and most of the Great Plains and is the fourth longest river in the world and the tenth most powerful. Throughout its history, the Mississippi has always been a major navigation route through the center of North America. The river serves as partial boundaries for ten states.

The next stop is St. Louis, Missouri, the gateway to the West. Many of the settlers that were westward bound departed from here, or St. Joseph Missouri. I will describe the journey that lies ahead as they journeyed into the vast and dangerous spaces of the western frontier.

Then there is the Great American Plains. America was growing and most of this land was now populated, even though sparsely in most areas west of the Mississippi River. The Great Plains is the broad expanse of prairie and steppe grassland which lie west of the Mississippi River and east of the Rocky Mountains in the United States and Canada. This area covers many states as it stretches northward from the southern tip of Texas, across the Canadian border into Northwestern Canada. Most of the region was home to American Bison "Buffalo" herds that were so large, it could take two days for a herd to cross a trail. With the westward movement of settlers and the need to feed the workers on the railroad, they were nearly hunted to extinction. Men like William F. "Buffalo Bill" Cody, killed them not just for their meat, but also for profit from their hides. The loss of this great natural resource as a roaming herd of plains animals diminished a God given natural beauty and American treasure.

When the settlers saw the opportunity to settle a land that was almost treeless, this represented a great boon to farmers. There were no need to clear the land of trees and tree stumps, but this land had a natural enemy for farmers, wind. In general, the Great Plains have a wide variety of weather throughout the year with very cold winters and very hot summers. In addition, it was home to the Plains Indians. Over the next one hundred years, the founding of the fur trade brought thousands of ethnic Europeans into the Great Plains. Fur trappers from all over made their way across much of the region making regular contact with the Plains Indians. So did fur traders following Lewis and Clark's expedition of 1804-1806, to explore and map the Louisiana Purchase. By the 1870's, the Plains Indians were forced to leave the plains and were placed on reservations.

Having no trees, the settlers would build homes made of sod. They would use Buffalo chips (droppings) for firewood. Farming the grassy plains of North America would prove to be a challenge to those who dared tackle the elements and all of its fury. What was green today could be a dust bowl tomorrow. America was growing up.

The Railroad and its Influence

Transportation was improving, most of this new nation had been settled and the number of states to join the union had grown substantially. There were many business ventures designed to narrow the gap that separated much of the populace in this country.

Wells Fargo & Company and the Overland Stage lines transported people and light cargo. The Pony Express was started in the 1870's to carry the mail on a two thousand mile journey across the country and to do it within ten days. But of all of the great ideas, the railroad would prove to be the most important development of the Industrial Revolution in America. According to the book "The Americans". Statistics bear out the immense importance of railroads in the new industrial age. In 1870, the railroads employed 163,000 persons. In 1900, they employed more than a million. By 1880, they were the largest industry in the nation and the value of their stocks and bonds was more than the national debt.

The first railroad locomotive arrived in the United States from England in 1829. For the next twenty-five years, the railroad would advance it's reach to the Mississippi River at Rock Island, Illinois. A few years later, work would begin on the first transcontinental railroad in America. When the idea of running a railroad from the Atlantic Ocean to the Pacific Ocean was first discussed, it was mostly ignored. President Abe Lincoln decided that the first line should run from Omaha, Nebraska, to Sacramento, California. In 1862, Lincoln signed the Pacific Railroad Act. A second Railroad Act was passed in 1864. Under these acts, the Union Pacific and Central Pacific Railroad Companies received about 20 million acres of land, as well as, federal loans of $60 million dollars. Individuals and small towns made an investment as well, fearing that the railroad would pass them by.

The Union Pacific faced an array of problems and difficulties in its attempt to cross hundreds of miles of hostile and unforgiving land. It was necessary to transport materials, workers and food to feed them. The railroad would also have to provide shelter to house them under certain conditions. There were illnesses and accidents that killed many men during this venture.

The Central Pacific faced many of the same difficulties. There were few men available for hire, so they hired their crew from the Chinese that came to the gold fields of California seeking wealth. The question was, how could men of such small stature, approximately 110 pounds, perform such difficult and strenuous work? They worked from sunrise to sunset for less pay than their white counterparts who worked eight hours a day.

To spur them on, a competition developed between the workers of both railroads to see who could lay the most track in one days work. Jack Casement's men of the Union Pacific layed 7.5 miles of track in twelve hours. Charlie Crocker of the Central Pacific said his men would lay ten miles in one day. The Vice President of the Union Pacific bet Crocker $10,000 that it couldn't be done. They were successful and that record still holds today.

This huge construction project and probably the greatest engineering feat ever attempted in this country to date, finally ended on May 10, 1869. The two rail lines were joined together at Promontory Point, Utah, connecting the rails that joined the country from coast to coast with a golden spike. This set in place the most wonderful transportation system known to man for land transport.

The Indians called the railroad "The Iron Horse". The cattle drivers saw it as an easier way to get their herds to market. Businessmen saw a means of transporting goods from far distances more efficiently, and customers saw long distance travel made easier. America was coming together and growing as a viable and productive nation. The railroad provided a method of commercial travel that was far more comfortable than a stagecoach, or horseback. The trains were rickety and smoky, but had sleeping cars that were used by politicians and others. It also provided jobs for thousands of Americans. The need for jobs and housing would continue to mushroom as more and more people sought the shores of the nation that was called the land of plenty, of opportunity and freedom. The business opportunities would continue to explode as American cities and towns grew in population.

Business Developement

With the growth of America came problems different from the earlier settlers. The new America needed housing, food stores, water, law and order, transportation and a miriad of business ventures to service the needs of a developing and ever growing nation. There were a need for every kind of goods and services available. With the introduction of reasonably priced manufactured goods in the market place, merchants began to explore new methods and tactics to bolster sales and gain market share. There were many manufactured goods available to the consumer, so the good businessman found ways to deliver them at affordable prices.

The 5 and 10 cent store was an idea of a clerk named Frank W. Woolworth. His stores would grow into a chain of thousands across America. Others would copy the business idea developed by Woolworth, such as Niesner Bros. 5 and 10 cent stores. Americans needed much more, and to accommodate their needs, shops and stores of all sorts began to spring up across the landscape.

Out of the industrialization of this growing nation, steel mills and factories, cement producers, furniture manufactures, garment districts, loggers, electrical engineers, master plumbers, car manufactures and many others began to produce goods and provide services for this growing economy. The boom of a nation was at hand and America was the place to be.

Labor Union's

Along with the great manufacturing development and improved goods and services growing by leaps and bounds in America, came worker discontent. The workers faced abuses from managerial personnel and bosses that ruled with an iron fisted mentality. This kind of workplace erosion often breeds confrontation. Out of the workplace toils and strife, the inevitable came as workers grew weary of disrespect and poor working conditions. They began to develop a protectionist mentality. The answer to this kind of discontent was the re-birth of labor unions that started in the 1600's. The labor forces of this great nation were exploding as immigrants continued to land on these shores. In addition to the businessmen of earlier years, many brought a different set of skills and became businessmen themselves. America's ever expanding economy was a gold mine.

The disgruntled workers were growing as well and organized labor was the vehicle that would take them to a place called worker justice. The unions were bridge builders to justice in the workplace, they were bridge builders to labor peace and they were bridge builders to respect and self-determination. They became a buffer in the face of an unscrupulous foe, the workplace manager.

This new urban-industrial scene brought with it unforeseen challenges. An economy that had survived on skilled labor provided by individuals, had now grown into a new and different form of work called mass production. In the 1890's, the assembly line had been introduced in the American workplace and management needed workers to man the lines and machinery for mass production of its product. The repetitive work and the low wages and long hours, began to destroy the pride and self worth of the factory worker. Labor union's were already in full bloom in this country. In those days, they were organized by skills. There were carpenter unions, seamstress and pipe fitter unions and many others. There was even a labor union formed by black workers, the National Colored Labor Union (NCLU), under the leadership of ship-caulker Isaac Myers of Baltimore, Maryland. Frederick Douglass replaced Isaac Myers and after nearly becoming an affiliate of the Republican Party, disappeared from the American scene.

The first recorded work stoppage in North America was when Polish-born Immigrants in Virginia demanded equal pay for equal work in 1619. This was not an attempt to gain justice through organized labor, but the determination of a group of workers who stood up for fair and equitable practices in their workplace.

In 1792, journeyman shoemakers in Philadelphia organized the first permanent U.S. union. Shoemakers, bootblacks, or simple shoe repair shops provided a great service to the men and women of

America for many years. Shoe repair has now become a dying trade. It has all but disappeared from the business scene in America. In 1866, the National Labor Union was founded as the first attempt to link unions into one federation. As the years passed, it was evident that workers were not satisfied with their plight in the workplace. In 1869, The Knights of Labor was founded. Among its affiliates was the Carriage and Wagon Makers Union. This was probably the first union of vehicle workers, horse powered, or gasoline powered. In 1881, The American Federation of Labor (AF of L) was founded. In 1886, Workers demonstrated in Haymarket Square, Chicago, demanding eight-hour days. Police violence erupts; and four labor leaders were hanged without consideration of whether they were involved in the disturbance or not. In 1905, Industrial Workers of the World (IWW), attempts to organize auto and other workers into one big union. In 1913, the IWW calls the first auto strike at Studebaker's Detroit, Michigan plant. 1913, was also the year that the moving assembly line was introduced at Henry Ford's, Detroit, Michigan plant. In 1914, Ford announces a "$5-a-day" pay policy in response to growing union activity. In 1932, thousands of unemployed autoworkers marched on Ford's Rouge plant in Dearborn, Michigan, to demand relief. Four workers were killed. In 1935, The American Federation of Labor gives a charter to the International Union UAW, but to gain recognition from the auto companies, the workers at General Motors and Chrysler Corporation began sit down strikes in 1937, recognition was won at all three companies.

Workers have felt the sting of unjust business owners and their managers since the birth of this nation. To win the right to bargain collectively against these companies, was their only recourse for gaining labor peace and justice in the workplace.

Aviation

America was continuing to grow and develop as a country and the needs of her people were forever changing. Another one of the most important inventions ever discovered for moving masses of people, is the airplane.

Man has always been fascinated by the idea of human flight, and in his attempt to conquer flight, many devices were used. But it was two brothers from Kitty Hawk, North Carolina, that on December 17, 1903, built the Wright Flyer and became the inventors of the aireal age. The Wright Brothers, Wilbur and Orville, were two Americans who are generally credited with inventing and building the world's first successful airplane and making the first controlled powered and sustained heavier-than-air human flight. In the two years afterwards, the brothers developed their flying machine into the first practical fixed-wing aircraft.

Although not the first to build and fly experimental aircraft, the Wright brothers were the first to invent controls that made fixed-wing powered flight possible. The brother's fundamental breakthrough was their invention of three-axis control, which enabled the pilot to steer the aircraft effectively and to maintain its equilibrium. This method remains standard on fixed-wing aircraft of all kinds.

William Lendrum "Billy" Mitchell, was an American Army Brigadier General who is regarded as the father of the United States Air Force. He is one of the most famous and controversial figures in the history of American airpower. Mitchell served in France during the First World War and by the conflicts end, commanded all American air combat units in the country. After the war, he was appointed Deputy Director of the Air Service and began advocating for increased investment in air power, believing this would prove vital in future wars.

He argued particularly for the ability of bombers to sink battleships; then he organized a series of bombing runs against stationary ships designed to test the idea.

He antagonized many people in the army with his arguments and criticism and in 1925, was returned to his permanent rank of colonel. Later that year, he was court-martialed for insubordination after accusing Army and Navy leaders of an "almost treasonable administration of the national defense." He resigned from the service shortly afterwards.

Romanion inventor Henri Coanda, invented the first jet-propelled plane in 1910. This was just seven years after the Wright brothers performed their first flight. The prototype crashed on take off and the design was thought to be impracticable, but was a technological marvel for its time. Yet, it fell into relative obscurity because the gas-powered piston engine was proven capable.

With the advancement of man's ability to take flight, America would go on to become a military power and a force to be respected by the modern world. Transportation now had worldwide ramifications, and the world of transportation would never be the same. The ability to transport people and goods across land and oceans in mere hours, would have a profound effect on the world and business opportunities.

Population explosion

Immigrants were continuing to arrive at Ellis Island by the shiploads. The Europeans from many countries sought the opportunities that only the new America had to offer. The large cities along the Eastern Seaboard were experiencing tremendous population growth. Therefore, the need to provide goods and services to accommodate the new arrivals created business opportunities for entrepreneurs all over the country.

The immigrants were mostly Irish, Germans and English on the East Coast and the Chinese on the West Coast. There would also be immigrants from Austria, Hungary, Poland, Italy and Russia. The number of foreign-born people in the United States rose from 4 million in 1860, to 13 million by 1910. The overall population increased as well. The proportion of immigrants to native-born Americans were about the same.

There were controversy over the number of immigrants arriving in this country because of the great cultural differences between the new immigrants and those that arrived in earlier years. The other cause for friction was that they were mostly concentrated in already highly populated areas of the country. They began to look on the new immigrants as different and became disenchanted with their presence. The language spoken by so many different people caused concern. Most of the earlier newcomers to these shores spoke English. The later newcomers spoke many different languages and created problems with communication among the masses.

The idea and reality of mass production would become a necessity in the business community. The sweatshops were expanding and becoming more dangerous. There were no business regulations to control, or monotor them. Therefore, they were free to proceed at will and at their own discreasion, without regard to the safety of the workers that labored in hazardous conditions.

Family farms were growing and becoming the mainstay in the agricultural business. Families making a living from the land was proud and respected employment. The new arrivals brought with them the old skills learned in their homelands and would begin to apply them in America. This country became a greater nation because of their skills. Many brought with them seeds for plants and trees that would bare fruit.

America would grow into the most highly mechanized industrial manufacturing nation on the planet. This country was growing and blooming with new products and services for masses of Americans and the world. The nations progress would continue for decades to come.

National Parks

Some of this countries greatest wonders and natural beauty is its national parks. To see the breathtaking beauty of Yellowstone Park, "Montana/Wyoming" and the animals that live and graze on it's grasses, or hunt it's prey for survival, is awe-inspiring.

The main attraction is the fantastic "Old Faithful" and its hundreds of fellow gysers and hot springs. To travel through the park and gaze at the herds of Bison and Elk and the occasional moose and wolf in the wild free setting that they enjoy, is astounding. Walk the trails and pathways through wild country with its mountains and valleys teaming with wild life and wild flowers. The tree lined hilltops and the vastness of a land that only God could have envisioned and created.

Move on to Yosemite National Park, California, and enjoy downhill skiing in winter at the five-lift Badger Pass Area. There you will find Glacier Point Ski Hut. For those that love the outdoors in winter, this is a visit that you must take. Take hikes through the 8,000-feet high Tuolumme Meadows area, where Ansel Adams practiced his skills. See the grove of big trees and the cluster of giant sequoia trees that seem to touch the sky.

Ansel Adams was an American photographer and environmentalist best known for his black and white photography of the American west, especially in Yosemite National Park. He was a hyperactive child, but was prone to bouts of sickness and hypochondrial. He was not a very social person but took to nature at an early age. Some of the best photography work in the world belonged to him and was worth millions. Adams died in 1954, at the age of 82 years. America lost one of its finest contributors to her story.

Take the drive through the gateway community of Gardiner, Montana, toward the Roosevelt Arch, the century-old ceremonial north entrance to Yellowstone. You may see Bison crossing the road, or wondering among the cars in the parking lot. There are Elk and Pronghorn Antelope, Big Horn Sheep, Mule Deer, Coyotes, wolves and Bald Eagles. The Gray Wolf will follow anywhere grazing animals gather, predator looking for prey. You will hear the eerie howls of the coyote and wolves in the darkness of night.

This is the home of the largest gyser concentration in the world. You must see and explore this land of glorious beautiful and bountiful interest provided by the wonders of nature.

There are more than 390 parks in the system, included are 58 major parks. The American National Parks draw more than 270 million visitors each year. The prime-visiting season is from June through August.

Visit Washington's Olympic National Park located in the cool and often damp Pacific Northwest, where hiking through the rain forest is one of the park's top draws. The summer season is the dry season, but winter rains bring out the vigor and brilliant green lushness in the mosses, lichens, and liverworts.

Move on to the vast desert landscape of California's Death Valley National Park, it is the countries hottest location. The temperature hit 134 degrees here once and is the driest spot during the summer months. Visitors can't venture far into the desert without risking their lives. During the winter months is when daily high temperatures average 65 to 72 degrees. This is when the park's 3.5 million acres are opened fully for leisurely exploration. Stargazing is especially rewarding during the long winter nights. A few times in a decade, enough rain falls in winter that wild flowers bloom in February. One of the most rewarding aspects of these locations is to see the changes in the demographics of the people visiting the national parks.

The American leaders, the Presidents and the Congress, had pulled together for the making of a great nation. They knew in their infinite wisdom that the citizens would need recreational facilities to relieve them of the stresses of hard work and life's challenges. The National Parks system would provide a comfort and beauty that would answer and satisfy that need. The country was still young and many of the needs had been realized. Land ownership, home ownership, jobs, farming, manufacturing and banking, put in place a nation readily designed for progress. However, the problems were just beginning. America would be tested on many fronts and would overcome many obsticals. The growing pains of a nation are not far removed from the growing pains of man. New experiences bring about new and different challenges, but people of America were up to the task of problem resolution and improving this new land.

To have an opportunity to watch the growth of such a magnificent nation is a reward in itself, but to be a part of that development and subsequent growth, is truly refreshing. America could not have become the great nation that she is, had it not been for the continued perseverance of a determined people of all nationalities. The demographics are constantly changing and we must embrace it for the common good of America. We must join hands and make an effort to put an end to the degrading and devastating, Raping of America.

Part 8

ENVIRONMENTAL DISASTERS

Clear cutting Forest Timber

America, with all of her beautiful attributes, cannot withstand the onslaught of neglect and lack of concern perpetrated on her by individuals and American Corporations. Man is wreaking havoc on this land, water and air, in his quest for riches driven out of greed and his desire to profit at any cost. The environment has been severely damaged and the onslaught continues. Humans have not been spared from this ever-increasing encroachment on the health of mankind. Our children have been leaded from paint and other household and toy products. Our air is filled with smog and industrial chemicals that poison our lungs, damage our bodies and our minds and causes cancerous diseases. We have driven ourselves into a corner. The land is damaged, causing hundreds, if not thousands of plants and animals to become extinct each year because of the destruction of their habitat.

Clearcutting of American forestland causes devastating effects on the land, animals and streams in the immediate area. The environmental effects include a range of negative results, from loss of habitat, to an elevation in water temperatures which poses many difficulties to the fish and other water born animals that require cool water for survival, including birds, reptiles and mammals.

Clear cutting is a logging practice used by some companies to completely clear an area of trees, regardless of their size for the possibility of useful timber sales. The negative results reflect major changes to the land that can take decades to correct. Many activists have suggested more environmentally sustainable alternatives to clear cutting, such as selective logging.

Clearcutting completely clears all standing trees from the forest floor, leaving the remaining scrub and brush to be burnt in large burn piles that can cast a smoky haze over the area for several days. A clearcut area can be relatively small, or, can cover several miles. It can be clearly visible from the air, along with the scars of logging roads cut to access the area. The abrupt removal of trees in a clear cutting operation can cause serious environmental impact on the affected, as well as, the surrounding area. There are times when clear cutting may alter the coarse of local rivers. If logging comes too close to the banks of the river, as it often does, it eliminates the shady shield of trees which can cause the temperature of the river to elevate. Even a few degrees can make a huge difference to native plants, fish and amphibians, and can cause a significant population decrease. Numerous organizations monitor global rivers and have warned that extensive clear cutting could result in the extinction of some fish species, as they are driven out of their native habitat. Clearcutting also softens the banks of the river by enabling erosion, which can cause the banks to collaspse into the water.

In addition to harming rivers, clear cutting also alters the water cycle in general. While trees are growing, they help to trap and retain water along with precious topsoil. When trees are removed, water runs over the surface of the earth rather than filtering into the aquifer. The water runoff can cause flooding and take valuable topsoil with it. Read more about this on the internet where much of this information can be accessed.

We are the stewards of this earth; there is no replacement. We are bound by common sense and a duty to God and country to preserve it and to keep it in a life sustaining condition. We have sherked our duty and in time, we will pay the ultimate price, unless we correct our behavior and change our destructive practices.

Clearcutting in and of itself does not necessarily destroy a forest if the trees are replanted. When wild fires burn a forest, the results of the burn gives new life and clears the forest of greenhouse gases caused by the decay of organic materials.

Some logging companies use selective logging to harvest trees from a forest. With this method, trees are taged for cutting and selected by size and marketable value. The trees are replanted and the cycle continues. The biggest aide to our forest and their longevity is to recycle materials made from wood products. This is an environmental protective method that protects the planet and is cost effective as well.

Most forest recover from clear cutting, and over time, continue to provide oxygen. Over a period of years; the recovery can be healthy in areas where the forest genetics are bad. Even new forestation must fight for survival in competition with other new growth. The strongest and best of the new trees will gain advantage over weaker growth and the forest will be the better for it.

West Virginia and Eastern Kentucky Coal Sludge spill

In October of 2000, a great catastrophy took place in Eastern Kentucky and West Virginia. Retaining ponds, or huge reservoirs are used to store coal sludge by businesses such as Massey Energy Company. Coal sludge, or slurry as it is sometimes called, is the water left over when coal is washed free of dirt and other residue. The water is then stored in reservoirs. Many of these reservoirs are so large that they cover many acres. When they fail, everything down hill, or down stream of its onslaught, will be over run by hazardous material. In the case of this spill, the bottom of a coal sludge impoundment owned by Massey Energy in Martin County Kentucky, broke into an abandoned underground mine below. The slurry came out of the mine opening, sending an estimated 306 million gallons of sludge down two tributaries of the Tug Fork River. By morning, Wolf Creek was oozing with the black waste. In Coldwater Fork, a ten-foot wide stream became a 100-yard expanse of this sludge. Everything in the streams all the way to the Ohio River were killed.

The spill was over five-feet deep in places and covered nearby resident's yards; it polluted hundreds of miles of the Big Sandy River, and its tributaries. The Ohio River, the water supply for over 27,000 residents, was contaminated and all aquatics in Coldwater Fork and Wolf Creek, were killed. The spill was 30 times larger than the Exxon Valdez oil spill. United States Secretary of Labor, Elaine Chao, wife of Republican Senator Mitch McConnell of Kentucky, oversaw the

Mine Safety and Health Administration at the time. Choa placed a McConnell staffer in charge of the MSHA investigation into the spill. In 2002, a $5,600 fine was levied. In September 2002, Massey gave $100,000 to the National Republican Senatorial Committee chaired by non-other than Mitch McConnell. You do the math.

Politicians and CEO's of business entities have violated the trust of the American people since the beginning of the Republic, when will we ever learn? We must challenge wrongdoing in this country, no matter who the perpetrator might be.

We must ask ourselves, did President George W. Bush cover-up a major environmental disaster? When Bush took office, he decided that the country needed more energy and less regulation of energy companies. Years later, slurry remains on many of the properties that line the streams; it was never properly cleaned up.

Three Mile Island Nuclear Meltdown

The Three Mile Island accident was a partial core meltdown in unit 2, (a pressurized water reactor, manufactured by Bobcock and Wilcox) of the Three Mile Island Nuclear Generating Station in Dauphin County, Pennsylvania, near Harrisburg. The plant was owned and operated by General Public Utilities and the Metropolitan Edison Company. Metropolitan Edison pled guilty to falsifying reactor leak rates right before the emergency. If the reactor had been shut down for repairs, per regulations, the partial meltdown would not have occurred at that time. The Three Mile Island meltdown and disaster was the most significant accident in the history of the American Commercial Nuclear Power Generating Industry. This dangerous and destructive accident resulted in the release of radioactive gases and the forever-dangerous Iodine-131. On Wednesday, March 28, 1979, the facility began to sustain failures in the non-nuclear secondary system by a stuck open relief valve. With this valve failing to close, large amounts of reactor coolants began to escape. Poorly trained plant operators failed to recognize the accurring events as a loss of coolant so the coarse of events continued. The scope and complexity of the accident did not become clear for several days. The reactor was finally brought under control.

President Jimmy Carter ordered an investigation by a presidential commission to determine the reason for the failure and to find ways to prevent such an accident from ever happening again.

During the last week of March, 2009, the world marked the 30th anniversary of the Three Mile Island nuclear accident, which resulted in the release of up to 13 million curies of radioactive noble gases and remains the most notorious accident in the history of the American nuclear power industry.

Over the months that followed; the public was mislead and outright lied to about the extent of the accident and its potential effects on nearby resident's health. The federal government did not keep track of the health histories of the region's residents and some say that the state of Pennsylvania hid the health impacts of the accident, deleting cancers from the public record and misrepresenting the facts that it could not hide. Anecdotal evidence suggest a far greater toll, with large numbers of central Pennsylvanians suffering skin sores and lesions after being exposed to the fallout. Many residents developed visible tumors and breathing problems. While the nuclear industry maintains that "no one died at Three Mile Island", it has continuously refused to allow an open judicial hearing on the hundreds of cases still pending. "Information source, earthfirst.com".

The Monsanto Company Chemical Poisoning

PCB-Polychlorinated Biphenyl, are man-made chemicals once used for a diverse range of applications including flame-retardants, coolants, lubricants, politicizes, pesticides and sealants. It has been banned for most use in the United States since the late 1970's, but still persist in the environment in products before the ban.

They have been known to cause skin rashes, immunological and neurological changes. The (EPA), Environmental Protection Agency, has classified them as "probable human carcinogens".

It is said that Monsanto has been identified by the United States "Environmental Protection Agency", as being a potentially responsible party for 56 contaminated sites in the United States. Monsanto has been sued and has settled multiple times for damaging the health of its employees, or residents, near its Superfund sites through pollution and poisoning. Monsanto is the largest producer of herbicides through its popular brand "Roundup". They also produce genetically modified seeds for agriculture, along with many chemically laden products.

Monsanto was charged with life threatening environmental damage in Anniston, Alabama, 40 years ago. Plantiffs in a pending lawsuit provided documentation showing that the local Monsanto factory knowingly discharged both mercury and PCB-laden waste into local creeks for 40 years. It is said that in 1969 alone, Monsanto had dumped 45 tons of PCBs into Snow Creek, which supplies much of the areas drinking water. The company also buried millions of pounds of PCBs in open-pit landfills located on hillsides above the plant and surrounding neighborhoods. In August 2003, Solutia and Monsanto agreed to pay plaintiffs $700 million dollars to settle claims by over 20,000 Anniston residents related to PCB contamination. Monsanto never issued an apology to the people of Anniston, Alabama.

This company has been sued over the years for everything from Saccharin, which they won, to Agent Orange that was used to kill vegitation in the Vietnam War, to a 1979 dioxin chemical spill in Sturgeon, Missouri, as well as, corrupt business practices. This company has had, and continues to have, problems all over the world.

The damage caused to the American society and America as a nation, will take many years for her to recover from, if ever! The willful and systematic destruction of America for the sake of profit is shameful to those that feel shame. America continues to be raped and pillaged from the four corners of this land. How long can she sustain herself from such a wanton onslought? It is the duty of every American citizen to stand-up against these kinds of harmful business practices. We must demand redress and stiff regulations from our government, or suffer the long-term effects of this rape.

The Love Canal

William T. Love was a man with a dream and a vision to create and build a "model city". He started his project in the late 1800s. His plan was to build his city near a canal with the intent of connecting the two levels of the Niagara River that were separated by Niagara Falls. The plan was doomed to failure due to a lack of sufficient funding. The digging of the canal had barely gotten underway when William Love was forced to abandon the project. By the 1920s, his dream had become a dumping ground for the city of Niagara Falls. During the 1940s, Hooker Chemical, sought and was given permission to dump 21,000 tons of industrial chemicals at the site; in 1952, he covered it up with dirt and vegetation.

Hooker Chemical no longer had use for the site, so he sold it to the school board for one dollar. While this site hid extreme toxic dangers under the soil, the city built a school on the site. By 1955, a 25-foot area crumbled and exposed toxic drums, which filled with water during rainstorms creating huge puddles that the children liked to play in. Low-income housing was built near the site and the walls of the canal were breached during the construction of sewers to accomadate the new housing. The new residents had no knowledge of the history of love canal. During the 1970s, health effects began to plague the community.

Severe health problems were beginning to spread throughout the residents. Lois Gibbs, a local mother, began to investigate and discovered the truth about the chemical waste. Her curiosity took control when she discoveed that so many, including her son, had severe health problems. There were high incidents of asthma, miscarriages, mental retardation and other illnesses along with reports of strange odors and substances. A survey conducted by the Love Canal Homeowners Association found that 56% of the children born from 1974-1978, had a birth defect. Gibbs and other residents struggled through a three-year battle to call attention to the problem, finally making it a national media event in 1978. The proof of a major problem was in the results of the investigation. The government took control and relocated Love Canal families and held Hooker Chemical liable for the damages through the Superfund Act. Hooker, now Occidental Petroleum, was forced to pay $129 million in retribution, and the site was officially declared clean in 2004. "The above is a matter of public record".

What is the Superfund?

The Superfund is the common name for the Comprehensive Environmental Response, Compensation and Liability Act of 1980. A United States Federal Law designed to clean up abandoned hazardous waste sites. Superfund created the Agency for Toxic Substances and Disease Registry (ATSDR), and it provides broad federal authority to clean up releases or threatened releases of hazardous substances that may endanger public health or the environment. The law authorizes the Environmental Protection Agency (EPA), to identify parties responsible for contamination of sites and compel the parties to clean up the site. Where responsible parties cannot be found, the Agency is authorized to clean up sites itself, using a special trust fund. Superfund was inacted by Congress in response to the Love Canal disaster in New York.

Even though Hooker Chemical was forced to pay $129 million in retribution, Companies continue to destroy land and rivers that adversely impacts the lives of Americans in the name of profit. The raping of America continues.

The Great Pacific Garbage Patch

The Great Pacific Garbage Patch is a huge swirling mess of plastic in the North Central Pacific Ocean. It has been estimated to be the size of the United States. Seamen, sailors, and scientist, have referred to it as the world's largest garbage dump. The Algalita Marine Research Foundation found in 2008, that plastic outnumbers plankton in some areas of the patch. The pollution is just under the surface of the water and has been described as "plastic soup". Even though this marine pollution formed over time, it gathered together in this area by oceanic currents, and researchers believe that it may contain more than 100 million tons of debris. The vast majority of the garbage is believed to come from land-based sources, with the remainder coming from ships.

The Texas City Disaster

On the morning of April 16, 1947, a fire on board the French-registered vessel, the SS Grandcamp in the port of Texas City, detonated approximately 2,000 tons of ammonium nitrate, creating a chain reaction of fires and explosions that killed 581 people. These events also triggered the first ever class action lawsuit against the United States government, under the then-recently enacted Federal Tort Claims Act (FTCA), on behalf of 8,485 victims.

The Grandcamp was a 437-foot-long liberty ship. It was originally christened the SS Benjamin R. Curtis in Los Angeles in 1942. Along with ammonium nitrate, the ship was carrying small arms ammunition, machinery, and bales of sisal twine. The ship that intensified this disaster was the SS High Flyer that was in the harbor and about 600 ft away from the Grandcamp. The SS High Flyer was carrying an additional 961 tons of ammonium nitrate and 3, 600, 000 pounds of sulfer. The cargo was fertilizer on its way to farmers in Europe. A fire was detected in the hold of the Grandcamp and at 09:12 am, the ships cargo detonated. The blast was so devastating; it leveled nearly 1,000 buildings on land. The shock was felt as far away as Louisiana, a city that is 250 miles away. The High Flyer exploded as well. When the last claim had been processed in 1957, 1,394 awards, totaling nearly $17, 000,000 had been made.

What is the Federal Tort Claims Act? (FTCA)

The Federal Tort Claims Act, (FTCA), is a statute in-acted in 1948 by the United States Congress in which the United States authorizes tort suits to be brought against itself. With exception, it makes the United States liable for injuries caused by the negligent, or wrongful act, or omission of any federal employee acting within the scope of his employment; in accordance with the law of the state where the act or omission occurred. Three major exceptions under which the United States may not be held liable, even in circumstances where a private person could be held liable under state laws are, the "Feres doctrine", which prohibits suits by military personnel for injuries sustained incidental to service; the discretionary function exception, which immunizes the United States for acts of omission of its employees that envolves policy decisions; and the intentional tort exception, which precludes suits against the United States for assault and battery, among some other intentional torts, unless they are committed by federal law enforcement or investigative officials.

This report discusses, among other things, the application of the Feres Doctrine to suits for injuries caused by medical malpractice in the military, the prohibition of suits by victims of atomic testing, Supreme Court cases interpreting the discretionary function exception, the extent to which federal employees may be held liable for torts they commit in the scope of their employment, and the government contractor defense to products liability design defect suits. **TORT**--A civil wrong or breach of a duty to another person, as outlined by law. A very common tort is negligent operation of a motor vehicle that results in property damage and personal injury in an automobile accident.

Picher, Oklahoma Lead Contamination

Picher, Oklahoma, was once home to the world's richest lead and zinc mines. However, in 1981, the area was declared a superfund site. The mines of Picher were worked for decades; as a result, mine waste covered 25,000 acres of land in this community. This contamination devastated the Quapaw Indian tribal lands, as well as; the local economy. Acid mine water burned nearby Tar Creek and left the water red.

An alarmingly high percentage of local children were found to have toxic levels of lead in their blood. Even though the mines closed in 1970, sinkholes would open without warning, threatening the lives of children. The federal government's buyout program allowed most of them to move elsewhere. Many refused to leave regardless of the hazards. For all intents and purposes, Picher became a ghost town.

The Exxon Valdez oil spill of 1989

Man have proved to be his own worst enemy, whether it's due to experimentation, research, energy, profit, or just plain and simple greed. Much of the great American landscape has been damaged, scared, polluted, or left a devastated wasteland that will take decades to recover from, if ever. The cause of this systematic rape of a country that had the most perspective and promising future of any nation on the planet, is man. In his quest to improve his way of life and provide a social and business atmosphere that would catapult America into the forefront of world leadership, he has left a wake of environmental distruction and disaster.

The one of the most notorious man-made environmental disaster in America's history was the Exxon Valdez oil spill of 1989. This spill devastated the coast of Alaska when the oil tanker heading from the Valdez oil terminal in Alaska to Long Beach, California, on March 24th, 1989, struck Bligh Reef, accidentally releasing about $1/5^{th}$ of its total load of oil. This was caused due to the negligence of the supposedly sleep deprived pilots who put the ship on autopilot.

The huge spill caused wide environmental damage. Alaska's fisheries were severely damaged; thousands of seabirds were killed. The oil slick caused by this massive spill stretched for 1,300 miles along the Alaskan coastline. As scientist continue to study the effects of oil spills on the environment and animals, it has been documented that petroleum-based hydrocarbons can severly impact aquatic life at concentrations as low as one part per million.

Seabirds were immediately affected by the spill. The oil penetrated their plumage, reducing the insulating ability of their feathers, making them prone to hypothermia and rendering them less buoyant in the water. The oiled feathers also impair bird's flight, thus making it difficult, or impossible, to feed or escape from predators.

The Prince William Sound has always been abundant with water-loving birds. When the birds would attempt to preen or clean their feathers, they would ingest oil that coats their plumage, causing kidney damage, altered liver function and digestive tract distress. It is estimated by wild life biologists that 90,000 to 270, 000 birds died or disappeared in the Sound following the oil spill.

The Exxon Valdez disaster was the first major spill where field stablization and transport were utilized extensively. Stablization consist of warming or cooling birds to help maintain a normal body temperature, providing oral fluids to combat dehydration and providing them with much needed rest in a dark quiet place. The Oil Response Association that represents seven oil companies who operate in Valdez, including Exxon, assumed responsibility for the cleanup.

This battle had to be fought out in court, this was one of the longest cases in maritime history, and it finally wound its way through the U.S. Court system. In June 2008, the U.S. Supreme Court finally voted 5-3 to reduce $2.5 billion punitive damages award, to no more than $507.5 million. Earlier, a lower court awarded $5 billion in damages to area fishermen who lost revenue after the spill. Another court cut that award in half to $2.5 billion.

The spill consisted of 11 million gallons of oil that spread from Prince William Sound for 470 miles to the village of Chignik on the Alaskan Peninsula. More than 1300 miles of shoreline was coated. Exxon estimated that it spent $2.1 billion on cleanup over the following four summers. Many billions of dollars were spent to satisfy this great disaster, and evidence of oil still remains after 21 years.

The British Petroleum (BP) oil spill in the Gulf of Mexico

Every effort must be explored and every resource must be put into action to reverse this assault on the environment. There must be critical support from the Environmental Protection Agency (EPA), to clean up the many tragic and disastrous spoils left behind. There must be improved rules and regulations from the Minerals Management Service (MMS), in cases such as this. The time for change is now.

On April 20, 2010, a Deepwater Horizon drilling rig exploded in the Gulf of Mexico, 11 platform workers were killed. It is the largest marine oil spill in the history of the petroleum industry. This oil gusher from the sea floor, one mile below the surface, released an estimated 5 million barrels of oil before the leak was stopped on July 15, 2010, by capping the wellhead. About 800,000 barrels were captured by containment efforts that included burning, skimming, and chemical dispersants. This spill affected the livelihoods of thousands in the fishing, tourist, and vacation industry in the coastal states along the gulf.

BP, (British Petroleum), is held accountable for the spill and responsible for the clean up. President Obama forced BP to place into escrow 20 billion dollars to subsidize the lost income of the people of the Gulf States, and to fund the clean-up effort.

Five years following the BP oil spill, the citizens and business enterprises has not been fully compensated even though billions were released in 2015. The shrimp beds has been destroyed, the small islands are being eroded, the Pelicans has not returned in any large numbers, the tourist trade has been devastated along the shores of the gulf all the way to Florida. The recovery has not fully taken place, yet, BP is making every attempt at their disposal to circumvent their responsibility in making the people of the region whole. A foreign company allowed to rape America with impunity. This is a sad commentary on the United States Government.

Republican Senator Joe Barten, speaking on behalf of the energy policy and the Republican Party, said President Obama had instituted a Chicago shakedown when he demanded that BP put up the 20 billion dollars. He then issued an apology to BP. His concern was for the oil giant and not the American people. The extent that the members of the Republican Party will go in their hate for President Obama is tragic and shameful. The voters spoke up as loudly during election time and reelected Obama.

During the investigation into the cause of this tragic spill, the belief is that Vice President Dick Cheney's old company Halliburton, used inferior cement to cap a well, causing the blow-out of this well. If the findings are proven to be true, this company and its management should be charged with criminal activity and prosecuted to the fullest extent of the law.

The Environmental Protection Agency, and MMS, must continue to police all areas of possible environmental damage. Stricter laws and regulations must be put into place. The EPA has undercut many states at every turn. The funding has been reduced, the Clean Air Act has not been enforced, the controls and restrictions on air pollution has been relaxed, and the burning of coal to produce energy still produces far too many pollutants into our atmosphere.

America is not alone in the destruction of the environment. The Rainforest is disappearing at an alarming rate, when it's gone, it is irreplaceable, and the world will change forever. Thousands upon thousands of acres have been cleared for lumber and farmland. The weather patterns are changing, the planets temperature is raising, the ice caps are melting. The glaciers that supply fresh water has receded, thousands of plants and animals are going extinct each year, wild animals are encroaching upon our neighborhoods due to habitat destruction. Wake-up world!!

57 million trees are used each year making catalogs. hundreds of coal ash domes in this country are unsafe. The Grand Teton dome breached and 14 people died, this is in addition to those previously mentioned. There are 85,000 coal ash domes in the United States, 4,000 are unsafe while inspection programs have been cut. The state of Alabama has more than 2,000 coal ash domes, and has no inspections. The Federal Government has ceased funding many of these projects and the states can't afford to continue inspections alone, so we wait for certain tragedy.

Our problems are greatly magnified by a failing infrastructure. There are 4 million miles of roads in America; 3 trillion miles are driven each year on those roads. The highways and bridges are crumbling across this land. America's sewer system is cracked, rusted, and corroded. Over 1 million miles of sewage pipes support this system and 800 thousand miles nation wide needs replacement. This failed system leaks 6 billion gallons of drinking water a day at an astronomical cost to our citizens. 900 billion gallons of sewage pores into our rivers and streams each year, teaming with bacteria. Americans die because of microbes in the water. Our electrical grids are in serious trouble, without them everything shuts down. The grid is ageing and overwhelmed. There are 214 minutes of blackout time each year for the average American, and we will have more blackouts if we fail to address this most critical need. America can fight and fund two wars, Iraq and Afghanistan, yet, the republicans will not vote to fund the replacement cost.

The American people must stand up and let their voices be heard. They must demand industrial restraint, and political fortitude, to put forth the most effective technology available to prevent this environmental assault on the only home mankind has; the Planet Earth. The world community must mobilize to halt the destruction of what remains of the rainforest. The alternative is to witness the disappearance of mankind in this solar system.

What is the MMS?

The Minerals Management Service, (MMS), is the federal agency in the U.S. Department of the Interior that manages the nations oil, natural gas, and other mineral resources on the Outer Continental Shelf in federal off shore waters. The agency also collects, accounts for, and disburses mineral revenues from Federal and American Indian lands. MMS disbursed more than $8 billion in FY 2003, and more than $135 billion sence the agency was created in 1982. Nearly $1 billion from those revenues go into The Land and Water Conservation Fund annually for the acquisition and development of state and federal parks and recreation lands.

The MMS staff is to regulate and inspect the industry according to long established policies and protocols, and help relieve our national energy insecurity. In recent years, the U.S. has been struggling to increase its domestic production of natural resources to combat our insidious dependence on foreign imports. But we can't do this at all cost, it is imperative that we protect the citizens of this country with regulations that work.

The Republican politicians are opposed to regulations and have indicated that upon taking control of the white house, many of these departments will be eliminated, or greatly reduced in their responsibilities. The importance of these legislated departments are for the betterment of the health and wellfare of the American people, but their concern is for the richest Americans and want to eliminate any impediments to their progress, even at the expense of our health and safety. The raping of America is prevalent in all areas of environmental concerns, but oil and chemical spills has a long and lasting effect on the planet that we must protect for the sake of our very own survival. For now, the raping of America continues unabated.

Part 9

EDUCATION, CRIME, AND CORRUPTION

I continue to emphasize the fact that America is a great nation; I must continue to remind us all of that fact, but her greatness is predicated on her ability to educate her children. We must give them the opportunity and the educational ability to prosper in a global economy. Many discoveries, inventions and new technological advances have come from the minds of Americans. They have been innovators and determined stewards of change and advancement in our cultural and manufacturing development.

Today, the learning institutions in America are being challenged on many fronts. The educational systems have suffered many devastating changes. There was a time when schools participated in the building of our childrens character through prayer in schools; that was abolished. Schools provided an alternative for children with after school programs that kept them off the streets. There were glee clubs, the arts, plays and contest, sports and after school learning sessions. Today, in many school districts in America, children have to pay a fee to participate in sports.

What happened to the days when a teacher could teach the love for learning, and nurture the curiosity of our young peoples minds? We live in the information age where cities pass municipal bonds to purchase new technology for the benefit of other areas of municipality needs in order to function. How can we sustain a stable educational system, when we have lower standards, larger-class sizes, and higher at-risk populations than ever before? To compound this problem, lower funding inhibits it.

Getting a quality education in America seems to be hindered by a multitude of problems associated with students, parents, teachers, school boards, funding and administration. In some of our cities, such as Detroit, Michigan, up to 65% of students are dropping out of school. That means 2 out of 3 is left without a diploma and educational skills to challenge the job markets of today and tomorrow.

Our parents and our political leaders, must become more involved in the educational development of the children of America. We don't attend PTA meetings, we don't question our educators, we don't involve ourselves with our children, why?

In many areas of the country, our children attend schools without adequate supplies, such as books, computers, learning materials, and other necessities. They are housed in dilapidated buildings with leaking roofs and poor toilet facilities. In some of the inner city schools, they are walking through metal detectors and dealing with drug pushers. Our schools are half empty, while our jails are over flowing.

Segregated education is a sub-standard education. Many of the schools in this country are still segregated. Charter Schools has drained resources from the Public School System. The school vouchers for private or charter schools take dollars from the public school system, therefore, it is private schools with public dollars. Funding is reduced and schools are being closed while students are being relocated. Is re-segregation of schools the hidden and pre-designed agenda? Teachers are being laid off, school budgets are cut, 4 day school weeks with class sizes doubled; wake-up everybody!! State lotteries that were designed to support the funding of public education are putting the funds into the state general fund, breaking the trust of the voters who supported the lottery system. Should the formula used to fund education in America be changed? Should our educators receive more scrutiny? Should our lawmakers be held accountable? Yes! Then maybe we can stop the raping of our childrens future.

We need schools that are equally funded. We need to correct the wrongs that henders higher achievement. Put the computers in the classrooms. Broaden the corriculum to include music, atlethics, recreation, sports, and the arts. Build new schools that are student and learning friendly. Demand that our parents attend PTA meetings and involve themselves in their childrens lives.

We must provide them with the tools that will precipitate a solid foundation for success. Our children are the future of this country, we are their support system; lets not let them down any longer.

Crime and Corruption

Crime is a problem in any nation, whether it is developing, or the older countries of Europe. During the early years of a growing America, law and order was a rare commodity. Criminals and opportunist alike, victimized Americans. The Wild West is a prime example of a youthful nation struggling to gain its footing in the area of law and order. We have seen a growth in criminal activity over time. Look at the roaring 20's, with the prohibition era, and this countries attempt to control alcohol and the mobsters that defied the order. The 1930's, with famous villains such a John Dillinger, Pretty Boy Floyd, Bonnie and Clyde, Al Capone, Machine Gun Kelly, Willie "The Actor" Sutton, who when asked why he robbed banks, responded with, "that's where the money is", and many others. But crime is not always violent. Some of the worst villains committed their crimes with pen and paper. Some were men of the cloth, and provided guidance on Sunday mornings to their flock of worshipers. Many were businessmen of large firms, or CEO's of huge manufacturing companies or financial institutions. The biggest failure of all, is when crime is committed by heads-of-state.

Watergate

The Watergate scandal was a political scandal in the United States in the 1970's, resulting from the break-in of the Democratic National Committee headquarters at the Watergate Hotel and office complex in Washington, D.C.

This affair began on the evening of June 17, 1972, when Frank Wills, a security guard at the complex, noticed tape covering the latch and locks on several doors in the facility, (leaving the doors unlocked). He removed the tape and thought nothing of it. An hour later, he discovered that the locks had been re-taped. Wills called the police and five men were arrested inside the Democratic National Committee's office. The five men were Virgilio Gonzalez,

Frank Sturgis, James McCord, Eugenio Martinez, and Barnard Baker. The five men were charged with attempted burglary and attempted interception of telephone and other communications. On September 15, a grand jury indicted them, and two other men, (E. Howard Hunt, Jr. and G. Gordon Liddy), for conspiracy, burglary, and violation of federal wiretapping laws.

On September 29, 1972, it was revealed that John Mitchell, while serving as Attorney General, controlled a secret Republican fund used to finance intelligence gathering against the Democrats. On October 10, the FBI reported that the Watergate break-in was part of a massive campaign of political spying and sabotage on behalf of the officials and leaders of the Nixon re-election campaign. Despite the revelations, Nixon's re-election campaign was never seriously jeopardized, and on November 7, the President was re-elected in one of the biggest landslides ever in American history. However, as the events surrounding the break-in continued to surface, The Judge would eventually sentence E. Howard Hunt and G. Gordon Liddy to prison, and President Richard Nixon were forced to leave the office of the President of the United States of America in disgrace and shame. Frank Wills, the security guard was given a small job but years later, he was left unemployed and unnoticed, a forgotten figure who tried to stop the raping of the political system by criminal activity.

Some of those accused of, or found guilty of, a crime

Chandra Levy was a graduate student and intern who disappeared in 2001. Levy had just completed an internship with the U.S. Bureau of Prisons, when she went missing in May 2001, in Washington D.C.

U.S. Representative, Republican Gary Condit, was questioned by authorities in her disappearance, he was never considered a suspect in her death. Condit reportedly was having an affair with Levy. The negative publicity from the case was cited as a reason the California lawmaker lost re-election in 2002. Condit was unfairly looked upon, and pre-judged by the people and it cost him his seat in the House. In 2009, the authorities charged a Salvadorian immigrant, who was convicted of similar attacks in the park where the former intern disappeared. A young vibrant graduate student stolen from society and robbed of her future. The shameful thing as well, is that Gary Condit possibly lost a career unjustly. The media can destroy careers and reputations.

Idaho Senator Larry Craig pled guilty to the Minneapolis, Minnesota airport men's room sting that may have ended his political career. He was convicted of disorderly conduct when he sat in a stall and kicked feet with the person in the stall next to him. That person was a police officer working undercover. Senator Craig wanted to change his plea in the later months, but to no avail. He refused to step down from his position, but did not seek re-election of his office.

Judge Samuel Kent of the U.S. District Court, was found guilty of sexual harassment. The sexual misconduct was dropped as a plea bargain.

Edwin Edwards, former Governor of Louisiana, was sentenced to ten years in prison on racketeering and public corruption charges.

George Ryan, and Jim Thompson, both former Govenors of Illinois, have also been convicted on corruption charges.

Senator John Ensign, Republican of Colorado called Senator Larry Craig a disgrace, but had to admit his own indiscretions, but did not resign his office.

Spiro T. Agnew, Vice President of the United States under President Richard Nixon, was the 39th Vice President and the 55th Governor of Maryland. He was also the first Greek American to hold these offices. In 1973, Agnew was under investigation by the United States Attorney's office in Baltimore, Maryland, on charges of extortion, tax fraud, bribery and conspiracy. In October, he was formally charged with having accepted bribes totaling more than $100,000 while holding office as Baltimore County Executive, Governor of Maryland and Vice President of the United States. On October 10, 1973, Agnew was allowed to plead no contest to a single charge that he had failed to report $29,000 of income received in 1967, with the condition that he resign the office of Vice President. He is the only Vice President in history to resign because of criminal charges.

Newt Gringrich, Republican, was the Speaker of the House during the impeachment of President Bill Clinton. Gringrich was the driver behind this effort to remove the president. At the same time that Gringrich was pushing the ethics violation, the violation of the sanctity of the oval office, the infidelity of a sitting President and taking advantage of a young intern, he was far less than a perfect example of correct behavior. Gingrich has been married 3 times. He first married Jackie Battley, his former high school geometry teacher when he was 19 years old, she was 26. They had two daughters. Gingrich left Battley in the spring of 1980 after having an affair with Marianne Ginther. According to Battley, Gingrich visited her later that year while she was in the hospital recovering from cancer surgery to discuss the details of their devorce. Six months later; it was final. He wed Ginther in 1987. Gingrich began an affair with Callista Bisek, who is 23 years his junior, in the mid nineties, which continued during the Congressional investigation of Bill Clinton and the Monica Lewinsky scandal. In 2000, Gingrich married Bisek shortly after divorce from his 2nd wife Ginther, was finalized. Mr Gingrich has little room to criticize anyone's character. Now the inflammatory rhetoric he's using to criticize President Obama, is appalling and unbecoming a political figure seeking support for the office of the President of the United States. He is a pitiful sight of desperation and don't deserve consideration for the office of dog catcher. In my opinion, this is the lowest form of corruption in a political figure who held and violated the public trust. Gingrich won re-election during that time, but stepped down from office under the weight of scandal.

Sheila Dixon, Mayor of Baltimore, Maryland and a Democrat, was indicted on charges of accepting illegal gifts during her time as Mayor and City Council President, including travel, fur coats and gift cards intended for the poor that she allegedly used instead for a holiday shopping spree, "I am being unfairly accused" Dixon said. She was convicted on December 1, 2009, on one count of misappropriation of gift cards, she stepped down on February 4, 2010.

Mayor Marion S. Barry Jr., Democratic politician who served as the second elected Mayor of Washington D.C. from 1979 to 1991, and again as the fourth Mayor from 1995 to 1999, and later served on the D.C. City Council. Barry was the target of a high-profile 1990 Federal Investigation into his behavior. He was video taped using drugs in a hotel room. He was arrested and convicted on drug charges. Barry served six months in a Federal Prison. He died November, 2014.

Theodore Fulton "Ted" Stevens, Republican Senator from Alaska, serving from December 24, 1968, until January 3, 2009. Stevens was the longest-serving Republican Senator in history. Strom Thurmond served in the senate longer, but as a Democrat.

On July 29, 2008, Stevens was indicted by a federal grand jury on seven counts of failing to report gifts received from VECO Corporation and its CEO Bill Allen on his senate financial disclosure forms. He was formerly charged with violation of provisions of the Ethics in Government Act. Stevens pled not guilty and asserted his rights to a speedy trial, which began on September 25, 2008, in

Washington, DC, to have the opportunity to clear his name before the November election. On October 27, 2008, barely a week before the election, Stevens was found guilty on all seven counts. He lost the election, however, United States Attorney General Eric Holder, citing serious prosecutorial misconduct during the trial, decided to drop all charges against Stevens, an action that vacated his conviction. Stevens died in August 2010 in a plane crash in Alaska.

The long arm of crime apparently breaches all segments of society. Those that we perceive to be exempt from the lure of unsavory acts, fall into the trap of deceit and cover-up.

In the city of West Palm Beach, Florida, two priest were accused of embezzling hundreds of thousands of dollars from their church. Monsignor John Skehan 81, pled guilty to bilking parishioners at St. Vincent Ferrer Catholic Church in Delray Beach, for years. Skehan has been accused of taking $370,000 from 2001-2006.

During the years 2008, and 2009, the Catholic Church faced it's greatest and most devastating scandals as Catholic Priest were accused of sexual abuse and the raping of young boys in the church. The scandal raged on and on as the Pope failed to publicly address this most immoral and criminal issue. The church was finally forced to pay millions in the settlement of some of the charges. This terrible deed left many boys scarred for life. Many grew into manhood still keeping the secret that was destroying them from within. Many of the priest that committed this heinous crime on the children of the church, were left to continue to run their parish. The sins of man, and the raping of America's youth.

On January 13, 2009, prosecutors charged Racine, Wisconsin Mayor, Gary Becker, with sex felonies. He resigned days after being accused of trying to arrange a sexual encounter with someone he thought was an underaged 14 year old girl. He had gone to the mall to meet someone he had chatted on line with. Becker 51, resigned and stepped down as mayor.

Brian Doyle, Deputy Press Secretary for Home Land Security, went to prison for child porn.

Frank Figororoa, a senior Homeland Security employee who was the head of Operation Predator, was arrested for exposing himself to a young girl in a mall.

John Coarsmo, Chairman of the Federal Housing Board, pled guilty to lying about inviting banks that he regulated to a fund raiser for a congressional candidate. That cost his wife, Deputy Chief of Staff for the Labor Department, to lose her job as well.

The founder of New Life Church in Colorado Springs, Colorado, Ted Haggard, was brought down in the mist of a sex scandal involving a male who reported having a sexual relationship with Haggard.

Ronald Ferguson, 66, of Fairfield, the former Chief Executive of General RE Corp., was sentenced to two years in prison and fined $200,000 for his role in a scheme that cost shareholders of American International Group Inc., more than $500 million. He was convicted for conspiracy, securities fraud, mail fraud and making false statements to the Securities and Exchange Commission. He also must do two years supervised release after serving his prison time.

TIME magazine listed the names of some of the most scandalous businessmen in this country. The American people should be appalled at the greed and disrespect exhibited and carried out by these individuals.

Bernie Ebbers, Worldcom, was inducted into the Mississippi Business Hall of Fame in 1995. Ebbers was a graduate of the obscure Mississippi College. Mr Ebbers was the CEO of WorldCom. He started with a small telecommunications company that acquired smaller competitors, and eventually created one of the largest companies in the world. It turned out that as WorldCom exploded in profits, Mr. Ebbers amassed a personal wealth of more than $1 billion. This company was investigated in 2002, and the results of that investigation revealed that WorldCom had executed the largest accounting fraud in history to date. There were more than $11 billion in accounting misstatements. It was also alledged that Mr. Ebbers had taken $366 million in personal loans from the company. As a result, WorldCom's stock took a nosedive from more than $64 per share to just over $1.

Ebbers was found guilty in March, 2005, for his roll in the huge accounting scandal that led to the largest bankruptcy in U.S. history. A Federal Grand Jury, on it's 8th day of deliberations, convicted Ebbers on all nine counts that he helped mastermind an $11 billion accounting fraud at WorldCom, known as MCI. He had a right to appeal.

Even Martha Stewart was caught-up in insider-trading charges. Martha Stewart is CEO and Chairwoman of Martha Stewart Living Omnimedia. She was found guilty of conspiracy, obstrucrion of an agency's proceedings, and lying to federal investigators about an insider-trading deal. The multimillion dollar business woman had sold a few thousand shares of ImClone Systems stock to save just $45,000. She served five months in a Minimum-security prison camp in West Virginia and was released in March 2005.

To add insult to injury, teacher Mary Kay Letourneau, a level two sex offender, spent six years in prison for rape or child molestation of a student. She was placed on probation during her correctional period, but she would not stay away from the student, therefore, she was ordered back to prison to serve her term. Upon her release, she reconnected with the student and they were married with all of the fanfare of celebrities. The media covered the wedding and made her a star rather than the pedophile that she is. Where is our moral character?

There are different degrees of criminal activity, there are crimes that are carried out quietly and unnoticed until an event that exposes it suddenly appears on the scene. The perpetrators can range from the hoodlum on the streets of our cities, to heads of state. One of the largest crimes perpetrated on the American people was the Ponzi Scheme committed by Bernard Madoff over several years, but discovered in 2009. Madoff was the CEO of a Wall Street firm called Bernard L. Madoff Investment Securities LLC, started in 1960. In march 2009, Madoff pled guilty to 11 federal crimes and admitted to turning his wealth management business into a massive scheme that defrauded thousands of investors of billions of dollars. Federal investigators believe the scheme began as early as the 1980's, and that the investment operation may never have been legitimate.

The amount missing from clients accounts, including fabricated gains, was almost $65 billion. The court appointed trustee estimated actual losses to investors of $18 billion. On June 29, 2009, he was sentenced to 150 years in prison, the maximum allowed.

What is a Ponzi scheme ?

A Ponzi scheme is a fraudulent investment operation that pay returns to separate investors from their own money, or money paid by subsequent investors, rather than from any actual profit earned. The perpetuation of the returns that a Ponzi scheme advertises and pays, requires an ever increasing flow of money from investors to keep the scheme going. The scheme is destined to collapse because the earnings, if any, are less than the payments to investors.

There were many Ponzi schemes run by criminals in the past, but Madoffs was by far the biggest. The following are some examples: William Miller, of Brooklyn, New York, claimed in 1899, he had inside information on stocks. He defrauded investors out of $1 million.

Charles Ponzi, ran a bogus investment scheme in 1919-20 involving as many as 20,000 people who invested up to $10 million.

Lou Pearlman, the mastermind behind the Backstreet Boys and N Sync singing groups, operated a $300 million stock and investment scam. He was sentenced to 25 years in prison.

James Paul Lewis Jr., was sentenced to 30 years in prison for a scheme that ran from 1985 to 2003, and cost nearly 3,300 investors about $70 million.

Steven Hoffenberg, a bill collector who once briefly ran the New York Post, admitted he defrauded investors of $460 million. He pled guilty in 1995.

Reed Slatkin, co-founder of Earthlink Inc., and once a scientology minister, was sentenced in 2003 to 14 years in prison for swindling investors out of about $240 million over 15 years.

Daniel Heath, was sentenced to 127 years in prison for running an investment scam in southern California that bilked 1,800 people out of $187 million in the early 1990s. These culprits are from a list compiled by Associated Press.

On another front, one of the most terrible and dreadful practices in the criminal arena is the incarceration of drug abusers. The lowly junkies, or marijuana users, are arrested and prosecuted if they are caught with a designated amount of drugs that society deems excessive. If it is truly a disease, why are they prosecuted rather than treated? The jails and prisons are full of men and women arrested for this criminal infraction while the murderers, robbers and white collar criminals are set free to make room for new prisoners. There are no real treatment programs provided for these people. Thirty years in prison for 600 grams of cocaine is asinine and criminal within its-self. Therefore, the rape of Americans, even in the world of so called criminal activity, is still a form of rape.

There have been many periods of American political misjudgment. Let us revisit the period of alcohol prohibition in the 1920's and 1930's that grew criminal activity in this country on a massive scale. This era spawned the likes of Al Capone in Chicago, or the Mob in New York, or the Purple Gang in Detroit. This created the rise of illegal activity in many forms and the killings on our streets that left a bloody trail throughout many communities. Gambling, prostitution, the speakeasy, after hours joints, corruption of local and national politicians, and many other forms of criminal activity flourished during this era.

Then there were the mass discrimination by this country against Japanese, German and Italian American citizens during World War II; they were rounded up and moved to, and held at, the Wyoming Heart Mountain Relocation Center, until the war ended. These law abiding citizens lost everything they had due to this executive decision made by our government. They were in effect, imprisoned. The criteria was that they had not yet become American citizens.

During the Vietnam War, our soldiers were treated like they were infected with the black plague. American citizens marched in the streets in protest of the war, they rallied on college campuses and many faced arrest by the authorities. The most dreadful event was the Kent State University protest, when this nation turned its guns on its own students. When the smoke cleared, there were dead and wounded on the campus grounds. This event was deemed the May 4, massacre, or the Kent State massacre. This tragedy occurred on the campus in the city of Kent, Ohio, and involved the shooting of unarmed college students by members of the Ohio National Guard on Monday, May 4, 1970. The guardsmen fired 67 rounds over a period of 13 seconds, killing four students and wounding nine others, one whom suffered premanent paralysis. Some of the wounded were shot while walking nearby, or simply observing the protest.

There was a national response that involved hundreds of colleges, universities and high schools, that closed throughout the nation due to a student strike of four million. Public opinion was affected by this shameful event. The raping of America comes in many forms. The officers in charge of the Guard that day, was simply incompetent and used poor judgment against an unarmed crowd of students. Americans, under fire from the guns they pay to protect them from all enemies foreign or domestic. Sometimes the enemy is our protector and sometimes he walks among us.

During the Presidency of Rutherford B. Hayes, and in response to the Great Railroad Strike of 1877, when workers walked off the job and were joined by thousands across the country; the president called out federal troops to restore the peace and put down the unrest. For the first time in this country's history, troops fired on the striking workers killing more than 70. It was shameful then and it was shameful during the Kent State protest.

During the 1970's, the nation suffered from enormous cultural divisions. A cultural revolution was taking place in America. Normal inhibitions went out of the window, there were free and open sex. Drug usage and experimentation with drugs began to escalate. The flower children preached "Make love not war". The style of clothes changed, rallies were held at Woodstock. A change was sweeping across America. The word Hippies described the crowd that drove this change.

The plight of African Americans began to improve, the voting rights and civil rights laws were in place. Segregation in schools were ordered abolished, the busing of students that followed that order became the next big fight. The conditions that Blacks suffered in their community was not self imposed, but was the residue of many years of inequality. Affirmative action was supposedly designed to aleviate an injustice suffered by blacks, white women, and other minorities for the years they were denied equal opportunity in many areas of society. White women saw far better results than African Americans.

Nepotism is another big problem that society has failed to address. Segregation and exclusion was the law and not a standard, therefore, government should have made a correction because many Blacks met the standard and still was denied equal opportunity in jobs, schools, promotions and other areas of advancement. The necessity for change was evident and inevitable. To avoid equal employment opportunity and equal educational opportunity for all, relatives were hired to circumvent affirmative action. Due to the lack of total enforcement, the rape continues, but has improved.

Part 10

POLITICIANS, A BROKEN TRUST

The politicians of this country, in many cases, have failed their constituents on several fronts. Honesty and integrity in local, state, and federal government, has been lost or forgotten. Many of our representatives simply don't have a clue about the plight of poor people in America. The suffering endured by millions of Americans does not exist in the minds of these politicians. Therefore, they have lost their moral conscience. Many don't value the positions taken by the voter's, so they yield to the lobbyist that fill their campaign chest and sometimes their pockets with dollars. They fail to envision, or recognize, what our capabilities are. They have put aside, or, disregarded our ability to dream; they have lost their dedication to America and to the people that rely on them for justice. Some newspaper editors and radio and television pundits, have lost respect for their fellowman and have traded fairness for profit margins and ratings. They have the ability to amplify the positions taken by figures of authority, but they must do it with equal time on an agenda that will benefit all Americans. The issues must be relevant to the principles of the American people and not just those that are critical to a particular political party.

We still have a need for clarity on issues, or the settlement there of. We still have a need for courage, for conviction, and for allowing suffering voices to be heard. They must provide them an equal setting at the table of brotherhood and they must end their indifferences to poor Americans. They must be committed to truth and justice, morality and integrity, credibility and purpose, and end the narrow mindedness of me first. They must have a willingness to be truthful no matter the circumstances.

Under President George W. Bush, America stepped off the cliff of credibility with the Patroit Act. The government threw probable cause and due process out with the bath water. The use of this act gave the Bush administration the authority to violate the U.S. Constitution based on their personal judgment, when dealing with the citizens of this country.

They can enter the homes of our citizens without a warrant that once had to be granted by a judge. The CIA was not created and designed to operate within the borders of the United States, yet, they listen in on many of our phone calls. They used all of the technology available to them to violate our civil liberties. The government has stripped us of our freedoms. They look into every facet of our lives without our knowledge or permission. They use cameras, listening devices, spy satellites, eavesdropping capabilities, telephone access, cell phones, brainwashing and OnStar, to enter our private lives. The FBI, and Homeland Security, monitors everything in our lives, including our driving habits, our bank accounts, credit records and computer uses. They spy on our associates and friends, our workplace, our churches where we worship, our political party affiliation, our educational level and they make the determination as to whether or not we are political malcontents.

Under the Foreign Intelligence Surveillance Act, A (NSA) National Security Agency whistle blower Russell Tice, allegedly said that President George W. Bush spied on all Americans with wire tapping, eavesdropping and warrant-less wiretapping programs; he said that the NSA spied on average Americans and journalist, with no criminal investigation ever ordered.

Our Republican President blessed all of these measures. This is no longer the land of the free, but the land of federal checks and balances. We are being watched, abused, directed and we don't even know it. We are told when and where to smoke, to buckle up, to wear helmets, when to grow crops and what crops to grow. Cameras line some of our street corners and look right into our daily lives. The Bill of rights went out of the window with George W. Bush, Dick Cheney and their Republican criminals.

This country is soaked in a sea of wasteful spending and crippling bureaucracy. Criminals within the system have displaced ethics and credibility. Corrupt politicians reject us; we suffer from bank fraud and open borders, predatory lending and sub-prime mortgages. This country is being raped of its character and its legacy of the people first.

In 2010, the United States Supreme Court ruled that big business could donate as much money as they want to political candidates, giving way to buying elections. They killed the regulations that provided information on how much we could give, or from whom, or where it came from and some form of transparent control. They were previously restricted and limited to a certain dollar amount.

While our politicians bicker over bills in the House and the Senate that would ease the pain of the citizens, there are high times on Wall Street and hard times on Maine Street. People are losing their jobs, their homes are going into foreclosure, thousands are filing for bankruptcy, their belongings are being repossessed, millions were without healthcare until The Affordable Care Act, while we provide the best healthcare in the world to the members of the United States Congress. The leaders are well paid while they fight against raising the minimum wage for the poorest Americans. There is a re-distribution of wealth in America, from the lower class to the upper class.

In March 2010, President Obama signed the healthcare legislation into law. The Republican Senators were opposed to the bill and as a result, voted no while 45,000 Americans die each year because of a lack of healthcare. This bill is funded and will not increase the deficit.

In 2003, President George W. Bush signed into law the totally un-funded prescription drug plan that cost the taxpayers hundreds of billions of dollars and will continue to cost them. The republicans supported this legislation, why? As a result of the Affordable Care Act, some Democratic Party offices were being smashed, windows were broken, threats were issued and Democratic Congressmen had to hire extra security. An idiot in Alabama bragged that guns were being cleaned all over.

Republican politician Sarah Palin said, "We must reload and put them in our cross hairs", but what can you expect from an airhead like Palin. When interviewed by Fox News during her campaign as John McCain's running mate for Vice President of this country, she didn't know that Presidents don't declare war, Congress does. The so-called fair and balanced Chris Wallace didn't call her on it. Because the Fox (no news) Network is so biased towards President Obama. It is obvious that Sarah Palin is mentally bankrupt, extremely inept and borders on being an idiot. She was caught with written cheat notes on her hand to remind her during an interview to speak on energy, tax cuts and lifting Americans spirit. Even though her shortcomings are obvious, she still had a huge following in America, until now.

Republican Michelle Bachmann of Minnesota, stood on a podium urging on the fools that issue threats to our elected officials. She calls for the abolishment of Social Security and Medicare, the two most important pieces of legislation ever signed into law for older Americans; she didn't run for office again.

A militiaman in Alabama openly advocates violence while he sits on his butt enjoying his Social Security checks. To threaten the lives of Democratic Congressmen and Senators, with vicious name-calling and death threats, is beyond reasonable thinking. The Tea Partiers and the Republican Party condones and advocates this dangerous behavior. The Birthers contend that the President was not born in America, regardless of evidence to the contrary. It is evident to a thinking person that both the Birthers and the Tea Partiers are race driven; the signs at their rallies are a clear indication of that. There are signs calling Obama a Nazi, and comparing him to Hitler. There were signs with horns calling him the devil. During the Presidential campaign a woman in attendance at a rally, told Senator John McCain that Obama was an Arab, Senator McCain assured her that he was not.

When George W. Bush was president, they called it aiding and abetting the enemy to criticize a sitting president doing wartime. When President Barach Obama became president, the Fox News Network and its announcers did a 180-degree turn and criticizes everything he does while two wars were still raging. Is it racism? Yes!

On September 9, 2009, while President Obama addressed the nation, Republican Representative Joe Wilson yelled out, "You lie," in response to remarks made by the President. Republican Randy Neugebauer from Texas shouted out, "Baby Killer," as Democrat Bart Stupak of Michigan read an executive order by President Obama to assure that no federal funds would be used for abortion in the healthcare bill. Rush Limbaugh, a radio personality and a member of, if not the leader of the Republican Party, used a racial slur when he called President Obama, "Barach the magic Negro," the Republican

Party leaders said nothing, silence is complicity. Republican Senator Richard Behney of Indiana made the statement that if he doesn't see new faces after the 2010 election; he is cleaning his guns and getting ready for the big show. Glenn Beck, formerly of the Fox News Network, owned by Rupert Murdoch, called President Obama a racist and said he hates white people. The network says nothing, nor does Murdoch.

White America must accept the fact that President Obama is in the white house. This is no longer a nation of white majority rule, nor, only white leaders in business and government. There is a changing demographic in this nation, a Black President, more non-white immigrants than white, Jews in top leadership roles, and Hispanics growing in power. White America must accept this rendezvous with reality that someday soon they will be in the minority.

The house members have moved 290 pieces of legislation to the Senate and it is just sitting there with no action, though it may be justified. Some Americans believe that the government is broken. Is this what the founders intended, or does racism play a roll because of Barach Obama? While 81% believe that it can be fixed, can we really continue to send the same republicans to Congress and expect a different result? That is the definition of insanity?

President Obama has had more death threats than any other president in U.S. history. The threats are up 400% from when President George W. Bush was in office.

During the Bush Presidency, we had criminals in the white house. Both Bush and Dick Cheney admitted to water boarding Khalid S. Muhammed over 185 times. This is a violation of the laws of this country and the Geneva Convention.

There was a double standard in the Bush administration; many believe our enemies may have used this information to recruit new terrorist. President Bush convicted and sent to prison, the soldiers involved in the torture at the Abu Ghraib prison in Iraq. The ten involved were either convicted, or reduced in grade. He and Cheney should be prosecuted for war crimes; are they above the law? He said he would do it again if it would save lives. There is no evidence that any lives were saved as a result of this illegal torture. The President's admission to these crimes came in June of 2010. When you can't be held accountable for facilitating war crimes because the Justice Department says torture by water boarding was justified judgment, we're in trouble. With this rationale, the judgement at Nuremberg set the standard and this threw that ruling out of the window.

The lies and corruption in the George W. Bush administration didn't stop there. In 2007, the Justice Department was investigating whether Attorney General Alberto Gonzales lied, or, otherwise misled Congress in sworn testimony about the Bush administrations domestic terrorist spying program. The Senate Judiciary Chairman, Democrat Patrick Leahy, asked for the inquiry two weeks before Gonzales answered by saying he was stepping down. The question was whether Gonzales gave inaccurate testimony about the firing of several U.S. Attorneys in 2006. Gonzales had said he would leave the Justice Department on September 16, 2007. The case was about the department allowing the National Security Agency to eavesdrop on domestic terror suspects without court review. His departure ended without justice being served.

The Poor People's Struggle for Economic Justice

America has fought many battles in the building and growth of a stable economy in this nation. The battles were fought on many different fronts. The dust bowl and the drought of the plains states, the great depression of the 1920's and 1930's, the catastrophic weather that destroyed crops and raised the prices of food and other consumer goods, but the biggest economic disaster of all has been the greed of mankind.

The reduction of the economic status of this country has always been an anvil around the necks of poor Americans. When the rich call the economy a recession, the poor are in a depression. 70% of Americans are living from paycheck to paycheck. More homes have gone into foreclosure than ever before, cars and motor homes are still being repossessed at a higher rate than at anytime in our history. Americans are borrowing themselves into financial oblivian. Less are saving than ever before; many are living on credit cards and are debt ridden and desperate beyond recovery. This is a financial crisis of tremendous magnitude

When Ronald Reagan was in the white house, his answer to the economy he inherited was called trickle down economics. On his arrival, the deficit was $994 billion, when he left it was $2.8 trillion. The trickle never got down to the poor people of this nation. When Bill Clinton became President, he changed the policy and left office with a budget surplus of nearly 237 billion dollars.

The Republican Party gave Reagan credit for the biggest tax cut in history, but for poor people, it was the biggest tax increase ever imposed on this nation's poorest citizens. Before Reagan, interest paid on any item such as homes, personal loans, cars, credit cards, etc. could be written off our income taxes, he also increased social security taxes to a continuous yearly increase that could reach 90% of taxable earnings. Before Reagan, poor people had a chance to reach the cutoff point in social security taxes; today, that opportunity does not exist for the poor.

The Savings and Loan Crisis

During the early years of the Reagan administration, "the 1980's", America suffered through a savings and loan crisis that we have yet to recover from. This was a crisis in which 747 institutions failed. The survivors had to be rescued with $160 billion of taxpayer's money.

The payout still continues today and the amount of the rescue continues to grow. Ronald Reagan eliminated the loopholes in the tax code, including the elimination of the "passive loss" provisions that subsidized rental housing. Because this was removed retroactively, it bankrupted 747 savings and loans, many of which were operating more or less as banks, thus requiring the FDIC to cover their debts and losses with taxpayer's money. This, with some other "deregulation policies", ultimately led to the largest political and financial scandal in U.S. history to date.

Some have called it the largest theft in the history of the world and U.S. taxpayers were the victims of unarmed robbery. If Reagan had not deregulated the industry and eased the restrictions so much that abuse and misuse of funds became easy and went unchecked; this theft may have been averted. The expense is on going and has exceeded $1 trillion; the end is not in sight.

The Keating Five: were five United States Senators accused of corruption in 1989, igniting a major political scandal as part of the larger Savings and Loan crisis. The five senators, Alan Cranston, Democrat of California, Dennis DeConcini, Democrat of Arizona, John Glenn, Democrat of Ohio, John McCain, Republican of Arizona, and Donald Riegle Jr., Democrat of Michigan, were accused of improperly intervening in 1987 on behalf of Charles Keating Jr., chairman of the Lincoln Savings and Loan Association, which was the target of a regulatory investigation by the Federal Home Loan Bank Board. The board subsequently backed off taking action against Lincoln. What happened to the shareholders could have been one of the cruelest frauds in banking history.

The substantial political contributions that Keating had made to each of the senators, totaling $1.3 million, attracted considerable public and media attention. After a lengthy and full investigation, the Senate Ethics Committee determined in 1991, that Alan Cranston, Dennis DeConcini, and Don Riegle Jr., had substantially, and improperly, interfered with the FHLBB in its investigation of Lincoln Savings, with Cranston receiving a formal reprimand. Senators John Glenn and John McCain were cleared of having acted improperly, but were criticized for having exercised poor Judgment. All five served out their terms, only Glenn and McClain ran for re-election and both succeeded.

Presidents and politicians have caused the citizens of America massive economic losses, but private citizens, or CEO's of large companies or corporations, are not exempt from this economic deluge.

Kenneth Lee Lay, CEO and chairman of Enron Corporation, was best known for his role in the widely reported corruption scandal that led to the downfall of Enron. This Corporation became synonymous with corporate abuse and accounting fraud when the scandal broke in 2001. Lay was the CEO and chairman from 1985 until his resignation on January 23, 2003.

On July 7, 2004, Lay was indicted by a grand jury on 11 counts of securities fraud and related charges. Lay was found guilty on May 25, 2006, of ten counts against him. Lay could have faced 20 to 30 years in prison; however, he died while vacationing in Colorado on July 5, 2006. Lay dumped large amounts of his Enron stock in September and October 2001 as its price fell, while encouraging employees to buy more stock, telling them the company would rebound. Lay liquidated more than 300 million in Enron stock from 1989 to 2001. The lies and fraud of Kenneth Lay and the subsequent bankruptcy that followed, cost 20,000 employees their jobs, and many of them their life savings. Lay's wealth had grown to over 40 million dollars.

The nineteen nineties called for more oversight into the banking industry, so the Federal Reserve Board looked into a quagmire of discriminatory lending practices by banking institutions in this country. There was an obvious and concerted effort to discriminate against minorities in America. The outcry from critics against these discriminatory practices directed at minorities who were denied mortgages at a far higher rate than other Americans by mortgage lenders, were deafening.

The Federal Reserve Board recognized the need to examine these charges and found that the practices were true. Black applicants were twice as likely as whites to be denied the same opportunity to gain access to home ownership, that practice still exist in some areas. The solution to this problem was to give consideration to anyone seeking mortgage financing. Their ability to re-pay the loan was not of great importance, therefore, the federal governments position and the subsequent debacle to follow in the American housing market, was devastating to the American economy.

In the waning days of the Bush presidency, a new type of storm, a financial storm, hit America hard. Several weeks prior to this disaster, the president had predicted good economic weather ahead and stated "The Fundamentals of the Economy is Strong". On Wednesday, September 17, 2008, just days after investment giant Lehman Brothers went bankrupt; Americans went on a bank run. On that day, Wall Street stood still. On that Wednesday alone, over $140 billion were withdrawn; people were scared, they just wanted out. They clutched the cash like food in a famine. The President disappeared from sight, the next day he finally spoke simply saying the American people could be sure that he would act to strengthen and stabilize our financial markets and improve investor confidence. That was his total message as the worst financial crisis since the Great Depression was looming.

Sub-prime lending destroyed the housing market and caused the property values to go into the tank. During the collapse of the housing market, Americans by the hundreds of thousands were losing their homes to foreclosure. As the property values continued to decline, the property taxes in many states continued to rise creating additional hardship for many Americans. This unfair and unjust tactic is disgraceful. The loss of homes to foreclosure and the loss of jobs in this country caused America to become a debtor nation to a magnitude unheard of before. In addition to that, the banking system and the large financial institutions on Wall Street, failed. This required a bailout from the Federal Government of 798 billion dollars to right a sinking ship. The American citizens were raped again.

President George W. Bush borrowed this country into trillion-dollar debt owed to China to fight two unjust wars. He signed into law the Medicare Drug Benefit Plan that was un-funded, adding the biggest cost in decades to the American taxpayers. The Bush administration did not fully fund "No Child Left Behind", therefore, the states were given the responsibility of implementation, while Bush cut taxes on the top 2% of America's wealthiest wage earners. The weight of this problem is crushing this nations economy. The TARP bill was signed into law by President George W. Bush to save the banking industry and the investment firms on Wall Street, prior to his leaving office, however, most Americans blamed "TARP" on President Obama.

What is TARP?

The Troubled Asset Relief Program, commonly known as TARP, is a program of the United States government to purchase assets and equity from financial institutions to strengthen its financial sector, which was signed into law by U.S. President George W. Bush on October 3, 2008. It is the largest component of the government's measures in 2008 to address the subprime mortgage crisis. Originally expected to cost the U.S. government $356 billion, the most recent estimates of the cost, as of April 12, 2010, was down to $89 billion, which is 42% less than the tax payer's cost of the savings and loan crisis of the 1980's. This reduction is due to the pay back by most of these institutions along with interest.

A Violated Trust

The American people exercises their voting rights to select the candidate of their choice to represent them in the halls of government, whether it is local, state, or federal. This is done through the voting process guaranteed by the Constitution. We expect our candidates to be honorable men and women with impeccable character. We need men and women of integrity, intelligence and even valor. However, we have experienced crippling bureaucracy, corrupt politicians, criminals within the system, ethics gone awry, dedication forgotten, bank fraud, open borders, two unjust wars and a host of other betrayals. The most devastating betrayal is the Republican Party and its "just say no" attitude taken for political gain. They would do anything to bring down President Obama and get this Black man out of the white house.

The impurity of politicians is made apparent through their broken promises and the pledges they forfeit. They have weakened the confidence of the American people.

On March 24, 2010, the Republicans shut down all committee meetings because of President Obama's victory with health care; they just shut down government's ability to function.

Politicians must learn to serve the public interest and not their personal agenda. Many states have, or have had, politicians that are accused of using their power to make money. Some states are worst than others. Illinois, New Jersey and Louisiana, have been in the forefront of political corruption with many elected officials serving time in prison. These states have long been considered hot beds of public corruption. Congressman Jefferson of Louisiana was found to have $90,000 in his freezer and was later convicted for taking bribes and kickbacks. There were reports surfacing of an investigation into Senator Norm Coleman's finances in Minnesota. Political careers can lead to lucrative private sector jobs; therefore, the temptation to use it as a stepping-stone is very strong. Much of their time is spent around the rich people of this country and fund-raising makes asking favors so common that all politicians face that struggle, but not all succumb to its temptation.

Governments Wasteful Spending

We have all heard of wasteful spending by the Department of Defense with the purchase of $700.00 hammers and toilet seats. There are warehouses around this country filled with obsolete parts for military purposes. Many parts are still being ordered and stored. Many cannot be accounted for. In the home district of Republican John Beohner, the F-85 aircraft is being built with two engines for each plane, the Pentagon don't want it, yet we continue to waste the money because it's in his district. A man who does not take, or believe in earmarks and pork barrel spending, please!!

Senator Tom Coburn, Republican from Oklahoma says the government waste more than $385 billion dollars a year. Senator Coburn is an Oklahoma physician who has a reputation of fighting earmarks and pork barrel projects where ever he finds them. He has fought to block bills with no apology; some have been fixed, hidden and gotten through.. Senator Ted Stevens, the Republican from Alaska started to resign when Coburn proposed an amendment to the 2006 fiscal appropriations. This bill would have rerouted funding for Alaska's bridge to nowhere that was in the bill that funds transportation projects. Instead, Coburn wanted it allocated to rebuilding the twin bridge spans in New Orleans, Louisiana, that was damaged by Hurricane Katrina in 2005. Most of his colleagues fought to defeat Coburn's efforts.

Coburn released an overview in 2008, called "the Worst Waste of the Year". The following are some of his listings.

1) $3.2 million for an unwanted Pentagon Blimp
2) $9.4 million in grants to a California Institute to fund the continued search for extraterrestrials.
3) $24.6 million for the National Park Services 100th birthday celebration, 8 years before the anniversary.

Coburn says that career politicians are behind most government waste. He was still in his first term and said he would not serve a second term. He did not run in 2015.

The Iran-Contra Scandal

The Republican Party has always, in modern history, leaned towards the rich and dealt the poor in this country a bad hand. They have projected themselves to be a party dedicated to America and all of its citizens. They are not, nor have they ever been since reconstruction. The great party of ethical standards that they proposed to be, is tainted with prejudice and disrespect.

The presidency of Ronald Reagan was not free from scandals. During the EPA, (Environmental Protection Agency) scandals, over twenty high-level EPA employees were removed from office during the first three years of Reagan's presidency. Additionally, several agency officials resigned amidst a variety of charges ranging from being unduly influenced by industry groups, to rewarding, or punishing employees based on their political beliefs. There were multiple scandals resulting in investigation, indictment, or conviction of over 138 administration officials; the largest number for any president up to this point in history. In addition, several agency officials resigned amidst a variety of charges. Sewergate was the most prominent EPA scandal during this period. Rita Marie Lavelle, Assistant Administrator of the EPA appointed by Reagan, was found guilty of fraud and misuse of the Superfund monies and irregularities at the StringFellow Acid Pit. Lavelle was found guilty of one count of wire fraud and 2 counts of making false statements to the FBI; she got one-year probation and a $3,000 fine.

One of the great scandals for the American presidency was the Iran-Contra scandal, carried out under the watch and leadership of President Ronald Reagan. The Iran-Contra affair was a political scandal in America that was exposed in November, 1986. This during the Administration of the so-called great communicator, or as some called him, the Teflon President. Many U.S. leaders agreed to facilitate the sale of weapons to Iran, the subject of an arms embargo. The intent was to possibly gain the release of American hostages and allow the CIA to provide monetary support to the Nicaraguan Contras. The U.S. would use Israel as a middleman in this activity as a supplier and the U.S. would resupply Israel. The Lebanese Shia Islamist group, Hezbollah, was holding six American hostages, but they were unknowingly connected to the Army of the Guardians of the Islamic Revolution. The plan deteriorated into an arms-for-hostages scheme in which members of the executive branch sold weapons to Iran in exchange for the release of the American hostages.

Lieutenant Colonel Oliver North of the National Security Council, modified the plan in 1985, and diverted a portion of the proceeds from the sale. The remainder went to fund Anti-Sandinista and anti-communist rebels, or Contras, in Nicaragua. North was tried as a result of his involvement and wrote in a book that he was sure Reagan knew and approved what went on with the initiative and private efforts on behalf of the Contras. It is believed by many that the illegal drug trade was a large part of this Contra effort. There are those in the "ATF" Alcohol, Tobacco and Firearms Department, who insist that drugs were used to provide additional funding. All the while, Nancy Reagan was telling America's children to "Just say no to drugs".

During North's testimony before Senate and House investigating committees in July of 1987, North said he assumed that President Reagan was in the loop on what he was doing and had given his approval through his superiors. He said that he had repeatedly sent memoranda on several occasions to Admiral John Poindexter, Reagan's security adviser, seeking permission to divert money from the Iran arms sales to the Contras.

On May 4, 1989, Oliver North was convicted in federal court on three of twelve counts charged against him. His punishment, a $150,000 fine and a 3 year suspended sentence and 1,200 hours of community service. This was minimal in light of the charges that were directed against, and in defiance, of the laws set by Congress that prohibited the sale.

The Tower Commission appointed by the Congress to investigate this affair, found no direct evidence that Reagan knew the extent of the programs. Who believes the Tower Commission? In the end, fourteen administration officials were indicted, including the Secretary of Defense, Casper Weinberger. Eleven convictions resulted, some of which were vacated on appeal. The rest of those indicted, or convicted, were all pardoned in the final days of the George H. W. Bush Presidency; Bush had been Vice President during the affair.

The Impeachment of President Bill Clinton

This broken trust was not restricted to just one political party, but crossed all political lines. Trouble was brewing in the Democratic Party as well. William Jefferson "Bill" Clinton, the President of the United States, was impeached by the House of Representatives on December 19, 1998, and acquitted by the Senate on February 12, 1999. The charges were perjury, obstruction of justice, and malfeasance in office, that arose from the Monica Lewinsky scandal and the Paula Jones lawsuit. It was only the second impeachment of a President in American history, following the impeachment of Andrew Johnson in 1868.

Independent Counsel Kenneth Starr, was the investigator ordered by Attorney General Janet Reno to look into a wide range of charges including Bill Clinton's conduct during the sexual harassment lawsuit filed by former government employee, Paula Jones. Linda Tripp, a friend of Monica Lewinski and former white house intern, provided Starr with taped telephone conversations in which Monica discussed having oral sex with Bill Clinton. During the proceedings, Clinton stated "I never had sexual relations with that woman". He contended that oral sex was not a sexual encounter.

Linda Tripp encouraged Lewinski to keep a blue dress that she said was soiled when she had an encounter with Clinton. She put it in a plastic bag and never cleaned it. This was concrete proof.

President Clinton allowed himself to succumb to temptations that induced and attracted him to the touches of a younger woman. He sacrificed his character and allowed himself to disregard the importance and sanctity of the oval office. He failed to realize the consequences of his actions and he destroyed the trust of the American people. He went on to complete his term and leave office with a balanced budget and a 237 billion dollar surplus. In the end, he became a very popular president. Temptation can often times contribute to the defects of the human character and lays bare the enormity of the transgressions. Man has continued to illustrate joy and gratitude in the excellence of his achievements, but fail to see the deformity of the persuit of excellence when his only consideration in public office is to himself.

There are many modern day politicians that have violated the oath of office in favor of personal gain or gratitude in other forums.

The following are a few: Gary Hart, former United States Senator and Democrat. In April 1987, Hart announced his candidacy for the office of President. This was his second presidential campaign. Less than a month later, the Miami Herald published a photo of a young woman leaving Hart's residence. Hart expressed outrage at the paper; within a week the Herald received tips that Hart had visited Bimini Island with a woman who was not his wife. They published photos showing a 29-year-old model, Donna Rice, sitting on Hart's lap on a boat called, "Monkey Business". Less than a week later, Hart announced he was dropping out of the race.

David Vitter, Republican Senator from Louisiana, was a staunch advocate of the conservative platform of abstinence only education, to a Constitutional ban on same sex marriage. It appears that he had no problem with high-class call girls because his phone number was revealed to be part of a list of a company owned by the infamous "D.C. Madam". He issued a public apology for his sins and managed to retain his seat in the U.S. Senate.

Senator John Ensign, Republican of Colorado, called Senator Larry Craig a disgrace, yet on June 16, 2008, he admitted to having an affair with a former campaign staffer, Cindy Hampton, from December 2007, to August 2008. The Las Vegas Sun reported June 19, that Hampton's husband Doug, who was incidentally a former administrative aide in Ensign's Senate office, had sent a letter to Fox News five days before Ensign's press conference asking for help in laying bare the senator's "heinous conduct". "Senator Ensign's conduct and relentless pursuit of my wife, led to our dismissal in April of 2008," Hampton allegedly wrote. "The actions of Senator Ensign have ruined our lives and careers and left my family in shambles". Fox denied the report and Ensign's camp said he had come clean because the Hamptons were trying to extort money from the Senator. Citizens for Responsibility in Ethics in Washington, filed a complaint against the Senator on June 24, alleging that Ensign's actions had violated the Senate's ethics rules, and called for an investigation into the affair.

Ensign apologized and remained in the Senate, but in June 2011, he did step down.

Mark Adam Foley, Republican, resigned from Congress on September 29, 2006, acting on a request by Republican Leadership after allegations surfaced that he had sent suggestive emails and sexually explicit instant messages to teenage males who had formerly served and were at that time, serving as Congressional Pages. As a result of the disclosures, the Federal Bureau of Investigation (FBI), and the Florida Department of Law Enforcement, conducted investigations of the messages to find possible criminal charges. Each ended with no criminal findings. Mr Foley resigned from the Congress.

The shameful deeds of men in positions of trust, contribute greatly to the continued disgrace and the reality of the Raping of America.

Part 11

AMERICA RAPED, FLEECED, AND BROKEN

An American stands alone on a cold desolate December morning, watching the horizon with welcome eyes. Watching, as the sun breaks the darkness with the light that gives warmth and life and maybe another day of survival in his concrete jungle. The struggles of the poor and homeless, of the street people sleeping under bridge overpasses in large American cities, the thriving of the Wall Street money makers and the slow death of the desperate in this land of plenty, is shameful, confusing and puzzling.

The rising sun brings with it the noise of the awakening city, the joy of new life and the sadness of death. The hope of the down trodden is that this new day will bring a change in a life of continued turmoil, hopelessness and poverty.

God has given us this wonderful gift of life and a glorius and wonderful planet on which to nurture it and man has found a way to decimate and destroy, much of this place that gives us its life sustaining necessities. The once clear and picturesque rivers, lakes and streams, are poluted and stripped of much of its life. The land is ravaged and fleeced for the sake of profit. The skies are poluted and choked with smog and unsafe chemicals. Pollution exacerbates the existing health issues of residents living in the shadow of the culprit that produces it. There are water, sewer and garbage disposal plant's that incinerate their sludge and trash in residential neighborhoods. There are businesses that emit high levels of methyl ethyl ketone, a chemical that at high levels can irritate the lungs and affect the nervous system. Toxic air pollutants cause cancers and other diseases. Even though cities have zoning laws, industrial sites that emit toxic waste into the air surround some neighborhoods and the citizens are forced to breath it. The forest is clear-cut and erosion claims the hillsides. I wonder how long can this earth sustain us while man works diligently to destroy it?

The Bible says that there will be wars and rumors of wars. That prophecy has been true ever since man saw his brother as a competitive threat. Untold millions have died in its wake. Wars have been fought over women, territories, power, profit and lies. If man doesn't put an end to this terrible trend, it will leave this world desolate and bare, bloody and scarred, with the end of life at deaths doorstep. Crime, drugs, corruption, greed and deceit, have invaded this country. As a result of that invasion, criminals patrol our streets, while the citizenry stay behind closed and locked doors. There are more African American males in prisons than there are in college institutions. Prisons are overflowing to the point where convicts are given early release to provide space for the incoming traffic. Some politicians have become criminals and have broken the trust of the people that put them in office with the duty of making laws that governs and protects the American people and their way of life.

The educational system has failed our children and in some cities across America, less than half graduate. Guns are in the belts of our teenagers, they are killing each other for coats, shoes, money and drugs. Gangs divide our cities, police corruption fan the flames of descent and hatred. Single parent homes have devastated our youth, as their fathers walk away leaving mothers struggling in a vice of economic destitution. It is said that one in three American children live in a home without a father; it is nearly twice that for African Americans. Homes where there is no father, increases a child's chances of committing a crime, getting hooked on drugs, going to jail, or being destined to dwell in the scrap heap of poverty. We must vigorously attack this problem with all available resources.

Racism that white authority has declared dead, is alive and well, it merely takes on a new look, or new face. The hatred that exists by some extremist and many ordinary American citizens for the first Black American President, is evidence of this fact. White men armed near a presidential rally is unheard of, yet, not declared outrageous by the people, or the politicians that witness it. If a Black man had brought a loaded or unloaded gun near a white president, or any president, he would have been on the ground, beaten to a pulp with handcuffs on. Hateful rhetoric by our political leaders drives this point home. Republicans Sara Palin, Michelle Bachmann and others, fan the flames of hate with their thoughtless words. As a result of this senseless onslaught of stupidity, I am in great fear for the safety of President Barach Obama. The thought that someday a shot will ring out, awakens me at night, for I know the aftermath of such an act would destroy what's left of the sanity in America. If tragedy struck this nation as it has in the past, the streets of this country would become bloody battlegrounds, cities would burn, assaults would be merciless and many lives would be lost, as Black Americans would launch an assault on white society. When people are provoked by senseless rhetoric, emotions can often times trivialize logic and reduce common sense to the ridiculous.

The unthinkable happened on Saturday, January 9, 2011, in Tucson, Arizona, when a suspect identified as Jared Lee Loughner, 22, of Tucson, walked into a Safeway grocery store where Democratic Congresswoman Gabrielle Giffords was meeting with her constituents. He opened fire with a hand gun that held a 30 round clip. This madness killed 6, including a 9-year old girl and a Federal Judge, leaving 20 others wounded. Gifford was the first to be shot in what appeared to be an assassination attempt. A bullet struck the Congresswoman in the head, leaving her critically wounded. Sarah Palin had put cross hairs on her district along with the districts of many other Democrats. Giffords had mentioned this fact before she held this rally. Did this rhetoric, being so inflammatory, push this deranged man over the edge? I don't know. However, we can remove this kind of irresponsible speech from the equation and thereby eliminate the possibility. Congressmen, Congresswomen and potential candidates, should exercise some level of civility and suspend the heated rhetoric of Sarah Palin's "reload and put them in the crosshairs," or Sharon Engles "resort to second amendment remedies," or the fool that said, "we will use bullets if ballots don't work," or, "lock and load." Where will it stop?

When ever elected or potential political leaders stand on a podium and repeatedly lie to the American people to encourage outrage, they should be held accountable if violence erupts. Republican Michelle Bachmann, the blooming idiot of Neanderthal thinking, called the Obama administration "A gangster Government". Sarah Palin deliberately lied when she said there were death panels within the body of the 2010 healthcare bill. If she had spent more time being that "MOM" she talks about, she wouldn't be a grandmother today. Republicans Dick Army and J.D. Hayworth orchestrates this explosive non-sense as well.

When Americans, or politicians, lose respect for the institution and the processes of democracy, the reality of that disrespect can become political violence. When we learn to go forward as one nation, joined together in brotherhood, locked hand-in-hand in the democratic culture, America will become the great nation envisioned by her founders. If we unite together and embrace the common good and attack the forces that seek to destroy us, if we enforce the concept of liberty and justice for all, then America will glisten like a shinning star in the dark skies of world opinion.

The joblessness has escalated in the early 21st century. Long lines of unemployed workers line the streets of cities across this land. America has seen millions of jobs leave its shores due to unfair trade legislation; while the Chinese, the Mexicans, the Tiawanese, the Indians, and many other foreigners do the jobs we once did. As a result of this outsourcing, America is left with the afflicted, the jobless, the hopeless, the homeless and the oppressed. They are struggling to survive with nothing and have become the children of miserie and distress with no dreams, no hope and no opportunity to make that final "up hill climb to the bottom". One out of six Americans doesn't know where their next meal is coming from on any given day. We have become a country of consumers, we were once the manufacturing mecca of the world, now we merely consume the products and goods of foreign countries while Americans suffer the degrading existence of unemployment benefits to survive.

Americans are losing their homes to foreclosure and bank deals designed for failure, while the CEO's of lending institutions enjoy multi-million dollar bonuses. If they chose to retire, they receive golden parachutes worth millions of dollars on their departure from their company.

The American government and its political leaders boast that we are the great melting pot of the world. Every nationality is within our borders. We are a country of immigrants; only African Americans and the American Indians do not succumb to that discription. The American Indians owned this land; Blacks were brought here in chains. America has humanitarian scars that will never heal; history will not be kind to her. In the hearts and eyes of many, the suffering and heartless treatment of a people and the shame on those who caused it, will live forever in the annals of American history. The only true Americans, the American Indian, are the poorest and most destitute people in this great land of plenty. They were the landlords of this great nation, now they are tenants living on reservations carved out of desolate and worthless terrain that America didn't want. They are lost in the wilderness of third world citizenry and worse. A rape personified!!!

America's waterways are invaded by foreign species that threaten our natural wild life. The invaders are brought to this land in the belly of foreign vessels, or in its ballast water that is dumped in our rivers and lakes. The Japanese beatle destroys our forest. The Sea Lamprey is a prehistoric creature that invaded the Great Lakes over 80 years ago. The eel-like lampreys are one of the Great Lakes most destructive invasive species, devouring fish by sucking out their insides. The invasion took place in the 1920s and by the 1950s, lake trout had been wiped out. Eurasian water milfoil is an invasive weed that has taken over many large lakes in the state of Michigan, forming dense mats that damage boat motors and disturb fish habitat. Emerald Ash Borer: this Chinese invasive pest has killed millions of ash trees in the state of Michigan and has spread to other states. It arrived in Southeast Michigan in 2002 in a packing crate. The Zebra and Quagga mussels: can clog water pipes, which cost millions of dollars per year to cleanup. The Spiny Water Flea: eat plankton that young native fish species need. The Bloody Red Mysid: eat plankton as well. The Eurasian Ruffe and the Round Goby: out compete native species of fish for food and habitat. The Asian Carp and others bring damage to our aquatic animal life, changing our waterways forever.

Some of the citizens of this country contribute to the destruction of the eco system by buying exotic animals and releasing them into the wild when they become too large are aggressive to control. As a result of this, many foreign-born animals have invaded the Florida Everglades. Feral hogs were brought to Florida by the explorers from Spain hundreds of years ago. They have spread out across this country in great numbers, and are causing severe damage to the eco system, crops and farms. The Burmese Python has the ability to reproduce and lay as many as fifty eggs in the process. They are spreading across Florida and other states in great numbers. They have the ability to devour any animal in the everglades, if they go unchecked, the rare

Wood Rat that number only 200, will be extinct. The giant rat is also a foreigner.

America the beautiful is being raped at every turn. Can she overcome this illicit attack on her systems that give life to her inhabitants, both human and animal? America is raped of her treasures through greed, raped of her children through war and raped of her dignity by some members of the Legislative, Judicial and Executive Branches of government.

The Economy

America has been raped of her children's future with a $17 trillion dollar deficit that continues to grow, while other countries benefit from our small-minded stupidity. The politicians of America and participating countries have signed into law so called free trade agreements that have stripped us of our manufacturing base, leaving us with an unemployment situation that is disgraceful and was forever growing, until Obama turned things around.

America does not support her manufacturing industries, while other countries do. On Friday, June 25, 2010, hundreds of people worked their final shifts at a whirlpool refrigerator factory in Southern Indiana. The plant shutdown production after turning out refrigerators for 54 years; this caused the loss of 600 jobs. 450 workers were laid off previously in March of this year. The company announced last year that it would shut down the factory and move the operation to Mexico. The executives of the Benton Harbor, Michigan based company said, "it was needed to reduce cost and streamline its operation." This is another case of greed over humanity. Workers that served this company for many, many, years were simply discarded to the economic trash heap. This is another wound on the American workforce caused by NAFTA, the so-called "North American Free Trade Agreement." The American worker rarely see jobs coming into America from Mexico, so where is the fair trade? Most of our products such as televisions, textiles, steel, autos, toys, and others, have been outsourced from this country. America has taken no action to protect our jobs. 80% of the toys sold in this country are made in China, while millions of toy's and other items have been recalled because they are contaminated with lead paint. They even had a recall on Chinese made toothpaste because antifreeze was found in the ingredients.

Each year, 18 million containers of imported goods arrive at our nations ports, but there are only 400 federal inspectors assigned to check on the safety of their content. "Toys "R" Us" recalled thousands of art sets made in China in 2007, due to excessive levels of lead in some of it's black water color paints. Chinese imports to the United States in 2006, totaled $288 billion, a figure surpassed by only Canadian products. More than 60% of the recalls announced in 2007 by the Consumer Product Safety Commission, involved Chinese goods and all 40 toy recalls were in connection with products made in china. They are killing our children.

The U.S. deficit for goods and services for 2006 was a staggering $763.4 billion, leaving our nation and American workers vulnerable. We have the most open market in the world. Consider the South Korean-U.S. free trade agreement. In 2006, South Korea exported 695,134 vehicles to the United States, and in turn, America exported 5,732 vehicles to Korea. If the citizens of this country consider this fair trade, I would be appalled. The playing field is not level by any stretch of the imagination. Americans must face the reality of this job loss crisis and start buying the few American made products we do have. Our grown- up children are living in our basements while we drive foreign made cars. We must re-examine our common sense and our dedication to America, while we blame the President for job losses.

President George Herbert Walker Bush signed into law the NAFTA agreement. President George W. Bush inacted the last section that allowed Mexican or Canadian truck drivers to deliver their loads throughout America causing thousands of American truck drivers to lose their jobs. Previously, they would drop their loads at the border and American drivers would make the delivery. Now, even that has been taken away from American workers.

What is NAFTA?

The North American Free Trade Agreement, or NAFTA, is an agreement signed by the governments of Canada, Mexico, and the United States, creating a trilateral trade bloc in North America. The agreement came into force on January 1, 1994. It superseded the Canada-United States Free Trade Agreement between the U.S. and Canada. In terms of combined purchasing power parity GDP of its members as of 2007, the trade block is the largest in the world and second largest by nominal GDP comparison.

The North American Free Trade Agreement (NAFTA) has two supplements, the North American Agreement on Environmental Cooperation (NAAEC) and the North American Agreement on Labor Cooperation (NAALC).

Under the mobility of person's provisions of the agreement, according to the Department of Homeland Security Yearbook of Immigration Statistics, during fiscal year (October 2005 through September 2006), 73,880 foreign professionals (64,633 Canadians and 9,247 Mexicans) were admitted into the United States for temporary employment under NAFTA. Additionally, 17,321 family members (13,136 Canadians, 2,904 Mexicans, as well as a number of third-country nationals married to Canadians and Mexicans), entered the U.S. in the treaty national's dependent status.

There is far more to this agreement and the effects on employment in this country are astounding.

What is the WTO?

The World Trade Organization (WTO) was born out of the General Agreement on Tariffs and Trades (GATT), which was established in 1947. A series of trade negotiations, GATT rounds began at the end of World War II and were aimed at reducing tariffs for the facilitation of global trade goods. The rationale for GATT was based on the Most Favored Nation (MFN) clause, which, when assigned to one country by another, gives the selected country privileged trading rights. As such, GATT aimed to help all countries obtain MFN-Like status so that no single country would be at a trading advantage over others.

How it functions: Decisions are made by consensus, though a majority vote may also rule, (this is very rare). Based in Geneva, Switzerland, the Ministerial Committee, which holds meetings at least every two years, makes the top decisions. There is also a General Council, a Goods Council, a Services Council, and an Intellectual Property Rights Council, which all report to the General Council. Finally, there are a number of working groups and committees as well.

There have been many questions raised relative to the value of these agreements to American workers and consumers. The two are related. If we consume foreign goods, we lose American jobs. That is common sense, not rocket science.

Americans contribute to the demise of meaningful employment in this country, while they scream for an end to unemployment. American parents continue to house their unemployed offspring in the basements, attics and garages of their homes, as stated earlier, while the streets are filled with Kia's from Korea, Volkswagens from Germany, and cars and trucks from many foreign lands. They ask why their kids can't get a job, when the answer is sitting in their driveways. If Americans would only buy cars and trucks built in this country, that includes some Honda's and Toyota's and others, this country would see up to 3 million jobs created almost immediately. If we would seek out the few products that are currently produced in America, we would improve upon our jobless plight.

I know that American businessmen are manufacturing cars in foreign lands; I have already mentioned that tragedy precipitated by the quest for lower wages, to the detriment of American workers, but as in sports, sometimes the best offense is a good defense. Meaning that maybe we should consider Americans first and in this instance, let the world fend for itself. Many would say that this is not practical in a global market when we are trying to find a market in foreign lands for American products. American manufactured goods are miniscule compared to the past. Some American companies have outsourced their telephone services to India and other countries. If you call your company's headquarters for information, you are likely to speak to someone in India that you can barely understand. Where does it stop? When does Americans stop blaming President Obama and take a look at the man in the mirror, the answer will be evident.

America may never return to employment levels of yesteryear, while the before mentioned foreign countries continue to provide our lost jobs to their workers. NAFTA, Cafta, and the WTO should be revisited. The textile mills of the south and the automobile plants of the Midwest are now located in South America, Mexico and other foreign lands, sadly our jobs went with them. The free-trade era did not live up to its promise of job creation. In the wake of the civil war, technology transformed America into a mechanized giant of innovation and production. The goods we invented and produced are now offshore with the blessing of our so-called American leaders. Free, but unfair trade, is killing the American dream for workers seeking employment, while denying others the opportunity for advancement.

Manufacturing jobs build nations and provide products that generate sustainable wages for middle class living. Service jobs simply provide a personal, or sometimes a necessary need, such as, janitorial service, lawn care, or washing cars, but they seldom generate a middleclass livable wage. The global market that presidents and politicians base their trade logic on, is not free and fair to the American worker. The Japanese sale cars in this country on a playing field that is not only not level, but also unfair. They come to our shores and build plants that provide some jobs, but we can't build plants in Japan, nor can we build and own automobile dealerships in Japan. We must sale our cars in a Japanese dealership along side our Japanese competitors. The tariffs that are added on to our cars by the Japanese government, doubles the cost of American products. The American government does not apply equal restrictions to our competition; therefore, the playing field is not level. Fair trade legislation and a change in government policy, need to be enacted to undo the horrific imbalance in our manufacturing trade policies.

While Japan and it's car manufacturing companies sold 3 million cars in America last year, Ford and General Motors totaled 10,000 cars sold in Japan. Why? Because of mock-ups and restrictions applied to American imports; a $25,000 American car can sell for near $50,000 in Japan. No one in Japan calls that protectionism, but that is exactly what it is. Our laws should require Japanese and Korean car manufacturers to sell the same number of cars in the United States that they reluctantly import into their countries; it would limit Japan to 5.5 percent and Korea to 2 percent of the U.S. market.

Middle class jobs continue to disappear to foreign shores, while businessmen call it cost effective. I call it the raping of America. They should be stockholders in America, not just on Wall Street. Corporations take advantage of the greatest consumer market in the world at the expense of its citizens. Greed is the bottom line. They want to maximize shareholder profits. The question of what are you going to do for America, is set aside?

Many of the big businesses have moved their business address to the Cayman Islands where they pay no taxes. Transocean, the biggest oil drilling company in the world is there. It is their rig that blew up in the Gulf of Mexico on April 20, 2010, causing the biggest oil spill in the history of the world to date and the death of 11 workers.

The free trade laws of this country are destroying the American middle class. We are now a nation of the rich and the poor. The middleclass as we knew it, no longer exist in this great nation. When this country lost it's manufacturing base, the middle class went with it and we became a nation of 2% rich and 98% poor. We are approaching the status of a third world country; we are no longer the richest country in the world.

The steel producing companies in the rust belt of Pennsylvania and other states of the Midwest, were going out of business as foreign made steel flooded our shores with cheaper and inferior products. The American steel industry could not compete, therefore, they began to succumb to bankruptcy and American steel workers joined the ranks of the unemployed. As a result, foreign workers gained employment and raised their standard of living at the expense of American workers jobs.

President George W. Bush gave China Most Favored Nation status, which, when assigned to one country by another, gives the selected country privileged trading rights as I previously mentioned. The results of that gift to China were a flood of jobs and businesses leaving America for Chinese workers who receive extremely low wages. They live in a Communist country that provides for many of their needs. Therefore, the cost to sustain a living for themselves and their families is relatively low in comparison to our workers. The businesses that left this country seeking to pay lower wages for more work, are profit driven and have no concern for America, or the plight of her workers.

The Republican interest is still geared to the continued successful earnings of the millionaires, billionaires, and big oil that fill their coffers with millions of dollars for their election campaigns. There are no fair tax rates for these individuals, or these companies. General Electric, the seccond largest company in America, earned 14 Billion dollars in profits in 2010, and paid $0 in taxes. They have 975 people that do nothing but work on avoiding income taxes. Many companies that left this country for foreign shores put their profits in foreign banks to avoid taxes. The Congress will not impose restrictions on their earnings and bring them to the table of fairness. The Raping of America!!

The American workers have become victims of events beyond their control. Their budgets reflect the same economic illness as the federal government. They spend more than they take in, creating a budget deficit that they sustain with credit cards. This country continues to borrow from the Chinese to finance the last of two wars that is raping us of our potential to quell this on going depletion of our economic resources. Our national debt has reached $45,000 dollars per every man, woman, and child in this nation, but is on the downturn. We need millions of new jobs for tax-paying workers to counter this continued regression on our national wealth. America is ill and the prognosis is dire. We need to end this war, we need to cut federal spending, we need to curb borrowing from other countries and we need to stop selling off American property and businesses to foreigners. We no longer own many of the landmarks in this country that represent the successes of its people. Americans no longer control Capitol records, Pebble Beach, Rockefeller Center, the Sears Tower and many others. Self-preservation should be the law of the land. Someone said, "God bless the child that's got his own".

While America continues to borrow billions of dollars from China, the Chinese are making massive investments in this country that could allow China to exact a powerful influence over U.S. business and government policies. Thanks to its vibrant export markets, China has amassed nearly 2 trillion dollars in foreign funds to invest in the U.S. through its Sovereign Wealth Fund. China already has investments in Blackstone Group, Morgan Stanley and others. Bejing West Industries bought Delphi; now this American company is Chinese owned as well. Yet, to open any business in China, the investor must face 13 levels of government review. A report by the U.S. China Economic and Security Review Commission says, China could quietly buy up companies critical to the U.S. economy. Controlling interest could be gained so that some agency, or authority in China could have 10 or 15% of a U.S. company. Foreign Wealth Funds controlled by China and the Gulf States could grow to 2.5 trillion dollars in the next four years. With China being a non-democratic communist country, whose interest may not always align with that of the United States; they could apply pressure, gain access to sensitive technology, manipulate markets, or undermine economic rivals. They are not transparent, they don't report their holdings, they don't report true asset size and you can't contact them. Someone called it "A Red Storm Rising". China admitted to the WTO in 2001 that the manipulation of their currency gives them an advantage, are they opportunist, or a threat to America?

China has taken more than two million American manufacturing jobs. The U.S. trade deficit with China has reached 16.9 billion dollars, larger than with any other country. China has a business model that's based on cheating. Many of their practices violate the WTO. China, having an export driven economy, is hitting the skids. China's slowdown has generated concern that they may give out less money to buy piles of U.S. Treasury Bonds that Washington D. C. must sell to finance trillion dollar a year deficit spending, They point to other factors to test China's resilience as millions of workers get thrown out of jobs as factories shutdown, port activity slows and economic growth slows for the first time in a generation. China has amassed $1.9 trillion in foreign reserves. More than $1 trillion of that is in U.S. debt. China has used the savings from its trade surplus to buy U.S. treasuries and to finance U.S. deficits.

Political Strife

There is political unrest across this country, a congress with a Republican Party that has become the "party of no", under the republican minority leaders. Republican Mitch McConnell, the now Senate Majority leader from Kentucky, and Republican Speaker of the House John Beohner, has chosen to cause harm to this country rather than work with President Obama on any issue governing this nation.

I will say again that the hate for this president by the Republican Party is astounding. There is a certain decorum that must exist among our leaders in this so-called civilized nation. There is total disrespect for the holder of the highest office of the land and the leader of the free world. The Republican Party has lost its moral compass and is pitifully flawed by ignorance and disrespect. They still don't get the fact that the democrats won the Presidential election in 2008, and 2012. The politicians have left the Americans with a striking discord of uncertainty, we have endured major difficulties in this broken economy. We have suffered through fiscal irresponsibility and outrageous pork barrel spending. The taxpayer's have paid millions of dollars for projects such as the bridge to nowhere in Alaska. The politicians have no regrets, or remorse, for the fleecing of America and the hard working taxpayer's of this country. Greed was the engine that drove this financial Tsunami. Houses sold for 150% of its value. Speculators bought homes to be flipped, but the housing market bottomed out and they lost their investment. This country was saddled with record unemployment, until President Obama turned it around and grew the job market. Still 4.5 million food stamps are issued to the poor; but the Republicans are sure to make every effort to end it.

The Republican Party ridiculed President Obama for the stimulus package signed into law to help stimulate employment with projects that would create jobs. When the projects funded by the stimulus money were complete, the very republicans that opposed it went home to their districts and joined in the ribbon cutting ceremonies. John Boehner was one of them. They are pitiful and disgusting hypocrites

America's borders are not closed to illegal entry. Crime has followed the invaders through the tunnels and over the fences. The borders have not been closed since this country's existence, yet the Republicans blame President Obama for our porous borders. American citizens have become victims of those who trespass on their property as they avoid the border guards. Our ports are open to goods that are not fully inspected. The politicians refuse to in-act legislation that would change the immigration laws.

Many of America's elected representatives have lost their morals, dismissed the rule of ethics, abandoned a sense of respectability and shelved common sense in favor of racism just to bring down President Obama. They totally disregard the urgent needs of the American people for political reasons. What a revolting development this must be to the Americans that suffer in the wake of this hypocrisy and shameful display of leadership.

Our politicians should remain open to new ideas and progressive thought. The most innovative way of resolving many of these issues may be within the problem solving processes involving concerted effort and well-orchestrated think tanks. The leaders do not have a monopoly on brains and they may find that the answers they are seeking may come from the people that they least expect to have them, the American citizens.

During the general elections of November 2, 2010, the Republican Party and the out of control Tea Party was successful in their efforts to regain the House of Representatives by winning more than 80 new seats. They gained 6 additional seats in the Senate, but not enough to gain control. Republican John "the cry baby" Beohner, he'll cry at the drop of a hat, became Speaker of the House. Let us observe the actions of the politicians in this party, and the ship of fools that sail the rough waters churned by the likes of Sean Hannity, Russ Limbaugh, Glenn Beck, Sarah Palin and the Fox "No News" Network. The Fox News Network finally read the tea leaves and released Glen Beck and Sarah Palin, the only sensible move they've made in a decade.

The republican leaders continued their disrespect for the president by refusing to honor his invitation to the White House on November 17, 2010. They even had the audacity to suggest that the president must dance to their music, or come to them, or they will continue to reject him. The president still holds the power of the pin and can veto bills that he think is unjustified for the American people.

With all of the poisonous rhetoric from the GOP, the president was still able to reach a compromise on issues that was facing the American people. The Don't Ask Don't Tell Act, was repealed, The new Start Treaty with Russia was signed, The health bill to provide health care for the 9-11 first responders was passed after the Republican party said no, but was embarrassed into it by media coverage. The Unemployment bill was passed and signed into law, and of coarse the continued Bush Tax cuts remained in place for one more year. The Republican Party would not agree unless the top 2% of the riches people in America would receive nearly a trillion dollars in tax cuts at a time when the country is suffering and they don't need the money. If the tax cuts for the rich would create jobs, why didn't it creat jobs over the last ten years while the American people suffered 15% to 20% real unemployment rates? In 2014, the Republicans won both the house and the senate, now that they are in control, what will this bring.

America in crisis

I have written facts, figures and positions taken on the current condition of America and the lying, deceitful, dishonest and hypocritical politicians that were elected to serve us. Now, you must ask yourself, is America on the verge of self-destruction and economic implosion, have her morals and ideals and commitment to freedom been jeopardized to the point of no return? Have Americans become so selfish that we have forgotten, or simply disregard the principles on which our freedom was based? Have democracy suffered a destructive blow that has weakened her inner soul to the point of self-destruction?

The sky over America is not as blue, the sun does not shine as brightly and the air is filled with hate for those who are different from the white majority. Nothing in America is sacred anymore. The authorities have stripped us of our basic personal freedoms and every facit of our lives are examined and exposed to public and governmental inquiry, without our knowledge or permission.

There is an underlying and unjustified fear factor surrounding immigration while we are a nation of immigrants. What happened to our competitive drive in job creation and new technological advancement?

The Republicans don't have a clue as to the plight of the poor in America. They should take a walk on the wild side for a change and enter the poor neighborhoods of our large decaying inter-cities. They should walk where the homeless, the hungry and the dislocated families reside and face a reality that they can't even immagine. Let them leave the ivory polished halls of congress and walk the rat-infested streets of the ghetto. They are out of touch with the reality of millions of Americans struggling to stay alive, day-by-day. Let them touch the millions of children that go to bed hungry every night and cry themselves to sleep. Let them touch their bloated bellies caused by malnutrition. Let them visit the abandon, burned out and vacant houses in poor neighborhoods. Let them see the factories that stand deserted and chained on land poluted and poisoned by those industries that occupied them and left them never to be reclaimed by economicly strapped cities.

They should be ordered to walk the land of the poor as a pre-requisite to running for political office. Let them visit the soup kitchens, the flophouses and the people of the streets. Let them talk to the families torn apart by poverty. Let them dry the tears of the children lost in a world of confusion while living in fear and hopelessness. Let them see the poor people of a great nation of plenty and convince them that the door is open to riches. Let them visit the schools that are worn, torn and in disaray. Let them sit in cold classrooms with leaking roofs and no toilet articles. Let them visit the real California where marijuana has become this states largest cash crop. The politicians don't know anything about the true America where millions of struggling families reside everyday. The politicians are lost in a world of dreams that's void of reality.

The politicians of the Republican Party such as Newt Gingrich, Sarah Palin, Sean Hannity, Rush Limbaugh and Glenn Beck, even though they are not holding public office, do have a public audience of millions and are therefore political with there rhetoric. They said, the laid off workers don't deserve unemployment compensation. They should have to step into the shoes of the poor for 60 days. Charles Payne of the Fox Business Network on cable television said they should resort to cannibalism, a disgusting thought by an overpaid pig of humanity. They disregard the fact that they paid into unemployment compensation insurance for this protection. The silver spoon in their mouths may not always be so bright. They have never lived or learned, or maybe they have forgotten the plight of the 46.3 million Americans living in poverty in this country. Or maybe they just don't regard the poor in this country as true Americans, evidenced by the attitude of the Fox News Network.

The quest for equal treatment under the law in mainstream America is still an idea unrealized by most poor Americans. The culture of cronies is still a hindrance. African Americans and other people of color have had a remarkable cultural progression in this country and with the election of this country's first black president; the door of opportunity may have finely been opened. African Americans can now believe that nothing, or no political office is beyond their reach. We have finally achieved a status where we can honestly say that our opportunities may be unlimited; a black man is the leader of the free world. This was an achievement unforeseen in America's history. Does this mean that racism has finally been conquered? No! Does this mean that the playing field has finally been leveled? No! Maybe this means that the nation has realized that the supression, or the oppression of its citizens of any color, can only reduce dramatically the level of achievement that we can accomplish when equal treatment under the law and in humanity, is the blueprint for greatness?

Let me remind the newly elected Tea Partiers to Congress, who have decided that to have a pension and Social Security is un-American. Let me remind, or inform them, of the words of our greatest union leader Walter Reuther of the UAW, (The United Auto Workers Union), when he asked the question, "what do you do with a worker that's too old to work, and too young to die?"

I will answer that for the Republican Party, he deserves the same kind of benefits that the Congress recieves from the American citizens and the "Big Bosses" receive from the companies that they run. He deserves economic justice in the twilight of his life. He should have the opportunity to die with dignity and respect for his many years of turmoil in this country's workplaces. The Raping of America knows no boundaries.

Through it all, through all of the disrespect of the president and the office he holds, on November 6, 2012, President Obama won re-election over his Republican opponent, Mitt Romney, and destroyed the antiquated ideas of the GOP. Now they lanquish in the valley of defeat, licking their wounds wondering what happened to an election that they thought was an automatic victory for the Grand Old Party. They had a reprieve in 2014 when the GOP was able to regain many political offices, and take control of the Congress through their gerrymandering of their political districts. This was a dishonest arrangement but that is where this party lives, in the arm pits of America. The raping of America continues.

Part 12

THE PRESIDENTS OF THE UNITED STATES OF AMERICA

Under the terms of the Constitution of the United States of America, the President of the United States is the head of state, and the head of government of the United States of America. As chief of the executive branch, and head of the federal government as a whole, the presidency is the highest political office in the United States by influence and recognition. The President is also the Commander-in-Chief of the U.S. armed forces. An Electoral College indirectly elects the president to a four-year term, or by the House of Representatives should the Electoral College fail to award an absolute majority of votes to any person. Since the ratification of the Twenty-Second Amendment to the United States Constitution in 1951, no person may be elected to office of the president more than twice, or serve more than a total of 10 years. Upon death, resignation, or removal from office of an incumbent president, the Vice President assumes the office.

The information in this book was acquired from many sources, such as the History channel for the first 23 Presidents. the media, the internet, such as Wikipedia, history books, The Americans the History of a people and a Nation, American Citizenship, and my

personal experiences. In recognition of those sources, I express my thanks for the information provided, tune-in to the History channel for a great educational experience.

GEORGE WASHINGTON, Number 1, 1789-1797

Federalist, 57 years old from Virginia. Wife Martha. On April 30, 1789, standing on the balcony of Federal Hall on Wall Street in New York, he took his oath of office as the first President of the United States of America. "As the first of everything in our situation will serve to establish a precedent," he wrote James Madison, "it is devoutly wished on my part, that these precedents may be fixed on true principles."

The American Presidency existed because of one man who was twice elected unanimously, and got every vote in the Electoral College. Born in 1732, into a Virginia planter family, he learned the morals, manners and a body of knowledge requisite for an 18th century Virginia gentleman. Commissioned a Lieutenant Colonel in 1754, he fought the first skirmishes of what grew into the French and Indian War. The next year as an aide to General Edward Braddock, he escaped injury although four bullets ripped his coat, and two horses were shot from under him.

From 1759, to the outbreak of the American Revolutionary War, Washington managed his lands around Mount Vernon and served in the Virginia House of Burgesses.

When the Second Continental Congress assembled in Philadelphia in May 1775, Washington, one of the Virginia delegates, was elected Commander in Chief of the Continental Army. On July 3, 1775 at Cambridge, Massachusetts, he took command of his ill-trained troops and embarked upon a war that was to last six grueling years. Finally in 1781, with the aide of French allies, he forced the surrender of Cornwallis at Yorktown.

Washington longed to retire to his fields at Mount Vernon. But he soon realized that the nation under its Articles of Confederation was not functioning well, so he became prime mover in the steps leading to the Constitutional Convention at Philadelphia in 1787. When the new Constitution was ratified, the Electoral College unanimously elected Washington President.

He was the first man to take office and he added the words "In God We Trust". He feared that his countrymen would expect too much from him. The American people wondered what to call him,

The President, The High Mightyness, he solved their concern and said call me, Mr. President.

He refused to shake hands; he thought that was beneath the president. He rode a white horse named Nelson, he married a widow named Martha Dandridge Custis, and had no children.

First in war, first in peace, first in the hearts of his countrymen. Washington's cabinet was the best we ever had. John Hamilton was a brilliant man, and was the Secretary of the treasury. Thomas Jefferson was Secretary of State; Henry Knox was Secretary of War. Hamilton had many landmark achievements; he set the coarse of this countries economy. He built the framework of a National Banking System. He left after two terms; he was also the single largest distributor of alcohol in America with 11,000 gallons of whiskey at Mt Vernon.

Washington enjoyed less than three years of retirement at Mount Vernon, for he died of a throat infection December 14, 1799. For months the nation mourned him.

JOHN ADAMS, Number 2, 1797-1801

Federalist, 61 years old from Massachusetts. He was the eldest of three sons. He was born on October 30, 1735 in what is now Quincy, Massachusetts. Adams married Abigail Smith, his third cousin. Their children were Abigail, future president of the United States, John Quincy, Susanna, Charles, Thomas Boylston and the stillborn Elizabeth.

He was Harvard educated, he was ambitious but humble, one day up, one day down, but he craved fame. He was wracked with self; his personality was not suitable for the Presidency. He was America's first Vice President, and was a very opinionated man that was sure that he was right and did not accept council. He was prone to fits of anger and unleashed it on his subordinates.

Two issues defined his presidency, The XYZ affair and the Alien and Sedition Act. Both were caused by a crisis in foreign affairs, the escalating war between England and France. The French were seizing our shipping because they didn't want us trading with Britian. Hoping to quell the crisis, Adams sent a diplomatic team to Paris, the delagation was met with the demand for a bribe; they reported back to the American Congress. Instead of referring to the Frenchmen by their correct names, they were refered to as XYZ, so this became known as the XYZ Affair. Adams was extremely angry so he sent another delegation; he was offended. For this, the warmongers in

Congress vilified him. Adams had the courage to stand against these men and the men in his own party; he was firm and adament in reaching a peaceful solution. He would reach it in 1800.

Many were voicing their distress with the Adams Government, there were editors, businesses, politicians and others. Adams was sensitive to criticism and decided that the verbal attacks were sedition, so in 1798, Adams signed the "Alien and Sedition Act", making it a crime to falsely speak out against certain office holders including the President. This Act made it a crime to publish "false, scandalous and malicious writing," against a government or its officials. Punishment included 2-5 years in prison and fines up to $5,000. This was the single greatest blemish on an otherwise extraordinary carrier. He also signed into law, The Naturalization Act; this changed the period of residence required before an immigrant could attain American citizenship to 14 years. The Alien Friends Act and The Alien Enemies Act, allowed the President to deport any foriegnor he thought was dangerous to the country. These acts were passed to surpress republican opposition. John Adams was a one term President. He died on July 4, 1826, at the age of 90 years.

THOMAS JEFFERSON, Number 3, 1801-1809

Democratic Republican, 58 years old from Virginia. Wife Martha Wayles Skelton, they had six children, only the eldest daughter Martha lived beyond age 25. The Federalist had been defeated and he was moving into the White House. He was the first President inaugurated in Washington. He walked to the unfinished capitol to deliver his inaugural address. He thought the government was going down a very bad path under the Federalist, he thought he had saved it. He believed they had put too much power in the central government and vowed to reverse that. He was a casual man, he was also excentric and secretive. He presented himself as a man of the people. He was an effective manager and preferred working in the privacy of his office.

He did not give his annual messages to Congress as speeches, but sent them in writing instead. He was not a good public speaker with his soft voice, but was a brilliant politician. In 1802, a tabloid allegedly reported Jefferson's affair with Sally Hemmings, one of his slaves. He was mentioned by name by James Calendar, and that was the first time Sally Hemmings name appeared in the newspaper. Sally Hemmings is the half sister of Martha Wales Jefferson who was

Jefferson's wife. Jefferson never responded to the scandal. He simply ignored it.

The defining moment of Jefferson's Presidency was his expansion of executive power to make the Louisiana Purchase the mega deal of the 19th Century. It more than doubled the size of the United States for a mere 15 million dollars. He wasn't sure it was Constitutional, but he did it anyway and used Alexander Hamilton's system of finance to fund it. He was the one worried about the Federal Gonvernment doing too much and taking on too much power, yet he grabbed a third of the continent, and proposed to rule it by military Governors.

He also authorized a secret exploration of the territory called, The Lewis and Clark Expedition. When he sent a message to Congress requesting money for the mission; his opponents screamed that it was an unconstitutional military foray. In 1804, he was overwhelmingly re-elected, but he found no joy. He hated criticism, and felt as though he was a prisoner. By 1808 he was tormented by migrain headaches, the presidency had aged him considerably. He came to hate the presidency so much that he left it off his gravestone, yet his achievements remain unparalleled in American history.

Two Presidents signed the Declaration of Independence, John Adams, and Thomas Jefferson. Both died on July 4th 1826, the 50th anniversary of the signing.

JAMES MADISON, Number 4, 1809-1817

Democratic Republican, 57 years old from Virginia. Wife, Dolly Madison. He was immensely qualified, a veteran of the revolution, author of the Constitution, and a Jeffersonian Democrat.

James Madison was everything Thomas Jefferson wasn't. He was short in stature, but had a sense of humor, and was not given to rage or small talk. He also brought something else to the white house, a first lady, Dolly Madison. The Madison's became known for lavish parties and feast at the white house. As an executive, he had an abiding sense of fairness. He had a calm demeanor and was always prepared, except for war, though the War of 1812, ultimately defined his presidency.

He came into office with half the country pushing for war with England, the other half wanted to go to war with France. With this enormous problem on his hands, Madison was really pushed by events into the war with England. Shortly after his election, England began seizing American ships. Diplomatic efforts to solve the crisis went nowhere. Finally, on June 18, 1812, Madison became the first President in U.S. history to ask Congress for a declaration of war. We declared war on Great Britain. Our navy in 1812 numbered about 20 ships; theirs numbered about 1,000. It was a disaster; we would lose humiliating engagements in Detroit, and upstate New York. It was almost a Civil War in 1814, because New England threatened to secede from the union because they were so angry; their life's blood was commerce and shipping. Then in August 1814, the British raided Washington and burned the Presidents mansion. He was driven from his home. Madison became the first and only sitting president to face enemy fire. He personally took command of a battery outside Washington, but to his embarrassment, the Commander-in-Chief is forced to retreat. Our capitol is burned, we are defeated on land and sea and we definitely lost a war. Madison was burdened, he got us into this war and he was desperate to end it.

He sent James Monroe to negotiate peace with England. In December, 1814, he succeeded with a treaty that officially ended the war. Before news of the treaty reached Washington, America was rewarded with a belated victory at the battle of New Orleans. The man who benefited most was the defender of New Orleans, General Andrew Jackson. It did little for Madison; two important things came out of this war, Dolly Madison saved the portrait of George Washington and the star spangled banner composed by Francis Scott keys.

Madison was tarnished; he learned an important lesson about the office he helped create. It is not so much about the man, but the unforeseen events which define a presidency. A lesson learned by him and the presidents to follow.

JAMES MONROE, Number 5, 1817-1825

Democratic Republican, 58 years old from Virginia. Wife Elizabeth kortright, they had 3 children, 2 girls and 1 boy. Another founding father is elected to the Whitehouse.

The last of the revolutionary generation to hold high office. He was never thought particularly well of, except his character. He was a war hero, honest, patient, yet he was elected twice to the presidency by a crushing margin. He was unopposed when he ran for his second term. This was a period of peace and happyness in America. He was a hands off executive who hired great people for his cabinet and he delegated authority.

When Missouri applied for statehood, it should have added a star to the flag, in stead, it ignited a political debate over slavery. Would it be a free, or slave state? As Congress debated the explosive issue, Monroe, a slave owner himself, made it clear that he would veto any legislation that restricted self-determination for any state. Eventually, Congress passed the Missouri compromise of 1820. Missouri entered the union as a slave state, Maine entered as a free state. Monroe came up with his own plan; he proposed to return slaves back to Africa. It was called the American Colonization Society; this led to the founding of Monrovia Liberia, the only foreign capitol to be named for an American President. This did little to solve the crisis at home.

He also forced a border crisis in Florida. It was owned by Spain, but the Spanish did little to govern it. It was filled with pirates, outlaws and Indian tribes that were not under the control of the Spanish government. By 1818, border encursions were common and Seminole Indians were raiding white settlements in Georgia. In response, Monroe sent troops to the region led by General Andrew Jackson. Jackson was sick and tired of it so he invades Florida and captures the British and hangs them. It creates an international incident involving three countries, The United States, Spain and Britain. Jackson's raid caused an uproar in Monroe's cabinet. Secretary of War, John Calhoun, wanted to reprimand him. John Quincy Adams said what the British were doing was outrageous and the Spaniards should have stopped them, therefore, Jackson did what he ought to have done. So Monroe did not reprimand Jackson, he opened negotiations with Spain for the rights to the territory. In 1819, the Spanish ceded Florida to the United States without a fight.

Border incidents were common during Monroe's tenure; it was a border incident that led to his defining moment of his presidency. In December, 1823, the president delivered a message to congress and to the world. He addressed a minor dispute between Russia and the U.S. over Alaska. The speech contained a short paragraph that became his legacy; it stated "The American Continents are henceforth not to be considered for future colonization by any European powers." The Monroe Doctrine is our statement that we reject European countries coming in and trying to acquire further territorial gains in this hemisphere; you stay in your hemisphere, we'll stay in ours. It wasn't until 1852 that people began calling it the Monroe Doctrine. It was regarded as Monroe's greatest moment and yet, he was not the true author, it was written by John Quincy Adams, Secretary of State.

The end of his presidency marked a turning point of American political history. He was the last of the American revolutionary generation. The last of the architects of the American Republic. He died July 7, 1831 at the age of 73 in New York, New York.

JOHN QUINCY ADAMS, Number 6, 1825-1829

Democratic Republican, 57 years old from Massachusetts. Wife, Louisa Catherine Johnson. They had three children.

He came into the white house under a cloud of controversy. During the first year of the American presidency, the Secretary of State was the stepping-stone to the White House. Thomas Jefferson, James Madison and James Monroe, had blazed that trail. In 1824, John Quincy Adams was set to follow but in this election year, other ambitious men wanted the job. Treasury Sceretary William Crawford, Secretary of War, C. Calhoun, in congress, the Speaker of the House, Henry Clay and rising national hero, Andrew Jackson, "Old Hickory" was very popular.

1824 was the first election where states began to count the popular vote in presidential elections. In 1824, Andrew Jackson was the clear choice of the people, but the presidential election was still decided by the Electoral College, but with the popular vote a candidate could carry his states. Jackson received 151,271, Adams 113,112; Clay received 47,531, Crawford 40,856. He could measure his popularity with the common man. The way the four of them finished, Jackson 99, John Quincy Adams 84, William Crawford 41, and Henry Clay 37, Jackson does not get a majority of the electoral votes. According to the constitution, the top 3 go to the House of Representatives which must chose among them. Clay is dropped, then William Crawford had a stroke, so the contest came down to two men, Adams vs. Jackson with Henry Clay presiding from the pulpit of the House of Representatives. Clearly some deal was made, the house picks John Q. Adams on the first ballot and Adams picks Henry Clay as the Secretary of State. Andrew Jackson screams that this is a corrupt bar, it is a scandal and John Quincy enters office under this terrible cloud.

He had many goals; he wanted America to explore western territories. He wanted to fund public education. He promoted scientific advancement and discovery, along with vast internal improvements, such as roads and canals across this nation. He doesn't get to do any of it because the politics of his term is so rancid that he is unable to manage them. This would haunt his presidency and leave Adams with few accomplishments. His personality did nothing to help his agenda.

He was physically short and pudgy like his father and stuborn. He was the first President to wear long trousers instead of knee britches. He wanted to do better than his father. He would not kiss people who were for him, or fire those that were against him. The results were devastating; he endured what was probably the most miserable presidency that any president ever experienced.

It was four years of unrelenting attacks by the Jacksonites. In 1828, Adams ran for a second term but again Andrew Jackson stood in his way. The election of 1828, was the dirtiest campaign in history; it was brutal. Jackson campaigned on his impressive war record. He was the hero of New Orleans, the conqueror of Florida, a bonofied veteran of the American Revolution, but his past included some unsavory behavior which the Adams camp brazenly exposed. They accused him of being a gambler and a military tyrant; Adams called him a barbarian. In this election, character was the main issue, but in this case, they went beyond the pail. They attacked Jackson's wife Rachel with ruthless attacks. The dirt on Rachel was that she had married Jackson in 1791, before obtaining a legal divorce from a previous marriage. The charge was true, but so old no one expected it to be an issue.

In the heat of the campaign, a Cincinnati News-Paper published the story that Rachel had lived in bigamy and Jackson had lived in sin. It tore at his soul and Adams never believed his denial.

Jackson had responded with equally outrageous charges on Adams. They would reply that he lived with his wife before they were married and that he provided a young American virgin for the pleasure of a Russian Czar. Campaign rhetoric was virtually ignored. Instead, they focused on the personal lives of the candidates. However, the things that the people said about Jackson were true. The things that the Jackson people said about the Adams were lies. In this election, the truth hardly mattered. Jackson's popularity with the common man was overwhelming and he won in a landslide. The joy did not last, in December 1828, after buying her an inaugural gown, Rachel died suddenly of a heart attack, she was 67 years old. This would shape his presidency.

He did forgive those that attacked him personally, but he would never forgive those who attacked his wife. As for John Quincy Adams, like his father, he was not gracious in defeat, he refused to attend

Jackson's inauguration and instead, he went home to Massachusetts. Two years later he was elected to the House of Representatives becoming the only ex-president to do so. In this roll, he would be an out spoken congressional leader in the fight against slavery. That work, not his presidency, would become his greatest legacy. John Quincy Adams was the first president to have his photograph taken. He died February 23, 1848. He was the first president to follow his father into the white house. Like father, like son.

Andrew Jackson, Number, 7, 1829-1837

Democrat, 61 years old from Tennessee. His wife was Rachel; he had no children. She died of a heart attack during her preparation for his inauguration.

Old Hickory was a complex individual, he knew what he wanted to do and did it. Then he would try to enlist public support for what he wanted to do. He was called cantankerous, iron willed, a fighter for the people and an intimidating manager.

He was the first president to be born in a log cabin. He asked to be called general, not Mr President. He was a bar room brawler, a passionate Indian fighter and a gambler who brought his own racehorse to the white house. He was a duelist with two bullets in his body. He would fight at the drop of a hat. He considered personal honor above all else. He also had a furious temper but could use it as a management tool. Jackson's cabinet members did not want to socialize with Margaret Peggy Eaton, wife of Jackson's Secretary of War John Eaton, because she had dated her future husband while married to another man. Jackson hated this; he told them they had to socialize, but they refused for two years so he asked his cabinet members to resign, which they did.

After the Peggy Eaton affair, Jackson placed no trust in his secretaries; he went through four Secretaries of State and five Secretaries of the Treasury.

Jackson was determined to change Washington and America and he did so with lightening speed. The first peace of legislation he passed was the Indian Removal Act of 1830. This act empowered Jackson to forcebly evict all of the Indian tribes east of the Mississippi River. Many Indian Nations were directly affected, the Chocktaw, Chickasaw, Creek, Seminole and Cherokee. The five Cherokee tribes living in Georgia chose to fight the eviction; they took Georgia to court instead of the warpath. The case went all the way to the United

States Supreme Court. In a surprising and historic decision, Chief Justice John Marshall ruled in favor of the Cherokee saying they did not have to move, but Andrew Jackson thought differently. Jackson said of Marshall "he made his ruling, now let him enforce it". The result was that they were rounded up at gunpoint and forced to move. Their property was seized and they were sent west on the forced march called "The Trail of Tears". One out of four died along the way. This was one of the sadists chapters in American History, other than slavery and the most controversial decision of Jackson's career.

Soon after the Indian Removal Act, Jackson forced a dangerous issue that threatened the fabric of the Union, The South Carolina Nullification Crisis. South Carolina was angry about the high tariffs on imported goods, which helped England at the expence of southern planters. South Carolina declared it had a right to nullify the federal tax. John C. Calhoun, Vice President, articulated that theory most clearly. Calhoun believed Jackson would support him, but Jackson's personal hatred for Calhoun precluded any political sympathy. Instead, he responded with force; he threatened to raise an army and go into South Carolina and hang John C. Calhoun from the first tree. Calhoun was said to be genuinely afraid for his life. South Carolina backed down and Congress modified the tariff. Jackson made it clear that he was the supreme leader of the nation and it was not going to fall apart on his watch.

When Jackson ran for president in 1828, his opponents called him "Jackass". Jackson liked the image so much it became the mascot of the new Democratic Party. He was re-elected. Under Andrew Jackson, the U.S. Government was completely debt free for the first and only time in history.

His presidential legacy is the most complicated in American history; he changed the presidency by giving it more power by imposing his will on the economy, the government, the landscape and the people. By doing so, he forged the future of a nation. He called it "The Age of Jackson".

Martin Van Buren, Number 8, 1837-1841

Democrat, 54 years old from New York, Widower, 4 children. He was the father of the Democratic Party, witty, elegant dresser and poor decision maker. His reputation was that of a want to be aristocrat with the way he decorated the white house, perfumed his whiskers and wore a cosset.

He inherited Jackson's financial mess, high unemployment, bankruptcy and worse. He was faced with blight in the cotton market and when the price of cotton collapsed, the economy went into the ditch. He was not of the job. By 1844, the country was in a deep depression. It was believed that anybody could run and beat Van Buren. William Henry Harrison was nominated because he resembled Andrew Jackson. He was a frontier General and an Indian fighter and was nominated by the new Whig Party. This was the first election where the slogan and campaign materials were used. "Tippecanoe and Tyler Too" was used as his slogan. This was in reference to a victory in an Indian War. They called him too old and fake, but the economy decided the election.

He was the first President to be born an American citizen. He was the third President to serve only one term after John Adams and John Quincy Adams. His administration was largely characterized by the economic hardships of his time. The most harmful was the Panic of 1837, between the bloodless Aroostook War and the Carolina Affair. He was voted out of office. In 1848, he ran for president on a third party ticket, The Free Soil Party.

He was one of two people, the other being Thomas Jefferson, to serve as Secretary of State, Vice President and President. He died on July 24, 1862, at the age of 79.

William Henry Harrison, Number 8, 1841-1841

Whig, 68 years old from Ohio, his wife was Anna. He had 10 children. The last president born a British subject. The only Pre-Med President.

He was unpretentious and a consensus seeker. He was an aristocrat, college educated and only president to study medicine. He caught a cold while speaking at his inaugural on a very cold March day with no hat and no overcoat, just to prove he was not too old. The cold turned into phenumonia and he died just 31 days into his administration. He became the first President to die in office. Vice President John Tyler went to Washington to take the office, but there were no guidelines for this, so another fight ensued. His death fostered an argument over who should take over the Presidency. Harrison's death sparked the 25th amendment to the U.S. Constitution.

He was the oldest President elected until Ronald Reagan in 1980. He was the last President born before the United States Declaration of Independence. He died on April 4, 1841; He was 68 years old.

John Tyler Jr., Number 10, 1841-1845

Whig, 51 years old from Virginia, He had two wives, Letecia, and Julia and 15 children. He was called a stubborn, aloof, aristocratic, independent leader, but he was in charge.

He was a Southern Gentleman with a rich background in politics. He had served in the House of Representatives, in the Senate and as Governor of Virginia. He believed in states rights and that too much power had been vested in the Federal Government, yet, he expanded that power once he became President.

Many had the impression of him as being weak; this was a great misconception. He turned out to be his own man with his own political agenda, which surprised people. Many believed he was just an acting President until a new election could be called. Even the members of his cabinet, which was Harrison's cabinet, tried to muzzle his claim to power. In their first meeting, Secretary of State Daniel Webster, told Tyler how the cabinet would make all executive decisions by Congress. To that, Tyler responded by asking for their cooperation, or their resignations.

Tyler had reminded the Whigs that Harrison had promised to push Whig bills through Congress, including a new charter for the Bank of the United States, but Tyler did not share the Whig view. What happened was really unprecedented and it never happened since. The Whigs passed two laws authorizing a new National Bank and President Tyler vetoed both of them. After the second bill was vetoed, the Whigs held a meeting at which they expelled President Tyler from their party and from then on; he was a man without a party, politically isolated in the white house. Tyler pressed the business of the nation while imposing his will and his skill as President.

He wasn't given credit for his foreign policy achievements, and skill. He had The Webster Ashburton Treaty, a historic treaty between the United States and Great Britain. This treaty settled the disputed border between the United States and Canada, which was still a British possession. He also had the annexation of Texas, which was very controversial. Tyler took it upon himself to sign a treaty with the New Republic of Texas, but the Senate immediately rejected the treaty. That didn't stop Tyler, he cleverly asked for a joint resolution of Congress and that passed, but his political popularity was sagging.

By 1844, Tyler thought about a second term, but the Whigs didn't want anything to do with him and the Democrats didn't trust him, so he graciously bowed out. He died January 18, 1862. He was 71 years old.

James Knox Polk, Number 11, 1845-1849

Democrat, 49 years old, from Tennessee. Wife Sarah, no children, workaholic, devious, micro-manager. He was not a very likeable man, but was the most accessible.

Polk was a president who wanted to carry out the Doctrine of Andrew Jackson; his credentials were similar to Jackson's. He achieved a whole series of Jacksonian measures once he got into office. He believed very strongly in the idea of a level playing field for the American people.

He made himself available twice a week to the American citizens. The Marine Corp Band played on the white house lawn every Wednesday. He saw himself as the first servant of the people. He was often called the hardest working president in U.S. history. He was known for long workdays and had gaslights installed in the white house so he could work through the night. He was the first president to really get deeply into the budget. He told all departments to not send budget request straight to the Congress, send them to me. More than anything, Polk wanted to fullfill the idealogical promise of Andrew Jackson's presidency, what was then being called America's Manifest Destiny. The idea that the U.S. has a providential destiny to expand westward was something that he accepted implicitly, this was more than an idea; it was his presidential mandate.

He had four goals that he wanted to settle during his presidency, he said he would only serve one term. (1) He wanted to settle the controversy between the United States and Great Britian over the Oregon Territories. (2) He wanted to bring California into the United States. (3) He wanted to set up an independent treasury to the credit mess that had prevailed since Jackson. (4) And he wanted to lower tariffs on imports into the American economy. To achieve his economic goals, he pressured Congress to lower tariffs and to establish an independent federal treasury. He proceeded to achieve his territorial goals; he used force. First, he threatened war with Great Britian to gain the Oregon territory. The cry was 54/40 or fight - meaning the 54th parallel. To his credit, it ended up at the 49th parallel. Then he actually went to war with Mexico to settle the Texas border problem and acquired the Southwest and California. The Mexican War, fought between 1846 and 1848, came to dominate

Polk's administration. However, that along with the acquisition of the Oregon Territory, became the legacy of his presidency. He took the country from just west of the Mississippi River, all the way to the Pacific Ocean in 4 years. From sea to shinning sea, Polk gave it to us. He made us a Continental Nation. In less than 75 years, the country had grown from a colonial possession into a Continental Nation with liberty and justice for some.

This new land threatened to divide the nation, most Republics throughout the coarse of history, had not survived. The Americans throughout the first half of the 19th century were uncertain whether the Republic would survive a series of crisis, or, would it break apart.

Tensions were rising between the North and the South, each wanted to settle the west in their own distinct image. The north was far more popular and far more economically developed than the south, but it had not exercised its real political power. The south had a strangle hold on the Democratic Party, the President and the Supreme Court. The nation was at a crossroads; the power struggle between the North and South was escalating into a crisis that demanded an extraordinary president.

James Polk served one term as President. He died June 15, 1849 in Nashville Tennessee. He was 53 years old.

Zachary Taylor, Number 12, 1849-1850

Whig, 64 years old from Louisiana. Wife Margaret, 6 children, poor speaker, never registered to vote, relaxed manager.

Taylor was a celebrity, a Mexican War hero who helped to win over a million square miles of new land for the nation. He was also a political unknown. He was not seeking the presidency; both sides came to him and wanted him to be the candidate.

As a war hero, he appealed to the North. As a Louisiana landowner and slave owner, he appealed to the south. He had no obvious agenda, but in the end, he would surprise them all. He was called, "Old rough and ready"; this was attributed as much to his fighting spirit as it was to his sloven appearance. He had none of the polish of a professional politician and was not a great communicator. Taylor had never registered to vote and didn't even vote in his own election.

Dispite outward appearances, he was really a Washington insider. His 2nd cousin James Madison had arranged his army position. Robert E, Lee was a 4th cousin and Jefferson Davis had been his son-in-law. As president, Taylor differed from others going so far as to declare that he would not exercise his veto power. He didn't see the presidency as a very powerful office and was often influenced by members of his cabinet and by certain members of Congress. He did say that he believed Congress should decide the slavery issue and he would go along with whatever the body proposed. The slavery debate was beginning to get ugly; the fragile peace between the North and South established 30 years earlier by The Missouri Compromise, was starting to crumble.

The country was facing a serious crisis on the question of the expansion of slavery into new western territories. On one side, southern extremist were threating secession if Congress didn't rule in their favor. On the other side, the clamor of northern abolitionist was growing louder. In response, Senator Henry Clay, created the Compromise of 1850, a bundle of bills designed to link the admission of California as a free state with some slavery measures favorable to the South. This was a package that Clay put before the Congress giving some concessions to the slave states and some concessions to the free states, which he hoped would go through and satisfy everyone. The compromise didn't satisfy some people, including President Taylor. Taylor surprised a lot of people, he said there was nothing to compromise about, he said California should be admitted as a free state and that is it. Taking back his promise, Taylor threatens to veto the compromise. Taylor insisted on going ahead even at the risk of provoking Southern States secession. Taylor's solution for the secession was somewhat simplistic, "I'll hang em," and I might start with my son-in-law Jefferson, who was a Senator from Mississippi.

Barely a year into his administration, Taylor was evolving into an ardent unionist. On a hot 4th of July of 1850, Taylor took a break from the political infighting to preside over a groundbreaking ceremony for the Washington Monument. Scorched by the summer sun, Taylor sought relief with a pitcher of milk and a bowl of cherries, within hours he complained of severe stomach pain. People were proposing that he was actually poisoned by arsenic, that there was a conspiracy to get rid of him. Taylor died 5 days later. Most believed he succumbed to an inflamation of the intestines, but there were lingering suspicions of foul play. It would take more than a century before anyone would know for certain. In 1991, a historian convinced Taylor decendants to allow his body to be exhumed. Forensic analysis revealed no signs of foul play; instead, they confirmed that a form of cholera was the cause of Taylor's death. He died July 9, 1850; he was 65 years old. Taylor's Vice-President Millard Fillmore assumed the Presidency.

Millard Fillmore, Number 13, 1850-1853

Whig, 50 years old from New York, Wife Abigail, 2 children, modest, amiable, avid reader and delegates authority.

He was an accidental president; some called him the Gerald Ford of his day. He was a rather strong president considering that he was an accidental president and those usually have a very hard time establishing their mark. He had not met Zachary Taylor until after they were elected. He was seen as a Taylor opposite, he was picked to balance the ticket both geographically and politically. Fillmore was a northerner and was always dressed impeccably. He was a bookworm and hands off manager, he aimed to please and appease rather than lead. He was a colorless character who believed in compromise. He deferred the congressional leadership, according to most observers. He was bland, friendly and willing to make you feel that you had said something important. But behind this amiable personality, lurked a man with backbone. Bitter at feeling over looked by Taylor's cabinet; he fired all of them. He continued to exact his newfound power by reversing the policy of his predecessor and signing The Compromise of 1850 into law.

Fillmore supported slavery because he believed its abolition would lead to a collapse of the Southern economy. 60% of U.S. exports came out of the cotton states. By 1850, to obolish slavery was to abolish an economic system. He also believed that slavery was protected by the Constitution and by signing the compromise, he would somehow put the issue to rest forever. But he failed to grasp the moral consequences and he blamed abolishioners for making slavery an issue. He was opposed to the abolishionist and thought they were troublemakers and fanatics. He was content with the compromise because he thought it would preserve the status quo. For some however, it only served to strengthen their resolve against slavery. By supporting the compromise he hoped to please everyone, but in the end, pleasing no one including members of his own party.

In the election of 1852, the Whigs wouldn't nominate him so he went home to Buffalo, New York, leaving behind one of the most forgettable presidencies in American History.

He died March 8, 1874 in Buffalo, New York. He was 74 years old.

Franklin Pierce, Number 14, 1853-1857

Democrat, 48 years old from New Hampshire. Wife Jane, 3 children, (all died in youth), charming, alcoholic, deferential, indecisive manager.

It was 1852, and the tennuious strands of the compromise were barely holding the nation together. Franklin Pierce appeared to be the perfect feel good candidate. He was a Northern Democrat with strong ties to the south. Voters in both regions thought Pierce would bring both balance and peace to the nation. Everybody liked him.

Everybody called him handsome Frank. He was well known as a man about town with a passion for drinking, often to excess. However, he managed to stay sober during his presidency, but some believed he was not emotionally stable because of a terrible tragedy he suffered just weeks after his election. Pierce, his wife Jane and his son Benny, was in a train wreck; Pierce and his wife were unscathed, but their 11-year-old son was killed. Pierce and his wife had already lost two other children to disease. Benny was their last surviving child, to have their remaining son, the light of their lives, killed in a train accident; you could imagine the horror that that would instill in anyone. Added to Pierce's troubles was the death of his Vice President, William Rufus King, six weeks after the inauguration and things were about to get worse.

Early in 1854, Pierce received a visit from members of his own party including Illinois Senator Steven A. Douglas. He informed Pierce that he was sponcering a bill called The Kansas Nebraska Act. The act was designed to repeal the Missouri Compromise of 1820, which banned slavery in states above the southern border of Missouri. The intent was to let the new territories of Kansas and Nebraska, both north of the boundary, decide for themselves if they wanted slavery or not. Douglas promised to make Pierce's presidency a living nightmare if he did not support the scheme. The President should have said no, but he was weak and could be bullied and Douglas forced him to say the administration would support this. Pierce caved in to him. The bill found enough support to get through Congress. Slavery groups in the north went berserk over this bill. Among the outraged was a little known politician from Illinois named Abraham Lincoln. He was so angry at the blatant pro-slavery act; he helped create a radical new political party that apposed the expansion of slavery, The Republican Party.

The Kansas Nebraska Act, brings Lincoln back into politics and it brings him in as a spokesman against the expansion of slavery. Meanwhile, in the Kansas Territory, anti and pro slavery settlers were literally fighting it out. On May 21, 1856, pro slavery forces burned the abolitionist stronghold at Lawrence, Kansas, down to the ground. The whole political situation begins to desintegrate and Pierce is completely incapable of putting it back together again. Pierce failed to see his roll in the weakening of the union.

He thought he had a shot at a second term, but even his own party rejected him. Pierce returned home to New Hampshire, his reputation ruined. Several years later, after his wife Jane died, he returned to heavy drinking and lived his remaining years as a recluse, perhaps the saddist legacy of any president. As tragic as Pierce's presidency had been, it would pale in comparison to his successors. Pierce was considered one of the worst presidents in U.S. history. He died October 8, 1869, at age 64, in Concord, New Hampshire.

James Buchanan, Number 15, 1857-1861

Democrat, 65 years old from Pennsylvania. He was never married, generous, procrastinator, engaging, consensus seeker. James Buchanan was one of the most politically accomplished presidents America ever had. He had been a Congressman, Foreign Minister, Senator and Secretary of State. He would stay up late at night to attend to the smallest of details. He was different in another way; he was never married and was often referred to as America's only bachelor president. There are folks in this country that would say that Buchanan is our first homosexual president. The allegations arose from the intimate friendship he shared with Franklin Pierce's Vice President, William Rufus king. The man he had lived with for 16 years.

Buchanan had his charming niece, Harriot Lane, serve as the white house hostess. Since Harriot wasn't Buchanan's wife, she was called the First Lady, a term coined to describe her role. While Harriot presided over social life at the white house, Buchanan presided over a house rapidly dividing. His decision to endorse the constitution written by the pro-slavery settlers in Kansas, made Buchanan appear to be a supporter of the south and a traitor to the north. The idea that the President will try to force slavery into a territory where it's clear that the majority of the settlers don't want it, completely discredits his administration in the eyes of large numbers of northerners, including Northern Democrats and Replublicans.

Everything that Buchanan does during the last part of his administration is so pro-southern that he does not do it in the classic presidential oath; preserve, protect and defend the United States. Ultimately, Buchanan's management of the battle in Kansas did nothing to settle the slavery issue, it only made it worse. Slavery embedded in the montra of states rights, was now the defining issue in the historic election of 1860.

On November 6, 1860, Abraham Lincoln was elected president. It was now only a matter of months before the south would lose its ally in the white house. In anticipation of an anti-slavery president, South Carolina seceded from the union on December 20, 1860. As a lame duck president, Buchanan denied the legality of the secession, but did nothing to stop it. Within weeks, six more states left the union and 8 slave holding states sat on the fence becoming Border States. On Febuary 9, 1861, the Confederate States of America, now composed of 7 states, elected Jefferson Davis as their new president. One month later, Buchanan's presidency came to an end. On his last day, Buchanan said to Lincoln, "If you are as happy to be entering the presidency as I am to be leaving it, then you are a very happy man". Unknown to America at the time, Buchanan had quietly purchased several slaves and sent them north, granting them their freedom. He died June 1, 1868 in Lancaster, Pennsylvania; he was 77 years old.

Abraham Lincoln, Number 16, 1861-1865

Republican, 52 years old from Illinois. Wife Mary, 3 children, excellent sense of humor, liked to be photographed, obsessed with military strategy and a decisive manager.

Lincoln was a conservative in the sense that he wanted to preserve and restore the union as it had existed before the secession of the Southern States and the beginning of the war. But the events of the war pushed him step by step to the left, or to the more radical position that eventually became revolutionary. Lincoln was not the great emancipator. He became the great emancipator to some extent against his own intentions. He showed us what greatness is. It is the capacity to grow, to understand the situation and to change. In Lincoln's lifetime, people either loved him or hated him, but the one thing they couldn't do was ignore him. He was very magnetic; he drew people to him. Young people, especially young men, who were active in politics thought of him as a God. He had an amazing sense of humor; he had a storehouse of anecdotes and jokes for every occasion.

Hidden behind the humor was a very complex man. Lincoln obsessed over matters and often suffered long periods of sadness, frustration and even dispair. Campaign literature called him honest Abe, banking on his compulsion for seeking the truth; his other nickname, the rail splitter, was more a political marketing invention in the Jacksonian Tradition, capitalizing on Lincoln's working class roots to appeal to the common man.

Lincoln was very much a politician, he loved the game of politics and he played it very well. He was an extraordinarily ambitious man like most politicians that rise to the top are. From childhood, Lincoln was driven to make something of his life, to climb up out of poverty.

In the south, they attacked him as a scoundrel. Lincoln turned his appearance into a positive by disarming people with self-deprecating humor, for he was not a handsome man. Once after being called two faced, he said, if I were two faced, would I be wearing this one?

Lincoln was his own best spin miester, once elected president; Lincoln chose a cabinet of intellectual equals. Just as J.F. Kennedy did a century later. In Lincoln's case, 4 of his 5 secretaries had been his political rivals. He was a judicious delegator of authority, but he always reserved the ultimate decision for himself.

Lincoln's election had been a political disaster for the southern slave power. His initial intention was just to halt the expansion of slavery into the western territories. He said if I could save the union without freeing a single slave, I would do that. If I could save it by freeing some and leaving others in bondage, I would do that too. He never had anything but moral outrage about it. He felt that the way to destroy the institution was to contain it and let it sufficate from within.

Waiting for Lincoln on his first day in office was a letter from Major Robert Anderson, the commander of Fort Sumter, located on an island in the harbor of Charleston, South Carolina. Anderson warned that without a shipment of provisions, he would have to surrender to the rebels. Lincoln had 3 options, he could order a surrender, attack, or send provisions; he chose the latter. So basically, Lincoln said to Jefferson Davis; if you let this food go in peacefully, it will be a symbolic manifestation of our soverety over this fort, if you stop it, then the burden for starting a war will be on your shoulders. Before Lincoln's supply ships arrived, Confederate President Jefferson

Davis ordered his men to attack the fort. The 1st shot was fired on April 12, 1861; the civil war had begun.

The violence at Fort Sumter motivated 4 more states to join the Confederacy, 4 others remained on the fence. Fort Sumpter surrendered to the south, but Major Anderson saved the American flag that had flown above it and brought it to New York City. They took that tattered and ripped flag and displayed it all over N.Y. and the flag inspired the people. If it were not for Fort Sumter, Lincoln may not have stirred up the union to a move that was necessary to fight and preserve the union. By an act of shrewd calculation, Lincoln had baited the south into striking the 1st blow of the Civil War, but neither he nor Jefferson Davis had anticipated what was about to unfold. It would be the 1st and only American presidency completely defined by war. Lincoln, who made Thanksgiving a national holiday, was also the first to pardon a turkey at Thanksgiving. He named it "Jack".

In the spring of 1861, Abraham Lincoln became the Commamder-in-Chief at the helm of the military effort to save the union. Possessing no military expertise, and humbled at the prospect of making life and death decisions, he gave himself a crash coarse on military strategy. He also became fascinated with the technology of modern warfare. Within a year, he was well versed in military tactics and strategy. Yet, nothing prepared Lincoln for the problems he was to experience with his generals. In August of 1861, Lincoln was furious upon learning that Major General John C. Freemont, had issued an emancipation proclamation in the border state of Missouri becoming the first to free slaves owned by confederates. Fearing Freemont's action would incite slave owner's in all of the border states to join the Confederacy, Lincoln nullified Fremont's action and relieved him of duty.

In February 1862, Lincoln's war effort was suddenly rocked by personal tragedy. His 11-year-old son Willie died from Typhoid Fever. In an effort to properly mourn their son's death, the Lincoln's decided to leave the white house and move to the soldier's home, an asylum for wounded soldier's in northwest Washington. Finding themselves at peace there among the soldiers, Lincoln adopted the home as their summer residency, turning himself into a commuter for ¼ of his presidency.

From then on the war consumed Lincoln, he worked night and day seven days a week, 18 or more hours a day. He was so determined to stay on top of the war news; he would sometimes stay late, or even all night at the U.S. telegraph office.

In April 1862, exactly a year after Fort Sumpter, the union had a major and critically important victory at Shiloh, but it came at a horrendous cost. Nearly 24 thousand men were killed, wounded, or missing after the battle. The carnage triggered a turning point when Lincoln realized they were going to have to wage a total war. He privately recognized he needed to refocus the war from merely preserving the union, to addressing the greater moral issue of slavery.

In July of 1862, Lincoln confided to his cabinet that he was prepared to surpass the legal powers of the presidency and exploit his unique wartime power as Commander-in-Chief. He announced his intentions to abolish slavery in the rebellion states, not only under the Confederate economic strength, but to end slavery in America forever. On September 22, 1862, Abe Lincoln issued his Emancipation Proclamation to the public. This war had evolved into a revolunary war to destroy the old south and it's social economic system. That was the transformation movement in American history that was the second Declaration of Independence. That's where Lincoln reaches the level of the founding fathers, where he fulfilled the promise of the Declaration of Independence to millions that had been denied freedom. The problem is that the Emancipation Proclamation didn't win battles.

Throughout 1862, and 1863, the union enjoyed success in the west, but that was overshadowed by devasting loses in the east. By June 1863, the military situation in Virginia was desperate. Robert E. Lee's rebel army was on a winning streak and marching towards Pennsylvania; it came to a climax in the first days of July near the small farm town of Gettysburg. The battle was suppose to be the battle of all battles. It was suppose to end the civil war. Three horrorifying days of massacre insued, the battleground was soaked with blood. Photographers produced horrible photos of the carnage, exposing the nation to the horrors of war. These were America's sons, husbands and brother's, lying dead on the battlefield. Lincoln himself sank into despair, overcome by the terrible loss.

In November, Lincoln traveled to Gettysburg to help commemorate the battlefield as a national military cemetery. Lincoln spoke for two minutes and redefined the commitment to the principles of the Declaration of Independence, that all men are created equal. He believed America was fighting not just for the promise of today, but for what he called a vast future also. His vision was all Americans should have an equal chance and an unfettered start in the race of life. As inspiring as his Gettysburg address had been, Americans were weary of the bloodshed.

By 1864, most wanted to see an end to the war. That year, Lincoln ran for re-election against one of his former generals, George B. McCellan, who ran on a platform that promised to negotiate an end to the war if he were elected. This election would test the resolve of a nation, and it's President.

In the fall of 1864, Lincoln was running for his political life against General George B. McCellan. It was a time when American's could have ended the war by casting their ballots for McCellan. The General also advocated repealing the Emancipation Proclamation. But Lincoln is not willing to take those steps that some people say would guarantee his re-election. He would have to agree to repeal the Emancipation, agree to an armistice with the south and agree to recognize the Southern Confederacy when he didn't before. To back away looked like it would be at the cost of his re-election, because it looked as though he would be defeated. Looking back, it seems inevitable that Lincoln was going to win, but it didn't appear that way in 1864.

Two months before the election, the tide turned for Lincoln. General William Tecumseh Sherman had burned Atlanta and would ten weeks later, begin his infamous march to the sea. Suddenly, the union army had momentum and so did Lincoln. Even though America was engaged in a terrible bloody war, He still won 56% of the vote in the northern states. That alone was an extraordinary testament to the people's faith in Lincoln. It was bitter sweet; the war had taken its toll on Lincoln, emotionally and physically. It's hard to find an American President that aged more than Lincoln did in 3 1/2 years. Four years to the day that Lincoln first took the oath of office, he was taking it again on March 4th 1865. This time around, Lincoln was a changed man, his visits to the front lines, his experience of living among the wounded at the soldiers home and his commute to the white house, brought him face to face with average Americans and contraband slaves. It had all deeply affected Lincoln making him empathetic to the humanity of all men.

Speaking at his second inaugural, he signaled his growth as a politician and his compassion as a man. For what may be the most moving speech ever written by a president, he laid out his road map for peace and reconstruction of the nation. Pledging malice towards none and charity for all. He talked about democracy and liberty and the necessity to come to terms with slavery.

On April 9, 1865, just two weeks after Lincoln's inauguration, Robert E. Lee surrendered his Confederate Army of Northern Virginia to U. S. Grant; the war was really over. Soon after, in what would be his last speech, Lincoln showed no signs of vindictiveness. He called upon the nation to heal itself. He spoke about giving favorable terms to the south and for the first time in public, about giving the black man the right to vote. On April 14, Good Friday, the Lincoln's attended the Ford Theatre to see the comedy "Our American Cousin"; it was Lincoln's last night on earth. He faced the worst crisis this country had ever seen and he rises to the occasion. Lincoln came to see that everyone, no matter the race, color, religion, or creed, had a right to live the American Dream.

The evil surrounding the Lincoln assassination was all about. In Washington, it was an evening of general treachery. Lincoln was shot; Secretary-of-State William Steward was stabbed, General U.S. Grant was targeted but was fortunately, out of town. Vice President Andrew Johnson was on the hit list too. Johnson was offered tickets to attend the play at Ford's Theatre, but turned them down. But Lincoln's assassin John Wilkes Booth knew exactly where Johnson would be spending the night. He assigned a co-conspirator to go to Johnson's suite at the Kirkwood Boarding House. Johnson retired to his quarters and is completely unaware that anything is going on. If all had gone according to plan, Johnson would have been awakened a short time later by a knock on the door, at which point a knife would have been plunged into his heart. But it never happened. The man assigned by Booth to assassinate Johnson lost his nerve and started drinking, he wasn't going to go through with it. So because of it, Andrew Johnson was spared.

When Lincoln died of his wound the following morning, Andrew Johnson became the first American President to gain the office because of an assassin's bullet. That became a part of Johnson's problem; he assumes the presidency and was not elected to it. Lincoln died April 15,1865, in Washington, DC at age 56.

Andrew Johnson, Number 17, 1865-1869

Democrat, 56 years old from Tennesse. Married: wife Eliza, 5 children,. Stubborn, principled, ambitious, and uncompromising. Johnson was nothing like his martyred predecessor. Unlike Lincoln, he was a southerner and a democrat and at one point, had owned a small number of slaves. But during the Civil War, he was the only

Senator from a seceding state to remain with the union. He had been selected as Lincoln's running mate in 1864, to broaden the tickets appeal. Nobody anticipated Johnson becoming president, if they had, he would not have been on the ticket.

He was regarded as stubborn, or principled, depending on whether you agreed with him or not. Like Lincoln, he had risen from poverty to prominence through his own determination. Johnson's background and personality greatly influenced his management style. He had no formal education and was trained to be a tailor. He also had a righteous streak. Johnson was dogged and stubborn, once he took a position, he was not willing to compromise it. He had a tendency to see conspiracy on all sides against him. In all of these respects, he differed sharply from Lincoln. For a model on how to run his presidency, Johnson looked to a former president with whom he shared a home state and a similar name, Andrew Jackson. One of Jackson's greatest quotations were, "Our Federal Union must be preserved". Johnson picked that up and used it throughout his career.

Like Jackson, Johnson believed he was the voice of the common white man. He was probably the most racist president we ever had. He talked about blacks as savages and barbarians and he really thinks they should go back on the plantation and leave the public to whites.

When Johnson took the oath of office, the war was essentially over. It was up to the tailor from Tennessee to stitch the tattered union back together. His entire legacy would be staked on reconstruction. The reconstruction crisis was the greatest crisis in American history, other than the crisis of the Civil War itself. What was at issue was not simply bringing the south back into the union, but defining the esseance of the American Nation; who was going to be a citizen of the United States, what rights should citizens enjoy, who is an American?

Among the more eager to learn about Johnson's policies was the so-called radical Republicans, the vocal reform minded wing of the party. Men like Pennsylvania representative Thaddeus Stevens, and Massachusetts Senator, Charles Sumner. They believed the South should be punished and the freed slaves protected and made citizens and given the right to vote. Johnson played his role well and then Congress leaves Washington not to return until December. Johnson had that window of opportunity to take over as president. What he did with this opportunity was to come up with his own reconstruction plan. Many in the defeated south were prepared for the worst. In April 1865, the south was so shell shocked that they would be willing to accept almost any terms of reconstruction.

Johnson came in thundering revenge and punishment, but Johnson had a pleasant surprise in store for the dispirited southerners. The south is a conquered region, but Johnson didn't want to treat them as a conquered region. These are his people after all. Nobody knows what Lincoln would have done, but Johnson's plan was for amnesty for most ex-confederates and quick acceptance for the seceded states into the union. The freed slaves got little protection; they weren't guaranteed citizenship or the right to vote. Johnson was on the wrong side of history, on morality and politics, he was unable to recognize that the Civil War had changed the nation, that the emancipation of the slaves carried with it some basic rights for them.

When Congress came back into town in December 1865, Johnson Announced that the restoration of the south had been completed. That is startling news to the members of Congress. Therefore, they immediately started to pass reconstruction acts of its own, beginning with the extension of the Freedman's Bureau, a measure begun by Lincoln to aid the transformation of Blacks from slavery into freedom. Johnson vetoed it, and from that point on, that would be the story of the relationship between Congress and the president. Congress would pass, and the president would veto.

The 29 vetoes by Johnson would shatter the previous record of 12 by Andrew Jackson. When a president rules his office with vetoes, he's not going to be successful. Johnson, stubborn and defiant as he was, refused to see that.

Now it was Congresses turn to make history beginning with the Civil Rights Bill of 1866. They realized they had the numbers to overturn Johnson's veto. Their record of overturning Johnson 15 times still stands. Throughout 1866 and 1867, Congress hammered away at Johnson's authority. In March of 1867, they passed the Tenure of Office Act, limiting the president's ability to remove appointees without the Senate consenting. It was a trap and Johnson couldn't resist the bait. He suspended and later dismissed the Secretary of War, a holdover from Lincoln's cabinet. Take no prisoners were his attitude and that inspired the Congress to fight back in the same way. That's why he was impeached. Violating the Tenure of Office Act, gave the radicals in Congress an excuse to get rid of him.

Articles of impeachment were drafted, but his opposition only made him more stubborn, he was unwilling to meet his critics halfway. He was unwilling to listen to criticism, so he destroyed his own presidency.

In Feburuary of 1868, the House of Representatives made an unprecedented move voting to impeach the president. The charges were flimsy at best and clearly politically motivated. Johnson was the target of a vast left wing conspiracy. He thought the impeachment was an outrage. He said that the people who are violating the constitution are impeaching me for violating the constitution; it should be the other way around.

A trial in the Senate would determine whether Johnson's misdeeds would amount to high crimes and misdemeanors required by the constitution to remove him from office. If 2/3 of the Senate voted to convict him, the Johnson presidency would be over. Tickets to this trial were like tickets to a heavyweight championship fight, it was the social event of the day and everybody came to the Senate to see what was going on. In the end, Johnson avoided conviction and removal from office by a single vote. Following his run-in with Congress, Johnson passed the rest of his term quietly. After returning home to Tennessee, Johnson would become the only former president elected to the Senate.

The troubling relationship between Johnson and the Congress had a lasting impact on the executive office for the next thirty-five years. A series of relatively weak presidents would occupy the white house. Andrew Johnson did not attend a single day of school, he taught himself how to read. He died of a stroke on July 31, 1875, in Elizabethton, Tennessee; he was 66 years old.

Ulysses S. Grant, Number 18, 1869-1877

Republican, 46 years old from Ohio. Wife Julia Dent, 4 children.

He was the youngest man ever to be elected president. He was the first West Pointer and also the first to be elected without winning the majority of the white vote. That's because Blacks in the south were allowed to cast ballots for the very first time and roughly 700,000 did, 12% of the total vote. They voted almost to a man for Grant. He was hailed as the victor of Vicksburg, the hero of Appomattox, the savior of the union. No American's picture was more coveted than that of General U.S. Grant. He was as close to a star celebrity in the late 1860's and early 1870's as you could have had. He was almost a shoe-in to become the Republican Presidential candidate. Enough people told him that he should be president, that he was convinced.

Grant was military commander during the Civil War and post-war reconstruction periods. Grant began his lifelong career as a soldier after graduating from the United States Military Academy in 1843. While fighting in the Mexican American War, he observes the techniques of General's Zachary Taylor and Winfield Scott. In 1861, after the American Civil War broke out, he joined the union's war effort, taking charge of training new regiments and then engaging the enemy near Cairo, Illinois. In 1862, he fought a series of major battles and captured a Confederate Army earning a reputation as an aggressive general and allowing the union to seize most of Kentucky and Tennessee. In July 1863, after a long complex campaign, he captured Vicksburg, captured another Confederate Army and took control of the Mississippi River.

President Abraham Lincoln promoted him to the rank of Lieutenant general and put him in charge of all Union Armies. Grant confronted Robert E. Lee in a series of very high casualty battles known as the "Overland Campaign" that ended in a stalemate siege at Petersburg. Grant coordinated campaigns launched by William Tecumseh Sherman, Philip Sheridan, and George Thomas, finally breaking through Lee's trenches at Petersburg. The Union Army captured Richmond, the Confederate capital in April, 1865. Lee surrendered to Grant at Appomattox; the Confederacy collapsed and the Civil War was over.

Enormously popular in the north after the Union's victory, he was elected to the Presidency in 1868. When re-elected in 1872, he became the first president to serve two full terms since Andrew Jackson did so forty years earlier. As president, he led reconstruction by signing and enforcing civil rights laws and fighting the Ku Klux Klan violence. He supported amnesty for former Confederates and signed the Amnesty Act of 1872. To further this, he favored a limited number of troops to be stationed in the South. This was sufficient numbers to protect Southern Freedmen, suppress the violent tactics of the Ku Klux Klan, (KKK) and prop up Republican governors, but not so many as to create resentment in the general population.

He helped rebuild the Republican Party in the south, an effort that resulted in the election of African Americans to Congress and state governments for the first time. Despite these civil rights accomplishments, Grant's presidency was marred by economic turmoil and multiple scandals. His response to the panic of 1873, and the severe depression that followed, was heavily critized. Grant's low standards in cabinet and federal appointments and the appointees lack of accountability, generated corruption and bribery in seven government departments.

One of the noticeable characteristics in the Grant Presidency was his concern with the plight of African Americans and Native Indian Tribes, in addition to civil rights for all Americans. Grant's 1868 campaign slogan, "Let us have peace," defined his motivation and assured his success. Grant made many advances in civil and human rights. In 1869 and 1871, he signed bills promoting black voting rights and prosecuting Klan leaders. He won passage of the Fifteenth Amendment, which gave freedmen the vote and the Ku Klux Klan Act, which empowered the president to arrest disguised night marauders.

Grant continued to fight for black civil rights, when he pressed for the former slaves to be "possessed of the civil rights which citizenship should carry with it." Grant was the first president to sign a Congressional Civil Rights Act. The law was titled the Civil Rights Act of 1875, which entitled equal treatment in public accommodations and jury selection.

Grant's attempts to provide justice to Native Americans marked a radical reversal of what had long been the government's policy: "Wars of extermination are demoralizing and wicked," he told Congress. The president lobbied, though not always successfully, to preserve Native American lands from encroachment by the westward advance of pioneers.

Grant was obviously a humanitarian, but the Panic of 1873, which was a worldwide depression that started when the stock market in Vienna crashed in June 1873 and spread throughout Europe and America, caused the depression to last for 5 years.

Grant's presidency was injured by nepotism, more than 40 family members profited greatly during his administration. His inability to establish personal accountability among his subordinates and cabinet members, led to many scandals during his administration. There were 11 scandals directly associated with Grant's two terms as President of the United States. In 1869, it was Black Friday when speculators cornered the gold market and ruined the economy for several years, it was called the New York customhouse ring. There were three investigations, two Congressional and one Treasury, both looked into the alleged corruption ring set up at the New York Custom House under Grant's appointments in 1872, collectors Moses H. Grinnell and Thomas Murphy. Then there was the Salary Grab, when Congressmen received a retroactive $5,000 bonus for previous term served.

The many scandals left his presidency tarnished, had he been more forceful with his subordinates and had he selected more capable politicians to surround himself with, maybe he could have avoided some of these adversities.

Grant died on July 23, 1885, at Mount McGregar, New York. He was 70 years old.

Rutherford Birchard Hayes, Number 19, 1877-1881

Republican, 55 years old from Ohio, wife Lucy, 8 children. Hayes began his presidency in the highly disputed election of 1876.

Though he lost the popular vote, Hayes was elected President by just one electoral vote in the highly disputed election of 1876. A Congressional Commission decided the outcome of the election by awarding Hayes the disputed electoral votes. Historians believe that an informal deal called the Compromise of 1877, was struck between Democrats and Republicans where the Democrats agreed not to block Hayes from the Presidency.

During his presidency, Hayes ordered federal troops to suppress The Great Railroad Strike of 1877 and ended Reconstruction by removing troops from the south. After the removal of federal troops, all southern states soon returned to democratic control, signaling the start of the Jim Crow South.

On administrative affairs, he began gradual civil service reforms and advocated the repeal of the Tenure of Office Act. In foreign policy, Hayes renegotiated the Burlingame Treaty with China, granted the army the freedom to intervene in Mexico in order to fight lawless banditos and nearly saw the construction of a canal across Panama.

Hayes became president after the scandal-ridden years of the Grant administration. He was noted for his ability not to affend anyone. A political journalist asserted that Hayes was a third rate non-entity, whose only recommendation is that he is obnoxious to no one. Hayes won the presidency by one vote, 185 to 184, over his opponent Democrat Samuel J. Tilden. A popular phrase of the day called it an election without "a free ballot and a fair count". For the next four years, democrats would refer to Hayes as "Rutherfraud B. Hayes" for his allegedly illegitimate election, because he had lost the popular vote by roughly 250,000 votes. Key Ohio Republicans like James A. Garfield and the Democrats, agreed at a Washington hotel on the Wormly House Agreement. Southern Democrats were given assurances in the Compromise of 1877, that as President, Hayes would appoint one southerner to his cabinet. He would pull federal troops out of the south and end Reconstruction. This agreement restored local control to the southern states and ended national control over the state and local governments in former Confederate states.

Hayes intended for his Inaugural Address to soothe the wounds of a nation still scarred from the Civil War. With the phrase "forever wipe out in our political affairs the color line and the distinction between north and south, to the end that we may not have merely a united north, or a united south, but a united country..." Hayes signaled the end of the Reconstruction Era. Hayes also faced a Democratic House of Representatives that refused to fund Reconstruction.

Hayes believed that southern whites, motivated by paternalism, would protect the rights of African Americans if given back control of state governments.

Hayes most controversial domestic act, apart from ending reconstruction, was his response to the Great Railroad Strike of 1877. Employees of the Baltimore & Ohio Railroad walked off the job and were joined acrossed the country by thousands of workers in the railroad industry. When the labor disputes exploded into riots in several cities, Hayes called in federal troops, who, for the first time in U.S. history, fired on the striking workers killing more than 70. Although the troops eventually managed to restore the peace, working people and industrialist alike were displeased with the military intervention.

Workers feared that the federal government had turned permanently against them, while industrialist feared that such brutal action would spark revolution similar to the European Revolutions of 1848.

Perhaps one of the biggest political challenges Hayes ever faced in his administration was the so-called "Battle of the Riders". In the elections of 1878, the Democrats captured control of both houses of Congress. The Democrats, in an effort to strengthen their chances in the 1880 elections, began adding riders, pieces of legislation that "ride" to passage on another bill to necessary appropriations bills. The Democrats riders targeted federal election enforcement laws that prevented fraud and voter intimidation. Determined not to give in, Hayes vetoed the bills with the riders citing two reasons: 1) every citizen has the right "to cast one un-intimidated ballot and to have his ballot honestly counted" and 2) "the riders were an unconstitutional attempt to force legislation on the President". The

Democrats could not overcome Hayes vetoes and eventually gave up the fight. Their efforts also backfired because Hayes tenacity had united the Republicans heading into the 1880 elections. The "Battle of the Riders" thus ended with a victory for presidential power.

In 1880, he kept his pledge not to run for a second term and retired quietly. Hayes died January 17, 1893 from a heart attack; he was 70 years old.

James A. Garfield, Number 20, March 4 1881-September 19, 1881 the second U.S. President to be assassinated.

Republican, 49 years old from Ohio, wife Lucretia Rudolph, they had seven children, 5 boys and 2 daughters. President Garfield had only 4 months to establish his presidency before being fatally shot by Charles J. Guiteau, a deranged political office seeker, on July 2, 1881. During his limited time in office he was able to re-establish the independence of the presidency by defying the Republican stalwart boss, Senator Roscoe Conkling. His inaugural address set the agenda for his presidency; however, he was unable to live long enough to implement these policies. Garfield's call for civil service reform was fulfilled in the Pendleton Civil Service Reform Act, passed by Congress and signed by President Chester A. Arthur in 1883. Garfield's assassination was the primary motivation for the reform bill's passage.

Garfield had little time to savor his triumph, when he was shot at 9:30 a.m. on July 2nd. The President had been walking through the Sixth Street Station of the Baltimore and Potomac Railroad, currently the Pennsylvania Railroad in Washington D.C.. Garfield was on his way to his alma mater, Williams College, where he was scheduled to deliver a speech, accompanied by Secretary of State James G. Blaine, Secretary of War, Robert Todd Lincoln, (son of Abraham Lincoln) and two of his sons, James and Harry. As he was being arrested after the shooting, Guiteau repeatedly said, "I am a stalwart of the stalwarts! I did it and I want to be arrested!" Arthur is President now! Which briefly led to unfounded suspicions that Arthur or his supporters, had put Guiteau up to the crime. Guiteau was upset because of the rejection of his repeated attempts to be appointed as the United States Consul in Paris, a position for which he had absolutely no qualifications.

One bullet grazed his arm; the second bullet lodged in his spine and could not be found. Garfield became increasingly ill over a period of several weeks due to infection, which caused his heart to weaken. Garfield died of a massive heart attack, or a ruptured splenic ortery aneurysm, following blood poisoning and bronchial pneumonia, at 10:35 p.m. on Monday, September 19, 1881, in Long Beach, New Jersey. Guiteau was sentenced to death and was executed by hanging on June 30, 1882, in Washington, D.C.

Chester Alan Arthur, Number 21, 1881-1885

Republican, 50 years old, from Vermont. Wife Ellen Lewis Herndon, two sons and one daughter. His wife and one son died before he took office. Arthur said he would never re-marry.

Arthur, as Vice President, was sworn into office on the death of President Garfield, he would serve as President until March 4, 1885. President Arthur became a champion of civil service reform. His primary achievement was the passage of the Pendleton Civil Service Reform Act. The passage of this legislation earned Arthur the Moniker, "The Father of Civil Service", and a favorable reputation among historians.

Once in the White House, Arthur was determined to go his own way. He became a man of fashion in his manner of dress and in his associates; he was often seen with the elite of Washington, D.C., New York and Newport.

President Arthur took the oath of office twice. The first time was at his Lexington Avenue residence, when it was given just past midnight on September 20. New York Supreme Court Justice, John R. Brady, gave the oath. The second time was two days later after he returned to Washington. This time Chief Justice of the United States, Morrison Waite, gave it in the Capitol. This was to avoid any dispute over whether the oath was valid if given by a state official.

Acting independently of party dogma, Arthur also tried to lower tariff rates so the government would not be embarrassed by annual surpluses of revenue. Congress increased about as many rates as it trimmed, but Arthur signed the Tariff Act of 1883 anyway. The tariff issue started to emerge as a major political issue between the two parties.

Civil reform had been a burning issue since the Grant administration and both Hayes and Garfield took smaller steps to wrangle in the corrupt and inefficient Patronage System in

Washington. Arthur realized that reform was vital after Republicans lost seats in the mid-term election of 1882. The Pendleton Act was written by a Democrat, Senator George Pendleton and "banned salary kickbacks, apportioned federal appointments among the states and ruled that new employees must begin their service at the bottom of the career ladder, advancing only by merit exams. The passage of this reform became the single most important act in Arthur's presidency. This act was a huge leap forward, spelling the end of the Spoils System.

Chester Arthur signed the Edmunds Act that banned bigamist and polygamist from voting and holding office. The act was especially enforced in Utah, a highly populated Mormon territory and established a five-man "Utah commission" to enforce the act.

The Arthur administration enacted the first general Federal Immigration Law. Arthur approved a measure in 1882, excluding paupers, criminals and the mentally ill. In response to anti-Chinese sentiment in the west, Congress passed a Chinese Exclusion Act. The act would have made illegal the immigration of Chinese laborers for twenty years and denied American citizenship to Chinese Americans currently residing in the United States who were not already citizens and who were not born in the United States. Arthur vetoed this steep restriction on the grounds that it violated the Burlingame Treaty. Newspapers in California immediately denounced him. When a compromise restriction of ten years was proposed, Arthur agreed and signed the revised bill, however, the Chinese Americans residing in the United States were denied citizenship.

The Act was renewed every ten years until the National Origins Act of 1924, essentially eliminated Chinese because the quotas were based on the 1890 numbers. The Act was not fully repealed until 61 years later, in 1943, by which time the U.S. was an ally of Nationalist China in the fight against Japan during World War II. The Act had become an embarrassment to the U.S. necessitating its repeal.

President Arthur was reluctant to enforce the 15th Amendment in the United States Constitution and never attempted, while President, to overturn "Jim Crow" laws throughout the nation that prevented African Americans from voting.

President Arthur's legacy may have been his determined effort to rebuild the United States Navy after the Civil War. The U.S. Navy had not been upgraded, so twenty years later, it was considered a joke when compared to the mighty armadas of the European powers. The president sought the building of steam-powered steel cruisers, steel rams and steel-clad gunboats. He moved decisively to curb corruption and incompetency within the Navy. He also created the Naval War College and the Office of Naval Intelligence. For these achievements he was called the "Father of the Steel Navy".

President Arthur was suffering from Bright's disease, a fatal kidney disease. He clearly was not well even though he worked vigorously during the elections of 1879 and 1880. The disease accounted for his failure to seek the Republican nomination for president aggressively in 1884. Arthur was the last incumbent President to submit his name for re-nomination and fail to obtain it.

He died November 18, 1886, in New York, New York; he was 57 years old.

Stephen Grover Cleveland, Number 22, 1885-1889

Democrat, 48 years old from New York. Cleveland was a bachelor when he entered the White House. On June 2, 1886, Cleveland married Frances in the Blue Room in the White House. He was the second president to marry while in office and the only president to have a wedding in the White House. The Cleveland's had five children, four girls and one boy.

Cleveland was the only Democrat elected to the Presidency in the era of republican political domination that lasted from 1860, to 1912. Cleveland won praise for his honesty, independence, integrity and commitment to the principles of classical liberalism.

Soon after taking office, Cleveland was faced with the task of filling all the government jobs for which the president had the power of appointment. These jobs were typically filled under the Spoils System, but Cleveland announced that he would not fire any republican who was doing his job well and would not appoint anyone solely on the basis of party service. He also used his appointment powers to reduce the number of federal employees as many departments had become bloated with political time-servers. While some of his decisions were influenced by party concerns, more of Cleveland's appointments were decided by merit alone than was the case in his predecessor's administrations.

Cleveland also reformed other parts of the government. In 1887, he signed an act creating the Interstate Commerce Commission. He and Secretary of the Navy William C. Whitney, undertook to modernize the navy and canceled construction contracts that had resulted in inferior ships.

Cleveland angered railroad investors by ordering an investigation of western lands they held by government grant. Secretary of the Interior Lucius Q.C. Lamar, charged that the rights of way for this land must be returned to the public because the railroads failed to extend their lines according to agreements. The lands were forfeited, resulting in the return of approximately 81, 000,000 acres.

As a reformer, he worked deligently against political corruption, patronage and bossism. Cleveland took strong positions and in turn, took heavy criticism. Cleveland faced a Republican Senate and often resorted to using his veto powers. He vetoed hundreds of private pension bills from American Civil War Veterans, believing that if their pensions request had already been rejected by the Pension Bureau, Congress should not attempt to override that decision. When Congress, pressured by the Grand Army of the Republic, passed a bill granting pensions for disabilities not caused by military service, Cleveland also vetoed that. Cleveland used the veto far more often than any president up to that time.

One of the most volatile issues of the 1880's was whether the currency should be backed by gold and silver, or by gold alone. Because silver was worth less than its legal equivalent in gold, taxpayers paid their government bills in silver, while international creditors demanded payment in gold, resulting in a depletion of the nation's gold supply.

Cleveland and Treasury Secretary Daniel Manning stood firmly on the side of the gold standard and tried to reduce the amount of silver the government was required to coin under the Bland-Allison Act of 1878.

Another contentious issue at the time was the protective tariff. While it had not been a central point in his campaign, Cleveland's opinion on the tariff was that of most Democrats; the tariff ought to be reduced. The Republicans favored a higher tariff to protect American industries, but the government was running a surplus. In 1886, a bill to reduce the tariff was narrowly defeated in the House.

When it came to Civil Rights, Cleveland, like a growing number of northerners, (and nearly all white Southerners), saw reconstruction as a failed experiment and was reluctant to use federal power to enforce the 15th Amendment of the U.S. Constitution, which guaranteed voting rights to African Americans. Cleveland initially appointed no Black Americans to patronage jobs, but did allow Frederick Douglass to continue in his post as recorder of deeds in Washington, D.C.

When Douglass later resigned, Cleveland appointed another black man to replace him.

Although Cleveland had condemned the "outrages" against Chinese immigrants, he believed that Chinese immigrants were unwilling to assimilate into white society. Secretary of State Bayard, negotiated an extension to the Chinese Exclution Act and Cleveland lobbied Congress to pass the Scott Act, written by Congressman William Lawrence Scott. This act would prevent Chinese immigrants who left the United States from returning. The Scott Act, easily passed both houses of Congress and Cleveland signed it into law on October 1, 1888.

Cleveland viewed Native Americans as wards of the state, saying in his first inaugural address, "his guardianship involves, on our part, efforts for the improvement of their condition and enforcement of their rights."

Cleveland would go on to lose the 1888 presidential election, but would run again in four years, unsuccessfully. He died of a heart attack in Princeton, New Jersey on June 24, 1908; he was 71 years old.

Benjamin Harrison, Number 23, 1889-1893

Republican, 56 years old from Indiana, Wife Caroline Lavinia Scott. Two children, one boy and one girl.

Harrison was elected to the presidency in 1888, defeating the Democratic incumbent, Grover Cleveland. He is the only president from the state of Indiana. His presidential administration is most remembered for its economic legislation, including the McKinley Tariff and the Sherman Antitrust Act, and for annual federal spending that reached one billion dollars for the first time. Democrats attacked the "Billion Dollar Congress" and used the issue, along with the growing unpopularity of the high tariff, to defeat the republicans, both in the 1890 mid-term elections and in Harrison's bid for Re-election in 1892. He also saw the admittance of six states into the Union.

In his attempt to right the wrongs of civil rights issues of the day, Harrison endorsed the proposed Federal Elections Bill, written by Representative Henry Cabot Lodge and Senator George Frisbie Hoar, in 1890, but the bill was defeated in the Senate. This was to be the last civil rights legislation attempted by Congress until the 1920's. Following the failure to pass the bill, Harrison continued to speak in favor of African American civil rights in addresses to Congress. In

1892, Harrison went before Congress and declared, "The frequent lynching of colored people is without the excuse that the accused have an undo influence over courts and juries." While Harrison believed the constitution did not permit him to end the practice of lynching, he did question the states civil rights records, arguing that if states have the authority over civil rights, then, "we have a right to ask whether they are at work upon it."

Harrison is the first president to have his voice recorded. Harrison also had electricity installed in the White House for the first time, but he and his wife would not touch the light switches for fear of electrocution and would often go to sleep with the lights on.

The first international crisis Harrison had to face occurred over fishing rights on the Alaskan coast. Canada claimed fishing and sealing rights around many of the Aleutian Islands, in violation of U.S. law. As a result, the United States Navy seized several Canadian ships. In 1891, the administration began negotiations with the British that would eventually lead to a compromise over fishing rights after international arbitration, with the British government paying compensation in 1898.

In his bid for re-election for the presidency, Harrison would face Grover Cleveland again, this time Cleveland would be successful.

After failing to win reelection in 1892, he returned to private life at his home in Indianapolis where he remarried, wrote a book, and later, represented the Republic of Venezuela in an international case against the United Kingdom.

He died in Indianapolis, Indiana on March 13, 1901; he was 67 years old. Fort Benjamin Harrison was named in his honor.

Stephen Grover Cleveland, Number 24, 1893-1897

Democrat, 56 years old from New York. Wife Frances Folsom, they had 5 children, four girls and one boy.

The election of 1892 would be a rematch of the one four years earlier. Unlike the turbulent and controversial elections of 1884,1876, and 1888, the 1892 election was, according to Cleveland biographer Allan Nevins, "the cleanest, quietest and most creditable in the memory of post war generations", in part because Harrison's wife was dying of tuberculosis. Harrison didn't personally campaign and Cleveland followed suit out of sympathy to his political rival as not to exploit Mrs. Harrison's illness. Cleveland would go on to win the election.

Shortly after Cleveland's second term began, the Panic of 1893 struck the stock market and he soon faced an acute economic depression. The panic was worsened by the critical shortage of gold that resulted from the free coinage of silver and Cleveland called Congress into session early to deal with the problem. The debate over the coinage was as heated as ever, but the effects of the panic had driven more moderates to support repealing the free coinage provisions of the Sherman Silver Purchase Act. Even so, the silverites rallied their following at a convention in Chicago and the House of Representatives debated for fifteen weeks before passing the repeal by a considerable margin. With the passage of the repeal through the Senate, the Treasury's gold reserves were restored to safe levels.

Having succeeding in reversing the Harrison administration's silver policy, Cleveland sought next to reverse the effects of the McKinley Tariff Act. What would become the Wilson-Gorman Tariff Act, introduced by Virginia Representative, William L. Wilson in 1893; the bill passed the House by considerable margin. The short fall was to be made up by an income tax of two percent on income above $4,000. By the time the bill left the senate, it had more than 60 amendments attached that nullified most of the reforms. Cleveland was unhappy, but allowed it to become law without his signature.

Cleveland's administration faced labor unrest, but was successful in defeating the efforts of a group called Coxey's Army, led by Jacob S. Coxey that marched on Washington to protest Cleveland's policies. They were arrested for walking on the grass of the United States Capitol and the group scattered. Coxey's Army was never a threat to the government.

The Pullman Strike had a significantly greater inpact than Coxey's Army. A strike began against the Pullman Company over low wages and twelve-hour workdays. Sympathy strikes led by Eugene V. Debs, soon followed. By June 1894, 125,000 railroad workers were on strike, paralyzing the nation's commerce. Because the railroads carried the mail and because several of the affected lines were in federal receivership, Cleveland believed a federal solution was appropriate. Cleveland obtained an injunction in federal court and when the strikers refused to obey it, he sent in federal troops to Chicago and 20 other rail centers. "If it takes the entire army and navy of the United States to deliver a postcard in Chicago," he proclaimed, "that card will be delivered". The use of troops hardened the attitude of organized labor toward his administration.

In the midst of the fight for the repeal of free silver coinage in 1893, Cleveland sought the advice of the White House doctor, Dr. O'Reilly, about a soreness on the roof of his mouth and a crater-like edge ulcer on the left side of Cleveland's hard palate. The diagnosis was not a malignant cancer, but instead an "epithelioma". Because of the financial depression of the country, Cleveland decided to have surgery performed in secrecy to avoid futher market panic. The surgery was conducted through the president's mouth, to avoid any scars or other signs of surgery.

After leaving the White House on March 4, 1897, Cleveland lived in retirement until his health began to fail him in the autumn of 1907, he fell seriously ill in 1908, and he suffered a heart attack and died. His last words were "I have tried so hard to do right". He died in Princeton, New Jersey, on June 24, 1908; he was 71 years old.

William McKinley Jr., Number 25, 1897-1901

Republican, 54 years old from Ohio. Wife, Ida Saxton McKinley, they had one girl. He was the last veteran of the American Civil War to be elected to office. His signature issue was high tariffs on imports as a formula for prosperity, as typified by his McKinley Tariff Act, of 1890. McKinley presided over a period of prosperity after the panic of 1893, then he made gold the base of the currency.

He demanded that Spain end its atrocities against Cuba, which were outraging public opinion. Spain resisted the interference and in 1898, the Spanish-American War became inevitable. The war was an easy task for America as the weak Spanish fleets were sunk and both Cuba and the Philippines were captured in 90 days. At the peace conference, McKinley agreed to purchase the former Spanish colonies of Puerto Rico, Guam and the Philippines, then set up a protectorate over Cuba. McKinley also annexed the independent Republic of Hawaii and forced Hawaii to join the U.S., with all its residents becoming full American citizens. The Democrats were opposed to the annexation of the Philippines.

McKinley's inauguration marked the beginning of the greatest movement of consolidation that American business had ever seen. Such consolidation of business (what was back then called trust), was the culmination of a trend already far underway when McKinley took office. The administration did not actively use the Sherman Antitrust Act, therefore, trust were allowed to grow.

McKinley validated his claim as the "advance agent of prosperity", when the year 1897 brought a revival of business, agriculture and general prosperity. This was due to the end of the Panic of 1893, which was caused by deflation dating back to the Civil War and underconsumption. The end of the deflationary period was largely due to the Gold Standard Act of 1900, which set the value of the dollar.

The single event that came to define McKinley's presidency was the Spanish-American War. The conflict between the two countries grew from yellow journalist stories of Spanish atrocities in Cuba, namely Spain's use of concentration camps and brutal force to quash the Cuban's rebellion. The Spanish repeatedly promised new reforms and then postponed them. Democrats and the sensationalist yellow journalism of William Randolph Hearst's newspapers, pushed American public opinion against Spain through a media blitz for war.

To demonstrate growing American concern, the war ship U.S.S. Maine was dispatched to Havana harbor. On February 15, 1898, it mysteriously exploded and sank, causing the deaths of 260 men. No one was officially blamed, but the episode riveted the nation. Congress voted for war, even though they thought the U.S. Army was poorly prepared. The Navy was ready. Militia and National Guard units rushed to the colors, most notably, Theodore Roosevelt and his "Rough Riders". The naval war in Cuba and the Philippines was a success, the easiest war in U.S. history and after 113 days, Spain agreed to peace terms at the Treaty of Paris in July. The United States gained ownership of Guam, the Philippines and Puerto Rico, with temporary control over Cuba. Hawaii, which for years had tried to join the U.S., was annexed.

McKinley carried African American sympathies for their struggles under the "Jim Crow" laws throughout the nation while he was President. McKinley was unwilling to use federal power to enforce the 15th Amendment in the U.S. Constitution. During his Presidency there were many murders, torturing and civil rights violations throughout the country against African Americans. The 1896 U.S. Supreme Court decision, Plessy vs. Ferguson, declared that public facilities that were "separate but equal", could be used to segregate African Americans from white society. McKinley made several speeches on African American equality and justice, but despite McKinley's sympathetic rhetoric, the political realities prevented any real action on the part of his administration in regards to race relations. He did little to alleviate the backwards situation of Black Americans because he was unwilling to alienate the white South.

McKinley was re-elected in 1900 to a second term, this time with foreign policy being his most important issue.

The President and Mrs. McKinley attended the Pan American Exposition in Buffalo, New York. He delivered a speech about his positions on tariffs and foreign trade on September 5, 1901. The following morning, McKinley visited Niagara Falls before returning to the exposition. That afternoon, McKinley had an engagement to greet the public at the Temple of Music. Standing in Line, Leon Frank Czolgosz waited with a pistol in his right hand concealed by a handkerchief. At 4:07 p.m., Czolgosz fired twice at the president. The first bullet grazed the president's shoulder. The second however, went through McKinley's stomach, pancreas and kidney and finally lodged in the muscles of his back. The president whispered to his secretary, George Cortelyou "My wife, Cortelyou, be careful how you tell her, oh be careful." Czolgosz would have fired again, but he was struck by a bystander and subdued by an enraged crowd. The wounded McKinley even called out "Boys, don't let them hurt him!" because the crowd beat Czolgosz so severly it looked as if they might kill him on the spot.

One bullet was easily found and extracted, but doctors were unable to locate the second bullet. It was feared that the search for the bullet might cause more harm than good. McKinley began to go into shock. At 2:15 a.m. on September 14, 1901, eight days after he was shot, he died from gangrene surrounding his wounds. He was 58 years old. His last words were "It is God's way; his will be done, not ours." His remains were later entered in the Mckinley Memorial, Canton Ohio. He was the third United States President to be assassinated.

Theodore Roosevelt, Number 26, 1901-1909

Republican, 42 years old from Ohio. Married. His first wife, Alice Hathaway Lee, died in 1884. He married Edith Kermit Carow; he had 6 children, 2 girls and 4 boys.

On September 6, 1901, President William McKinley was shot while at the Pan American Exposition In Buffalo, New York. On September 14, he died as a result of his wounds and Vice President Roosevelt became President of the United States of America, when he arrived in Buffalo and was sworn into office at 3:30 p.m., Roosevelt became president at the age of 42, taking office at the youngest age of any U.S. President in history, at that time.

Roosevelt attempted to move the Republican Party in the direction of progressivism, including trust busting and increased regulations of business. Roosevelt coined the phrase "Square Deal" to describe his domestic policies, emphasizing that the average citizen would get a fair shake under his policies.

On the world stage, Roosevelt's policies were characterized by his slogan, "Speak softly and carry a big stick". He was the force behind the completion of the Panama Canal; he sent out the Great White Fleet to display American power and he negotiated an end to the Russo-Japanese War, for which he won the Nobel Peace Prize. He was the first American to win the prize.

One of his first notable acts as president was to deliver a 20,000-word address to Congress asking it to curb the power of large corporations called "trusts". For that he was called a "trust-buster".

Building on McKinley's effective use of the press, Roosevelt made the White House the center of news everyday, providing interviews with photo opportunities. After noticing the White House reporters huddled outside in the rain one day, he gave them their own room inside, effectively inventing the presidential press briefing.

In May 1902, United Mine Workers went on strike to get higher wages and shorter workdays. Roosevelt set up a fact-finding commission which stopped the strike and resulted in the workers getting more pay for fewer hours. Union's has had a presence since the 1600's with the Carriage Workers Union.

In August 1902, Roosevelt was the first president to be seen riding in an automobile in public, while his security force rode bicycles along side of the car.

In stating his position on immigration in a 1894 article, Roosevelt said, "We must Americanize in everyway, in speech, in political ideas, in principles and in their way of looking at church and state. We welcome the German and the Irishmen who become an American. We have no use for the German or Irishman who remains such... He must revere only our flag, not only must it come first, but no other flag should even come second." With regard to African Americans Roosevelt said, I have not been able to think out any solution of the terrible problem offered by the presence of the Negro's on this continent, but of one thing I am sure and that is that inasmuch as he is here and can neither be killed nor driven away, the only wise and honorable and Christian thing to do is to treat each black man and each white man strictly on his merits as a man, giving him no more and no less than that he shows himself worthy to have. In 1886 he said, "I don't go so far as to think that the only good Indians are dead Indians, but I believe nine out of ten are and I shouldn't like to inquire too closely into the case of the tenth". He later became much more favorable.

In the opinion of many, one of his most disgusting statements, if true, were made when in 1907, eugenicists in many states started the forced sterilization of the sick, unemployed, poor, criminals, prostitutes and the disabled. Roosevelt said in 1914, "I wish very much that the wrong people could be prevented entirely from breeding and when the evil nature of these people is sufficiently flagrant, this should be done. Criminals should be sterilized and feeble-minded persons forbidden to leave offspring behind them."

Roosevelt chose not to run for another term in 1908 and supported William Taft for the presidency, instead of Fairbanks. Fairbanks withdrew from the race and would later support Taft for re-election against Roosevelt in the 1912 election. At the Republican Convention in Chicago, with Taft's victory not immediately assured, Roosevelt, realizing he would not win the nomination outright, asked his followers to leave the convention hall. They did and he formed the "Bull Moose Party". It did not sustain itself.

While Roosevelt was campaigning in Milwaukee, Wisconsin on October 14, 1912, a saloonkeeper named John Schrank shot him, but the bullet lodged in his chest only after penetrating both his steel eyeglass case and passing through a thick (50 pages), single-folded copy of the speech he was carrying in his jacket. Realizing the bullet didn't enter his chest cavity; Roosevelt gave his speech with blood seeping into his shirt. He said, "Ladies and gentlemen, I don't know whether you fully understand that I have just been shot; but it takes more than that to kill a Bull Moose".

It is said that the death of his youngest son Quentin, a pilot in World War 1 who was shot down behind enemy lines, left him broken and despondent. He was his favorite; he never recovered from the loss. On January 6, 1919, Roosevelt died of a heart attack preceded by a two and a half month illness. He was buried near Youngs Memorial Cemetery. His son Archie telegraphed his siblings simply "The old lion is dead. Vice-Persident Thomas R. Marshall said, "Death had to take Roosevelt sleeping, for if he had been awake, there would have been a fight."

Roosevelt joined Presidents George Washington, Thomas Jefferson and Abraham Lincoln with his likeness on the Mount Rushmore Memorial designed in 1927 and approved by President Calvin Cooledge.

He was also awarded the Congressional Medal of Honor posthumously, by President Bill Clinton for his bravery when he led his Rough Riders in a charge up San Juan Hill in Cuba during the Spanish American War. This is the Nation's highest honor.

At the time of his death, Roosevelt was 60 years old.

William Howard Taft, Number 27, 1909-1913

Republican, 51 years old from Ohio. Wife Helen Herron, three children, two boys and one girl. President Taft would later serve as the 10th Chief Justice of the United States. He is the only person to have served in both offices.

In his first and only term, President Taft's domestic agenda emphasized civil service reform, strengthening the Interstate Commerce Commission, improving the performance of the postal service and passage of the Sixteenth Amendment.

Abroad, Taft sought to further the economic development of undeveloped nations in Latin America and Asia, through the method he termed "Dollar Diplomacy".

The Sixteenth Amendment allowed for a federal income tax, and he was in support of the 17th Amendment that mandated the direct election of senators by the people, replacing the previous system whereby they were selected by state legislatures.

Taft considered himself a progressive; he believed that the law was the vehicle that should be used by judges to solve society's problems. Taft lacked the broad base of public support that Roosevelt enjoyed. When Roosevelt realized that lowering the tariff would risk severe tensions inside the Republican Party, pitting producers against department stores and consumers, he stopped talking about the issue. Taft ignored the risk and tackled the tariff aggressively; on the one hand encouraging reformers to fight for lower rates and then on the other hand, cutting deals with conservative leaders that kept rates high. The resulting Payne-Aldrich Tariff Act of 1909, was too high for most reformers, but instead of blaming this on Senator Nelson W. Aldrich and big business, Taft took credit, calling it the best bill to come from the Republican Party, alienating all sides.

In his foreign policy initiatives, Taft actively pursued what he termed "Dollar Diplomacy," to further the economic development of less developed nations of Latin America and Asia, through American investment in their infrastructures. One of Taft's main goals while president was to further the idea of world peace. In 1910, and 1911, Taft secured the ratification of arbitration treaties that he had successfully negotiated with Britain and France and thereafter, was known as one of the foremost advocates of world peace and arbitration.

To resolve an impasse during the 1909 tariff debate, Taft proposed income taxes for corporations and a Constitutional Amendment to remove the apportionment requirement for taxes on incomes from property, (taxes on dividens, interest and rents), on June 16, 1909. In July 1909, a proposed amendment to remove the apportionment requirement was passed unanimously in the Senate, and by a vote of 318 to 14 in the House. It was quickly ratified by the states and on February 3, 1913, it became a part of the constitution as the Sixteenth Amendment, just as Taft was leaving office.

On Civil Rights, Taft was reluctant, as were the presidents that preceded him, to use federal authority to enforce the 15th amendment to the U.S. Constitution, which guaranteed African Americans the right to vote. As a result, state governments were able to enforce voter registration requirements that prevented African Americans from voting. Lynching by whites was common throughout the south at the time; however, Taft did nothing to stop the practice. Taft publicly endorsed Booker T. Washington's program for uplifting the black race, advising them to stay out of politics at the time. A supporter of free immigration, Taft vetoed a law passed by Congress that would have restricted admissions by imposing a literacy test.

During his post presidency, on June 30, 1921, following the death of Chief Justice Edward Douglass White, President Warren G. Harding nominated Taft to take his place, thereby fulfilling Taft's lifelong ambition to become Chief Justice of the United States. There was little opposition to the nomination and the Senate approved him 60-4 in a secret session on the day of his nomination, but roll call of the vote has never been made public.

He died March 8, 1930 in Washington D.C., he was 72 years old.

Woodrow Wilson, Number 28, 1913-1921

Democrat, 57 years old from Virginia. His first wife Ellen died in 1914, they had three daughters. He married his second wife Edith Galt that same year. They had no children.

During Wilson's first term, he was successful in persuading the Democratic Congress to pass several piecies of lagislation. The Federal Reserve Act, the Federal Trade Commission Act, the Clayton Antitrust Act, the Federal Farm Loan Act and America's first-ever federal progressive income tax in the Revenue Act of 1913. Wilson brought many white Southerners into his administration and supported their expansion of segregation in many federal agencies.

Wilson is the only President to hold a PHD. Degree. He was the first person identified with the south to be elected president since Zachary Taylor and the first Southerner in the White House since Andrew Johnson left in 1868. Wilson had a strong base of support in the south. He was the first President to deliver his State of the Union address before Congress personally since John Adams in 1799. Wilson was also the first Democrat elected to the presidency since Grover Cleveland in 1892 and only the second Democrat in the White House since the Civil War.

Wilson experienced early success by implementing his "New Freedom" pledges of antitrust modification, tariff revision and reform in banking and currency matters. He held the first modern presidential press conference on March 15, 1913, in which reporter's were allowed to ask him questions. Wilson also secured the Federal Reserve Act in late 1913. However, in 1913, the Underwood Tariff Act lowered the tariff. The revenue lost was replaced by a new federal income tax, (authorized by the 16th Amendment).

There were a series of programs targeted at farmers. The Smith-Lever Act of 1914, created the modern system of agricultural extension agents, sponsored by the state agricultural colleges. The agent taught new techniques to farmers. The 1916 Federal Farm Loan Act, provided for issuance of low-cost long-term mortages to farmers.

The Keating-Owen Act of 1916, curtailed child labor, but the U.S. Supreme Court declared it unconstitutional in 1918. No major child labor prohibition would take effect until the 1930s.

When it comes to anti-trust, Wilson broke with the big lawsuit tradition of his predecessors Taft and Roosevelt as Trustbusters, finding a new approach to encouraging competition through the

Federal Trade Commission, which stopped perceived unfair trade practices.

In 1912, an unprecedented number of African Americans left the Republican Party to cast their vote for Democrat Wilson. They were encouraged by his promises of support for their issues. The issue of segregation came up early in his presidency when, at an April, 1913 cabinet meeting, Albert Burleson, Wilson's Postmaster General, complained about working conditions at the Railway Mail Service. Offices and restrooms became segregated, sometimes by partitions erected betweeen seating for white and African-American employees in Post Office Department offices, lunch rooms and bathrooms, as well as in the Treasury and the Bureau of Engraving and Printing. It also became accepted policy for "Negro" employees of the Postal Service to be reduced in rank, or dismissed. Unlike his predecessors Grover Cleveland and Theodore Roosevelt, Wilson accommodated southern opposition to the re-appointment of an African-American to the position of Register of the Treasury and other positions within the federal government. This set the tone for Wilson's attitude toward race throughout his presidency, in which the rights of African Americans were sacrificed for what he felt would be the more important longer term progress of the common good.

During Wilson's first term in office, he managed to avoid the war that was driven by the Germans and threatened the lives of American citizens. The U.S. maintained neutrality despite increasing pressure placed on Wilson after the sinking of the British passenger liner RMS Lusitania, with American citizens on board. This neutrality would deteriorate when Germany began to initiate its unrestricted submarine warfare threatening U.S. commercial shipping in early 1917. Wilson decided that the war had become a real threat to humanity. Unless the U.S. threw its weight into the war, as he stated in his declaration of war speech on April 2, 1917, western civilization itself could be destroyed. His statement announcing a "war to end war", meant that he wanted to build a basis for peace that would prevent future catastrophic wars and needless death and destruction.

With 50 Representatives and 6 Senators in opposition, the declaration of war by the United States against Germany was passed by the Congress on April 4, 1917 and was approved by the President on April 6, 1917.

After World War I, Wilson participated in negotiations with the stated aim of assuring statehood for formerly oppressed nations and an equitable peace. On January 8, 1918, Wilson made his famous

"Fourteen Points" address, introducing the idea of a League of Nations, an organization with a stated goal of helping to preserve territorial integrity and political independence among large and small nations alike. For his peace making efforts, Wilson was awarded the 1919 Noble Peace Prize, however, he failed to even win U.S. Senate support for ratification. The United States never joined the league. A poll of historians in 2006 cited Wilson's failure to compromise with the Republicans on U.S. entry into the League as one of the 10 largest errors on the part of an American president.

On October 2, 1919, he suffered a serious stroke that almost totally incapacitated him, leaving him paralyzed on his left side and blind in his left eye. He was confined to bed for weeks, sequestered from nearly everyone but his wife and his physician, Dr. Cary Grayson. For at least a few months, he used a wheelchair. Later, he could walk only with the assistance of a cain. The full extent of his disability was kept from the public until after his death on February 3, 1924, in his S. Street home. He was buried in Washington National Cathedral. He is the only president buried in Washington, D.C.; he was 67 years old.

Warren G. Harding, Number 29, 1921-1923

Republican, 55 years old from Ohio. Wife Florence kling, one Stepson. Harding ran on a promise to "Return to Normalcy", a seldom-used term he popularized. The slogan called an end to the normal era of the Great War, along with a call to reflect three trends of his time: a renewed isolationism in reaction to the War, a resurgence of nativism and a turning away from the government activism of the reform era.

During the campaign, political opponents spread rumors that Harding's great-great- grandfather was a West Indian black person and that other blacks might be found in his family tree. In an era when the "one-drop rule", meaning one drop of African blood in a white man would make him black, would classify a person with any African ancestry as black and black people in the south had been effectively disenfranchised. Harding's campaign manager responded, "No family in the state (of Ohio) has a clearer, a more honorable record than the Harding's"; a blue-eyed stock from New England and Pennsylvania, the finest pioneer blood. Harding once made a statement to a newspaper man James Faulkner, that perhaps, meant to be dismissive: "How do I know, Jim? One of my ancestors may have jumped the fence. If the rumors were ever proven to be true, by some definitions, Harding would be considered to be the first African-American president.

Harding was elected by a landslide and felt the pulse of the nation and for the next 28 months in office, he remained popular, both nationally and internationally. Harding however, has constantly been viewed as one of the worst United States Presidents, due to administration scandals. Was Harding really a failure? His accomplishments included income tax and federal spending reductions, a reduction in unemployment by 10%, and a bold foreign policy that created peace with Germany, Japan and Central America.

Harding pushed for the establishment of the Bureau of Veterans Affairs, later named the Department of Veterans Affairs, the first permanent attempt at answering the needs of those who had served the nation in time of war. He also created the Office of Management and Budget (OMB), becoming the first president to have the executive branch take a role in federal expenditures.

On June 12, 1921, President Harding signed the Budget and Accounting Act of 1921, establishing the Bureau of the Budget was considered to be one of his greatest domestic achievements. The law also stipulated that the president must submit a budget annually before the U.S. Congress.

On September 21, 1922, President Harding signed the Fordney-McCumber Tariff Act. This was protectionist legislation. The act increased the tariff rates contained in the previous Underwood-Simmions Tariff Act of 1913. By 1922, Harding soon began to realize that the long-term effects of tariffs could be detrimental to the national economy. The tariffs established in the 1920's, have historically been viewed as a contributing factor to causing the Wall Street crash of 1929.

President Harding's Secretary of State, Charles E. Hughes, worked behind the scenes to formally make peace with former enemies, Austria and Germany. This was known as the Knox-Porter Resolution; subsequent peace treaties were signed with both countries and ratified by the Senate and signed by Harding on July 21, 1921. The signing officially ended WWI for the United States.

President Harding, in an effort to improve U.S. relations with Mexico, Latin America, and the Caribbean Islands, implemented a program of military disengagement. On April 20, 1921, the Thomson-Urrutia Treaty with Panama was ratified by the Senate and signed by Harding. The treaty awarded $25,000,000 as indemnity payment for land used to build the Panama Canal.

On May 21, 1921, violence broke out again between union mining strikers and company strike busters near Matewan, West Virginia. The miners cut down telephone and telegraph lines and trained their guns on mines, strikebreakers and buildings. The strike lasted three days. In order to quell this labor unrest, Federal troops arrived on September 2, forcing miners to flee to their homes. 50--100 miners had been killed, as well as, 30 strike busters in the fighting. After the battle, 985 miners were indicted for crimes against the State of West Virginia; some were imprisoned for years.

About one year after the 1921 Blair Mountain mining labor war in West Vurginia, another strike broke out during the summer of 1922 in the railroad industry. 400,000 railroad workers and shopmen, on July 1, 1922, went on strike over reduced hourly wages by 7 cents, and a demanding 12-hour a day workweek. Harding sent the National Guard and 2,200 deputy U.S.Marshalls to keep the peace. Attorney General Harry M. Daugherty, who opposed unions, ordered judge James H. Wilkerson to issue an injunction to break up the strike. This was known as the "Wilkerson" or "Daughtery" injunction that caused labor to be enraged against the government. The strike finally settled out on its own, however, tensions remained high between railroad workers and company men for years.

During a speech on October 26, 1921, Harding advocated civil rights for all Americans, including African Americans. He suggested appointing African Americans to federal positions and was in favor of a national anti-lynching bill. He also advocated the establishment of an international commission to improve race relations between whites and blacks; however, strong political opposition by the Southern Democratic bloc prevented any of these initiatives from coming to fruition.

Harding supported Congressman Leonidas Dyer's federal anti-lynching bill, known as the Dyer Bill, which passed the House of Representatives on January 26, 1922. The bill was defeated in the Senate by a filibuster.

Harding appointed many of his longtime allies and campaign contributors to prominent political positions in control of vast amounts of government money and resources. Some of the appointees used their new powers to exploit their positions for personal gain. The author, Charles Mee Jr., called them the "Ohio Gang". There is no evidence to date to suggest that Harding personally profited from such crimes, but he was apparently unable to prevent them. "I have no trouble with my enemies," Harding told journalist William Allen

White late in his presidency, "but my damn friends, they're the ones that keep me walking the floor nights!"

The Harding administration was riddled with scandals and crimes of all sorts. The most infamous scandal was the "Teapot Dome Affair", which shook the nation for years after Harding's death. The scandal involved Secretary of the Interior Albert B. Fall, who was convicted of accepting bribes and illegal no-interest personal loans in exchange for the leasing of public oil fields to business associates. In 1931, Fall became the first member of a Presidential Cabinet to be sent to prison after conviction on charges. Thomas W. Miller, head of the Office of Alien Property, was put on trial and convicted of accepting bribes. Harding's Attorney General Harry M. Daugherty, who had remained in his position during the early days of the Calvin Cooledge administration, resigned on March 28, 1924, amidst allegations of accepting bribes from bootleggers. Daugherty's personal aide Jess W. Smith, was involved with selling liquor licenses, granting paroles, and arranging fixes. After a heated exchange with President Harding over these activities, Smith destroyed papers and committed suicide the following day. Charles R. Forbes, Director of the Veterans Bureau, skimmed profits, accepted high kickbacks, and directed underground alcohol and drug distribution. Forbes was estimated to have defrauded the government of $225 million through hospital construction and supply kickbacks and selling hospital supplies at extremely low prices to corrupt contractors. Harding, who was informed of the scandal in January 1923, summoned Forbes to the White House; he angrily grabbed him by the throat and shouted, "You double-crossing bastard". Forbes eventually was convicted of fraud and bribery in 1925 and drew a two-year sentence. Charles Cramer, an aide to Forbes involved in the scandal, committed suicide.

On June 13, 1921, President Harding appointed Albert D. Lasker, Chairman of the United States Shipping Board. Lasker, a cash donor to the Harding campaign, had no previous experience with shipping companies. The Merchant Marine Act of 1920, had allowed the Shipping Board to sell ships made by the U.S. Government to private American companies. A Congressional investigation revealed that while Lasker was in charge, many valuable steel cargo ships worth between $200 and $250 a ton, were sold as low as $30 a ton to private American shipping companies without an appraisal board. J. Harry Philbin, a manager in the sales division, testified at the Congressional hearing that under Lasker's authority, U.S. ships were sold as is, take your pick, no matter which vessel you took." Lasker resigned from the

Shipping Board on July 1, 1923. The activities of these individuals would taint Harding's presidency forever.

In June 1923, Harding set out on a cross-country "Voyage of Understanding," in which he planned to meet ordinary people and explain his policies. During this trip he became the first president to visit Alaska. Harding's health prior to the Alaskan venture was poor; his personal doctor believed getting away from the stresses of Washington would help the president. Rumors of corruption in his administration were beginning to circulate in Washington. At the end of July, while traveling south from Alaska through British Columbia, he developed what was believed to be a severe case of food poisoning. While at the Palace Hotel in San Francisco, Harding developed a respiratory illness believed to be Pneumonia. Harding died suddenly in the middle of conversation with his wife in the hotel's presidential suite, at 7:35 p.m. on August 2, 1923. He was 57 years old. Vice President Calvin Coolidge succeeded him as President.

John Calvin Coolidge, Jr. Number 30, 1923-1929

Republican, 51 years old from Vermont. Wife Grace Anna Goodhue, they had two boys. Coolidge succeeded to the Presidency in 1923, upon the sudden death of President Warren G. Harding. Coolidge was a quite and serious man and was commonly referred to as "Silent Cal", even though he was known to be a skilled and effective public speaker. Coolidge restored public confidence in the White House after the scandals of his predecessor's administration and was able to leave office with considerable popularity.

The vice Presidency didn't carry many official duties, but Coolidge was invited by President Harding to attend cabinet meetings, making him the first Vice President to do so. With Coolidge being a man of few words, a story has it that Dorothy Parker, seated next to him at a dinner, said to him, "Mr Coolidge, I've made a bet against a fellow who said it was impossible to get more than two words out of you. "His famous reply: "You lose." It was also Parker who, upon learning that Coolidge had died, reportedly remarked, "How can they tell?" Alice Roosevelt Long- worth supposedly once commented that, "He looks as if he had been weaned on a pickle."

On August 2, 1923, President Harding died while on a speaking tour in California. Vice President Coolidge was in Vermont visiting his family home, which had neither electricity nor a telephone when he received word by messenger of Harding's death. Coolidge dressed, said a prayer and came downstairs to greet reporters who had assembled there. His father, a notary public, administered the oath of office in the family parlor by the light of a kerosene lamp at 2:47 a.m. on August 3, 1923; Coolidge then went back to bed. Coolidge returned to Washington the next day and was re-sworn in by Justice Adolph A. Hoehling, Jr. of the Supreme Court of the District of Columbia.

Coolidge decided to continue with Harding's cabinet appointees even though many were scandal-tarred; he announced that he would not demand any of their resignations, believing that the people had elected Harding, he should carry on Harding's presidency, at least until the next election.

Coolidge addressed Congress when it reconvened on December 6, 1923, giving a speech that echoed many of Harding's themes, including immigration restriction and the need for the government to arbitrate the coal strikes that were on going in Pennsylvania. The Washington Naval Treaty was proclaimed just one month into Coolidge's term and was well received. In May, 1924, the World War I Veterans Bonus Bill passed over his veto. Coolidge signed the Immigration Act later that year, though he appended a signing statement expressing his unhappiness with the bill's specific exclusion of Japanese immigrants. Coolidge also signed into law the Revenue Act of 1924.

During Coolidge's run for the presidency in the 1924 election, he developed a blister on his hand while playing tennis on the White House courts. Calvin Jr. developed blood poisoning and died. Coolidge became withdrawn. He later said, "When he died, the power and glory of the Presidency went with him".

During his presidency, the U.S. experienced the period of rapid economic growth known as the "Roaring Twenties". With the exception of favoring increased tariffs, Coolidge disdained regulation and carried about this belief by appointing commissioners to the Federal Trade Commission and the Interstate Commerce Commission who did little to restrict the activities of businesses under their jurisdiction. The regulatory state under Coolidge was almost non-existant.

Coolidge's taxation policy was that of his Secretary of the Treasury, Andrew Mellon; taxes should be lower and fewer people should have to pay them. Congress agreed and the taxes were reduced during Coolidge's term of office. In addition to these tax cuts, Coolidge proposed reductions in federal spending and retiring some of the debt. Coolidge's ideas were shared by the Republicans in Congress and in 1924, Congress passed the Revenue Act of 1924, which reduced income tax rates and eliminated all income taxation for some two million people. They reduced taxes again by passing the Revenue Acts of 1926 and 1928, all the while continuing to keep spending down so as to reduce the overall federal debt.

Perhaps the most contentious issue of Coolidge's presidency was that of relief for farmers. However, due to rising prices, many in Congress were convinced that the bill was not necessary, so it was defeated just before elections in that year. Coolidge vetoed several later attempts.

Coolidge has been criticized for his actions during the Great Mississippi Flood of 1927, the worst natural disaster to hit the Gulf Coast until Hurricane Katrina in 2005. Although he did eventually name Secretary Hoover to a commission in charge of flood relief, Coolidge's lack of interest in federal flood control has been criticized. He did not believe that personally visiting the region after the floods would accomplish anything, but would be seen as political grandstanding. He did not want to incur the federal spending that flood control would require; he believed that property owners should bare much of the cost. On the other hand, Congress wanted a bill that would place the federal government completely in charge of flood mitigation. When Congress passed a compromise measure in 1928, Coolidge declined to take credit for it and signed the bill in private on May 15.

In the area of civil rights, Coolidge spoke out in favor of the civil rights of African Americans and Catholics. He appointed no known members of the Ku Klux Klan to office; the Klan lost most of its influence during his term.

In 1924, Coolidge responded to a letter that claimed the United States was a "white man's country". I was amazed to receive such a letter. During the war, 500,000 colored men and boys were called up under the draft, not one of whom sought to evade it. As president, I am one who feels a responsibility for living up to the traditions and maintaining the principles of the Republican Party. Our constitution guarantees equal rights to all our citizens, without discrimination on account of race or color. I have taken my oath to support that constitution....

On June 2, 1924, Coolidge signed the Indian Citizenship Act, which granted full citizenship to all American Indians, while permitting them to retain tribal land and cultural rights. However, the act was not clear as to whether the federal government, or the tribal leaders retained tribal sovereignty. Coolidge, like several presidents before him, called for anti-lynching laws to be enacted, but most Congressional attempts to pass this legislation were filibustered by Southern Democrats.

Coolidge's best-known initiative was the Kellogg-Briand Pact of 1928, named for Coolidge's Secretary of State, Frank B. Kellogg, and French foreign minister Aristide Briand. The treaty ratified in 1929, committed signatories including the U.S., the United Kingdom, France, Germany, Italy and Japan to "renounce war as an instrument of national policy in their relations with one another." The treaty did not achieve its intended results, but did provide the founding principle for international law after World War II.

In the summer of 1927, Coolidge vacationed in the Black Hills of South Dakota; he made Custer State Park his summer White House. While there, Coolidge issued a statement that he would not seek a second full term as President in 1928: "I do not choose to run for President in 1928." After allowing them to take that in, Coolidge elaborated, "If I take another term, I will be in the White House till 1933, ... Ten years in Washington is longer than any other man has had, Too Long!" The presidential office takes a heavy toll on those who occupy it and those who are dear to them. While we should not refuse to spend and be spent in the service of our country, it is hazardous to attempt what we feel is beyond our strength to accomplish." After leaving office, he and Grace returned to Northampton, where he wrote his memoirs.

He died of a sudden heart attack at his home in Northampton, Vermont at 12:45 p.m., January 5, 1933. Shortly before his death, Coolidge confided to an old friend, "I feel I am no longer fit in these times". He was 60 years old.

Herbert Hoover, Number 31, 1929-1933

Republican, 55 years old from Iowa. Wife, Lou Henry Hoover. In the presidential election of 1928, Hoover won the Republican nomination despite having no previous elected office experience. Hoover is the last cabinet secretary to be directly elected president. The nation was prosperous and optimistic at the time, this led to a landslide victory for Hoover over Democrat Al Smith.

To gain Republican votes in the Southern states, Hoover pioneered an electoral tactic later known as the "Southern Strategy". Hoover ousted many African American leaders in the Republican Party and replaced them with whites. This outraged the black leadership, which largely broke from the Republican Party and began seeking candidates who supported civil rights within the Democratic Party.

Hoover began his presidency on an optimistic note, saying during his inauguration speech: "Given the chance to go forward with the policies of the last eight years, we shall soon, with the help of God, be in sight of the day when poverty will be banished from this nation".

When the Wall Street crash of 1929 struck less than eight months after he took office, Hoover tried to combat the ensuing Great Depression with volunteer efforts, none of which produced economic recovery during his term.

Hoover entered office with a plan to reform the nation's regulatory system, believing that a federal bureaucracy should have limited regulation over a country's economic system. Hoover saw the presidency as a vehicle for improving the conditions of all Americans by regulation and by encouraging volunteerism.

Hoover expanded civil service coverage of federal positions, canceled private oil leases on government lands and by instructing the Justice Department and the Internal Revenue Service to pursue gangsters for tax evasion; he enabled the prosecution of Al Capone. He appointed a commission that set aside 3 million acres of national parks and 2.3 million acres of national forests; he advocated tax reduction for low-income Americans, (not enacted).

While in Argentina on foreign relations, Argentine anarchists led by Severino Di Giovanni plotted to destroy the railroad car in which Hoover was traveling, but the bomber was arrested before he could place the explosives on the rails. Hoover never mentioned the incident.

When it came to the rights of all Americans, Hoover seldom mentioned civil rights while he was President. Hoover believed that African Americans and other races could improve themselves with education and wanted the races assimilated into the white culture. First Lady Lou Hoover, defied custom and invited an African American Republican, Oscar DePriest, a member in the House of Representatives, to dinner at the White House. Booker T. Washington was the last previous African American to have dined at the White House with Theodore Roosevelt in 1901.

Charles Curtis, the nation's first Native American Vice President, was from the Kaw tribe in Kansas. Hoover's humanitarian and Quaker reputation, along with Curtis as a vice-president, gave special meaning to his Indian policies. His Quaker upbringing influenced his views that Native Americans needed to achieve economic self-sufficiency. As president, he appointed Charles J. Rhoads as commissioner of Indian affairs. Hoover supported Rhoad's commitment to Indians assimilation and sought to minimize the federal role in Indian affairs.

With the onset of the Great Depression, Hoover claims in his memoirs that he rejected Treasury Secretary Andrew Mellon's suggested "leave-it-alone" approach and called many business leaders to Washington to urge them not to lay off workers, or cut wages. Lee Ohanian from UCLA, has argued that President Hoover adopted pro-labor policies after the 1929 stock market crash. He believed that this accounted for close to two-thirds of the drop in the nation's gross domestic product over the two years that followed, causing what might otherwise have been a bad recession to slip into the Great Depression.

Calls for greater government assistance increased as the U.S. economy continued to decline. Hoover rejected direct federal relief payments to individuals, as he believed that a dole would be addictive and reduce the incentive to work. Hoover believed in balanced budgets and was unwilling to run a budget deficit to fund welfare programs. However, Hoover did persue many policies in an attempt to pull the country out of depression. In 1929, Hoover authorized the Mexican Repatriation program to combat rampant unemployment, relieve the burden on municipal aid services and remove people seen as usurpers of American jobs. The program was largely a forced migration of approximately 500,000 Mexicans and Mexican Americans to Mexico and continued through to 1937. In June 1930, over the objection of many economists, Congress approved and Hoover sign into law, the Smoot-Hawley Tariff Act. This legislation raised tariffs on thousands of imported items. The intent of the Act was to encourage the purchase of American made products by increasing the cost of imported goods, while raising revenue for the federal government and protecting farmers.

By 1932, unemployment had reached 24.9%. A drought persisted in the agricultural heartland, businesses and families defaulted on record numbers of loans and more than 5,000 banks had failed. Tens-of-thousands of Americans who found themselves homeless began congregating in the numerous Hoovervilles, (also known as shanty towns or tent cities), that had begun to appear across the country. The name was coined as a sign of their disappointment with the perceived lack of assistance from the federal government.

In response, Hoover and the Congress approved the Federal Home Loan Bank Act, to spur new home construction, and reduce foreclosures. Then there was the Revenue Act of 1932, which was the largest peacetime tax increase in history. The Act increased taxes across the board, so that top earners were taxed at 63% on their net income. The Act also increased the net income on corporations. Hoover's final attempt to rescue the economy occurred in 1932, with the passage of the Emergency Relief and Construction Act, which authorized funds for public works programs and the creation of the Reconstruction Finance Corporation (RFC). Its goal was to provide government-secured loans to financial institutions, railroads and farmers. The RFC had minimal impact at the time. To pay for these and other government programs and to make up for revenue lost due to the depression, Hoover agreed to roll back previous tax cuts his administration had affected on upper incomes. In one of the largest tax increases in American history, The Revenue Act of 1932, also doubled the estate tax and a "check tax was added that placed a 2-cent tax (over 30 cents in today's dollars), on all bank checks. For this reason, year's later, libertarians argued that Hoover's economics were Sadist. Franklin D. Roosevelt blasted the republican incumbent for spending and taxing too much, increasing the national debt, raising tariffs and blocking trade, as well as placing millions on the dole of the government. Ironically, these policies pale beside the more drastic steps taken under Franklin D. Roosevelt's administration later as part of the "New Deal".

Concerning the army bonus, thousands of World War I veterans and their families, demonstrated and camped out in Washington, D.C. during June 1932, calling for immediate payment of a bonus that had been promised by the Adjusted Service Certicate Law in 1924, for payment in 1945. Although offered money by Congress to return home, some members of the "Bonus Army" remained. Washington police attempted to remove the demonstrators from their camp, but they were outnumbered and unsuccessful. The police fired shots in a futile attempt to attain order and two protesters were killed while many officers were injured. Hoover sent U.S. Army forces led by General Douglas MacArthur and helped by lower ranking officers, Dwight D. Eisenhower and George S. Patton, to stop a march. MacArthur, believing he was fighting a communist revolution, chose to clear out the camp with military force. In the ensuing clash, hundreds of civilians were injured. Hoover had sent orders that the Army was not to move on the encampment, but

MacArthur chose to ignore the command. Hoover was incensed, but refused to reprimand MacArthur. The entire incident was another devastating negative for Hoover in the 1932 election that led New York governor and Democratic presidential candidate Franklin Roosevelt, to declare of Hoover: "There is nothing inside the man but jelly!"

1932 was an election year and Hoover agreed to run even though he had come to detest the presidency. The Republicans nominated Hoover for a second term. Hoover suffered a large defeat at the election, obtaining 39.7% of the popular vote to Roosevelt's 57.4%. Hoover's popular vote was reduced by 26% from his result in the 1928 election. In the Electoral College, he carried only Pennsylvania, Delaware and four other Northeastern states to lose 59-472. The Democrats also extended their control over the U.S. House and gained control of the U.S. Senate.

After the defeat, Hoover's attempts to reach out to Roosevelt to help calm investors and begin to resolve the economic problems facing the country, were rebuffed; since Roosevelt was not inaugurated until March 1933, this "guaranteed that Roosevelt took the oath of office amid such an atmosphere of crisis that Hoover had become the most hated man in America". The relationship between Hoover and Roosevelt was one of the most severely strained in Presidential history.

President Hoover had the longest retirement of any President to date, 31 years. He died October 20, 1964 in New York, New York; he was 90 years old.

Franklin D. Roosevelt, Number 32, 1933-1945

Democrat, 51 years old from Hyde Park, New York. Wife Eleanor Roosevelt, children, five boys and one girl. He was the only American President elected to more than two term.

The election campaign of 1932 was conducted under the shadow of the Great Depression in the United States and the new alliances which it created. Roosevelt and the Democratic Party mobilized the expanded ranks of the poor as well as organized labor, ethnic minorities, urbanites and Southern whites, crafting the New Deal coalition. During the campaign, Roosevelt said: "I pledge you, I pledge myself, to a new deal for the American people", coining a slogan that was later adopted for his legislative program as well as his new coalition. He campaigned on the Democratic platform advocating "immediate and drastic reductions of all public expenditures," abolishing useless commissions and offices, consolidating departments and bureaus and eliminating extravagances.

Roosevelt won 57% of the vote and carried all but six states. Historians and political scientists consider the 1932-36 elections a realigning election that created a new majority coalition made up of organized labor, blacks and ethnic Americans, such as Italian-Americans, Polish-Americans and Jews for the Democrats. This, transformed American politics and started what is called the "New Deal Party System" or the fifth party system.

When Roosevelt was inaugurated March 4, 1933, (32days after Hitler was appointed Chancellor of Germany), the U.S. was at the mercy of the worst depression in its history. 25% of the workforce was unemployed. Farmers were in deep trouble as prices fell by 60%. Industrial production had fallen by more than half since 1929. Two million were homeless. By the evening of March 4, 32 of the 48 states, as well as the District of Columbia, had closed their banks. The New York Federal Reserve Bank was unable to open on the 5th, as panicky customers had withdrawn huge sums in previous days. Beginning with his inauguration address, Roosevelt began blaming the economic crisis on bankers and financiers, the quest for profit and the self-interest basis of capitalism.

Starting in his "First Hundred Days" in office, which began March 4, 1933, Roosevelt launched major legislation and a profusion of executive orders that gave form to the New Deal. A complex and interlocking set of programs designed to produce relief, especially government jobs for the unemployed, recovery of the economy and reform through regulation of Wall Street, banks and transportation. With his inauguration occurring in the middle of a bank panic, this became the backdrop for his famous words, "The only thing we have to fear is fear itself". The very next day, Congress passed the Emergency Banking Act that declared a "bank holiday" and announced a plan to allow banks to reopen. This was his first proposed step to recovery. To give Americans confidence in banks, Roosevelt signed the Glass-Steagall Act that created the Federal Deposit Insurance Corporation (FDIC). The economy improved rapidly from 1933 to 1937, but then went into a deep recession.

The most popular of all New Deal agencies and Roosevelt's favorite, was the Civilian Conservation Corps (CCC), which hired 250,000 unemployed young men to work on rural local projects. Through the Federal Trade Commission, he provided mortgage relief to millions of farmers and homeowners. In 1933, major new banking regulations were passed. In 1934, the Securities and Exchange Commission was created to regulate Wall Street, with Joseph P. Kennedy in charge.

Roosevelt also kept his promise to push for repeal of prohibition. In April 1933, he issued an Executive Order redefining 3.2% alcohol as the maximun allowed. That order was preceded by Congressional action in the drafting and passage of the 21st Amendment, which was ratified that year.

After the 1934 Congressional elections, which gave Roosevelt large majorities in both houses, there was a fresh surge of New Deal Legislation. These measures included the Works Progress Administration (WPA), which set up a national relief agency that employed two million family heads. However, even at the height of WPA employment in 1938, unemployment was still 12.5%. The Social Security Act established social security and promised economic security for the elderly, the poor and the sick. Senator Robert Wagner wrote the Wagner Act, which officially became the National Labor Relations Act. The act established the federal rights of workers to organize unions, to engage in collective bargaining and to take part in strikes.

While the First New Deal of 1933 had broad support from most sectors, the Second New Deal challenged the business community. Conservative Democrats, led by Al Smith, fought back with the American Liberty League, savagely attacking Roosevelt and equating him with Marx and Lenin. But Smith over played his hand and his boisterous rhetoric let Roosevelt isolate his opponents and identify them with the wealthy vested interests that opposed the New Deal, setting Roosevelt up for the 1936 landslide. The labor unions, energized by the Wagner Act, signed up millions of new members and became a major backer of Roosevelt's re-elections in 1936, 1940, and 1944.

Total employment during Roosevelt's term expanded by 18.31 million jobs, with an annual increase of 5.3%. Roosevelt did not raise income taxes before World War II began; however, payroll taxes were also introduced to fund the new Social Security program in 1937.

The main foreign policy initiative of Roosevelt's first term was the Good Neighbor Policy, which was a re-evaluation of U.S. policy towards Latin America. Since the Monroe Doctrine of 1823, this area had been seen as an American sphere of influence. American forces were withdrawn from Haiti and new treaties with Cuba and Panama ended their status as United States protectorates. He also signed into law the Fair Labor Standards Act of 1938, which created the minimun wage.

In the November 1938 election, Democrats lost six seats and 71 House seats. Losses were concentrated among pro-New Deal Democrats. When Congress reconvened in 1939, Republicans, under Senator Robert Taft, formed a conservative coalition with Southern Democrats, virtually ending Roosevelt's ability to get his domestic proposals enacted into law. The minimun wage law of 1938, was the last substantial New Deal Act passed by Congress.

When World War II broke out in 1939, Roosevelt rejected the Wilsonian Neutrality stance and sought ways to assist Britain and France militarily. He began a regular secret correspondence and developed a personal relationship with Winston Churchill who became Prime Minister of Britain in 1940. In April 1940, Germany invaded Denmark and Norway, followed by invasions of the Netherlands, Belgium, Luxembourg, and France in May. The German victories in Western Europe left Britain vulnerable to invasion. The fall of Paris shocked American opinion. A consensus was clear that military spending had to be dramatically expanded, even though the isolationist warned that FDR would get the nation into an unnecessary war with Germany. He successfully urged Congress to enact the first peacetime draft in United States history in 1940; it was renewed in 1941, by one vote in Congress.

Roosevelt used his personal charisma to build support for intervention. America should be the "Arsenal of Democracy", he told his fireside audience. On September 2, 1940, Roosevelt openly defied the Neutrality Acts by passing the Destroyers for Bases Agreement, which gave 50 American destroyers to Britain in exchange for military base rights in the British Caribbean Islands and Newfoundland. Roosevelt sought innovative ways to help Britain, whose financial resources were exhausted by the end of 1940. Congress voted to commit to spend $50 billion on military supplies from 1941-45; there would be no repayment after the war.

World War II, in Europe and the Pacific, dominated Roosevelt's third term. Roosevelt slowly began re-armament and by 1940, it was in high gear with bipartisan support, partly to equip the U.S. Army and Navy and partly to become the "Arsenal of Democracy", supporting Britain, France, China and after June 1941, the Soviet Union.

The military buildup spurred economic growth. By 1941, unemployment had fallen to under 1 million. There was a growing labor shortage in all the nation's major manufacturing centers, accelerating the Great Migration of African Americans from farms in the South and underemployed farmers and workers from rural areas and small towns.

When Nazi Germany invaded the Soviet Union in June 1941, Roosevelt extended Lend-Lease to the Soviets. Roosevelt also agreed that the U.S. Navy would escort Allied convoys as Far East as Great Britain and would fire upon German ships or submarines (U-boats), of the Kriegs marine, if they attacked allied shipping within the U.S. Navy zone. In July 1941, Roosevelt ordered Henry Stimson, Secretary of War, to begin planning for total American military involvement. The resulting "Victory Program," provided the President with the total mobilization of manpower, industry and logistics, to defeat the "potential enemies" of the United States. Roosevelt was firmly committed to the allied cause and the belief that the Empire of Japan had formulated these plans before the Attack on Pearl Harbor.

On December 7, 1941, the Japanese attacked the U.S. Pacific Fleet at Pearl Harbor, destroying or damaging 16 warships, including most of the fleet's battleships and killing almost 3000 American military personnel and civilians. Roosevelt went to Congress to give his famous "Infamy Speech" in which he said: "Yesterday, December 7, 1941-- a date which will live in infamy--the United States of America was suddenly and deliberately attacked by naval and air forces of the Empire of Japan." Despite the wave of anger that swept across the U.S. in the wake of Pearl Harbor, Roosevelt decided from the start that the defeat of Nazi Germany had to take priority. On December 11, 1941, this strategic Europe first decision was made easier to implement when Germany and Italy declared war on the United States.

The "Big Three", as they were termed, Roosevelt, Churchill, and Joseph Stalin, together with Generalissimo Chiang Kai-shek, cooperated informally on a plan for this war strategy.

When the war began, the danger of a Japanese attack on the coast led to growing pressure to remove people of Japanese descent away from the coastal region. This pressure grew due to fears of terrorism, espionage and/or sabotage. On February 19, 1942, President Roosevelt signed Executive Order 9066, which relocated the "Issei" (first generation of Japanese immigrants who did not have U.S. citizenship) and their children, "Nisei" (who had dual citizenship). After both Nazi Germany and Fascist Italy declared war on the United States in December 1941, German and Italian citizens who had not taken out American citizenship and who spoke out for Hitler and Mussolini, were often arrested or interned.

In the area of civil rights, Roosevelt's record has been the subject of much controversy. He was a hero to large minority groups, especially African-Americans, Catholics and Jews, while being highly successful in attracting large majorities of these voters into his New Deal coalition. African-Americans and Native Americans fared well in the New Deal relief programs. Sitkoff, (1978) reports that, the WPA "provided an economic floor for the whole black community in the 1930's rivaling both agriculture and domestic services as the chief source" of income. The civil rights section of Roosevelt's Justice Department worked closely with the NAACP, even though Roosevelt fell short by not pushing for anti-lynching legislation. He simply denounced it as "a vile form of collective murder".

Roosevelt, who had turned 62 in 1944, had been in declining health since at least 1940. The strain of his paralysis and the physical exertion needed to compensate for it for over 20 years had taken their toll, as had many years of stress and a life of chain-smoking. By this time, Roosevelt had numerous ailments including chronic high blood pressure, emphysema, systemic atherosclerosis, coronary artery disease, with angina pectoris and myopathic hypertensive heart disease with congestive heart failure. Dr. Emanuel Libman, then an assistant pathologist at Mount Sinai Hospital in New York City, reacting to Roosevelt's appearance in newsreels, remarked in 1944 that, "It doesn't matter whether Roosevelt is re-elected or not, he'll die of a cerebral hemorrhage within 6 months" (which he did, five months later).

Aware of the risk that Roosevelt would die during his fourth term, the party regulars insisted that Henry A. Wallace, who was seen as too pro-Soviet, be dropped as Vice President. After considering James F. Byrnes of South Carolina and being turned down by Indiana Governor Henry F. Schricker, Roosevelt replaced Wallace with the little-known Senator, Harry S. Truman. In the 1944 election, Roosevelt and Truman won 53% of the vote and carried 36 states against New York Governor Thomas E. Dewey.

After leaving the Yalta Conference on February 12, 1945, Roosevelt flew to Egypt and boarded the USS Quincy near the Suez Canal. The next day he met with Farouk I, king of Egypt and Haile Selassie, Emperor of Ethiopia. On February 14, he held a historic meeting with King Abdulaziz, the founder of Saudi Arabia. A meeting that holds profound significance in U.S.-Saudi relations, even today. While at Yalta, Lord Moran, Winston Churchill's physician, commented on Roosevelt's ill health: "He is a very sick man. He has all the symptoms of harding of the arteries of the brain in an advanced stage, so that I give him only a few months to live".

When Roosevelt returned to the United States, he addressed Congress on March 1, about the Yalta Conference and many were shocked to see how old, thin and frail he looked. He spoke while seated in the well of the House, an unprecedented concesssion to his physical incapacity.

On March 29, 1945, Roosevelt went to Warm Springs to rest before his anticipated appearance at the founding conference of the United Nations. On the afternoon of April 12, 1945, Roosevelt said, "I have a terrific pain in the back of my head." He then slumped forward in his chair, unconscious and was carried into his bedroom. The President's attending cardiologist, Dr. Howard Bruenn, diagnosed a massive cerebral hemorrhage (stroke). At 3:55 p.m. that day, Roosevelt died. As Allen Drury later said, "so ended an era and so began another." After Roosevelt's death, an editorial by The New York Times declared, "Men will thank God on their knees a hundred years from now that Franklin D. Roosevelt was in the White House".

He died in Warm Springs, Georgia on April 12, 1945; he was 63 years old. He was the only President elected to more than two terms. He was elected to four terms, serving three and a partial terms.

Harry S. Truman, Number 33, 1945-1953

Democrat, 60 years old from Lamar, Missouri. Wife, Bess Wallace Truman, they had one child, Mary Margaret Truman.

Harry Truman succeeded to the presidency at the death of President Franklin D. Roosevelt. Truman was the third Vice President of Roosevelt's, a man who was elected to four terms as President of the United States of America, a feat never done before, or since.

Truman was the democratic choice over the current V.P., Henry Wallace. Wallace was deemed too liberal and recognizing the failing health of Roosevelt, the Democratic National Committee believed that the V. P. would in all likelihood, become his successor.

With the unexpected surprise of a lifetime before him and his newness to office still fresh upon him, the tragic death of a President was about to greet him. Truman had only been in office for 82 days when he had adjourned the Senate and was preparing to relax when he was called to the White House. He knew that Roosevelt had been out-of-town and suspected that he had returned sooner than expected and wanted a meeting. When he arrived, the first lady

Eleanor Roosevelt informed him that the president had suffered a massive stroke and died. Feeling deep concern for the first lady, he asked if there was anything he could do for her, she replied, "Is there anything we can do for you? You are the one in trouble now."

After Truman was administered the oath of office, he spoke to reporters and said "Boys, if you ever pray, pray for me now. I don't know if you fellas ever had a load of hay fall on you, but when they told me what happened yesterday, I felt like the moon, the stars and all the planets had fallen on me."

Roosevelt had not had the opportunity to brief Truman on the world affairs he was faced with, nor the domestic difficulties faced at home. The war had been raging for several years and there were major initiatives in the works such as the top secret Manhattan Project surrounding the testing of the world's first atomic bomb. Truman walked into the presidency with a full plate of major concerns.

Upon assuming the presidency, Truman asked all of the members of Franklin D. Roosevelt's cabinet to remain in place, he offered an olive branch by telling them he was open to their advice and ideas; then he laid down a central principle of his administration. He would make the decisions and he expected their support. Just a few weeks following Truman's inauguration, America and her Allies in the European Theatre of Operations, achieved victory.

Secretary of War Henry L. Stimson, briefed Truman on the Manhattan Project on the day of Roosevelt's death. This was a highly secretive operation involving the development of the first atomic bomb. While in Europe attending a conference, Truman was told that the Trinity test of the first atomic bomb had been a success. Truman informed Joseph Stalin of the Soviet Union that the U.S. had developed a new kind of weapon and was considering using it on Japan. Stalin had never been informed of the weapon but had learned about it through espionage, in fact, he knew of it before Truman did.

In August 1945, after Japan turned down the Potsdam Declaration, Truman authorized use of atomic weapons against Japan. On the morning of August 6, 1945, at 8:15am, the B-29 bomber Enola Gay, dropped an atomic bomb, "Little Boy", on Hiroshima, Japan. Two days later, having heard nothing from the Japanese government, the U.S. military proceeded with its plan to drop a second atomic bomb. On August 9, Nagasaki, Japan was also devastated with an atomic bomb, "Fat Man", dropped by the B-29 bomber "Bockscar". Hiroshima suffered as many as 140,000 deaths and Nagasaki 80,000 by the end of 1945, nearly half of those deaths occurred on the day of the bombings. The Japanese agreed to surrender on August 14, 1945.

Those who supported the decision to go forward with the bombings argued that it saved hundreds of thousands of lives by avoiding a land invasion of mainland Japan. In 1954, in retrospect, or in hindsight, Eleanor Roosevelt said that Truman had "made the only decision he could and that the bombs use was necessary to avoid tremendous sacrifice of American lives". Still, many have argued that the use of nuclear weapons was unnecessary and inherently immoral. Truman wrote later in life that, "I knew what I was doing when I stopped the war.... I have no regrets and under the same circumstances, I would do it again."

The end of World War II was followed by an uneasy transition from war to a peacetime economy. Americans had made many sacrifices during the war. The automobile plants had halted car production and began to produce America's war machine. Instead of cars, the assembly lines were building planes, bombers, tanks and other military weapons. The American people had to suffer through a number of rationings such as sugar, gasoline and others. Many items had to be purchased with government issued tokens. The president was faced with labor management conflicts that had been held in abeyance during the war. There were a shortage of housing and consumer products along with wide spread inflation, which at one point, reached 6% in a single month.

In the spring of 1946, this country was hit with a national railway strike that brought virtually all passenger and freight lines to a standstill for more than a month. Truman siezed control of the railways to defy the workers refusal to accept a proposed settlement. Truman threatened to draft striking workers into the armed forces. Truman sought support for his plan from the Congress. The workers settled on his terms.

Truman strongly supported the creation of the United Nations. He included Eleanor Roosevelt on the delegation to the U.N.'s first General Assembly. The communist had began to abandon the commitments to democracy made at the Potsdam Conference and had begun advances in Iran, Greece and Turkey. This caused Truman and his advisors to take a hard line against the Soviets.

Truman was Vice President for only a few months prior to the death of Roosevelt; therefore, he had little or no foreign policy expertise. Even so, Truman won bipartisan support for both the

Truman Doctrine, which formalized a policy of containment and the Marshall Plan, which aimed to help rebuild postwar Europe.

As part of the U.S. Cold War strategy, Truman signed the National Security Act of 1947, and reorganized military forces by merging the Department of War and the Department of the Navy into the National Military Establishment, (later the Department of Defense) and creating the U.S. Air Force. The act also created the CIA and the National Security Council.

As Truman readied for the 1948 election, Truman made clear his identy as a Democrat in the New Deal tradition, advocating national health insurance, the repeal of the anti-union Taft-Hartley Act and an aggressive civil rights program. Taken together, it all constituted a broad legislative agenda that came to be called the "Fair Deal". Truman's proposals were not well received by Congress, even after Democratic gains in the 1948 election. Only one of the major Fair Deal bills, the Housing Act of 1949, was ever enacted.

Recognition of Isreal

Truman made the decision to recognize the establishment of the State of Isreal over the objections of the Secretary of State George Marshall, who feared it would hurt relations with Arab States. At a meeting in the White House on November 10, 1945, he told envoys to Saudi Arabia, Syria, Lebanon and Egypt: "I am sorry gentlemen, but I have to answer to hundreds of thousands who are anxious for the success of Zionism: I do not have hundreds of thousands of Arabs among my constituents." Rejecting warnings that this action would serve to destabilize the Middle East, Truman and Congress continued to support the establishment of a homeland for the Jewish people. Truman recognized the State of Israel on May 14, 1948. Truman wrote: Hitler had been murdering Jews right and left. I saw it and I dream about it even to this day. The Jews needed someplace where they could go. It is my attitude that the American government couldn't stand idly by while the victims of Hitler's madness are not allowed to build new lives.

On June 24, 1948, the Soviet Union blocked access to the three Western-held sectors of Berlin. There was no negotiated agreement to provide supplies deep within the Soviet occupied zone. The commander of the American zone in Germany, General Lucius D. Clay, made plans to cross the Soviet zone to West Berlin with an armored column, with instructions to defend itself from any aggression. Truman believed this would create a risk of war. He devised and approved a plan to supply by air, thus defeating the ground blockade. On June 25, the allies initiated the Berlin Airlift, a campaign that delivered food and other supplies, such as coal, using military airplanes on a massive scale. Nothing like this had ever been done and no other nation had the capability to have accomplished it. The airlift worked; ground access was again granted on May 11, 1949. The Berlin Airlift was one of Truman's great foreign policy successes as president.

Truman's 1948 presidential election is best remembered for his come-from-behind victory. His public approval rate was at 36% and he was regarded as incapable of winning the general election. The "New Deal" heads and Truman's son James, fought to have Dwight D. Eisenhower as the Democratic nominee, even though Eisenhower's political views and party affiliation were unknown. Eisenhower refused to accept the nomination and Truman prevailed.

During the Democratic National Convention of 1948, Mayor Hubert H. Humphrey gave an astounding addrerss that, with the support of the local political interest of a number of urban bosses, convinced the convention to adopt a stronger civil rights plank; Truman approved wholeheartedly. The Alabama delegates and a portion of the Mississippi delegates, walked out of the convention in protest.

Within two weeks, Truman issued Executive Order 9981, racially intergrating the U.S. Armed Services. Truman took considerable political risk in backing civil rights. Democrats were concerned that the loss of the Dixiecrats support, might destroy the Democratic Party. But Truman went on a 21,928-mile presidential odyssey, with an unprecedented personal appeal to the nation. Truman gave brief speeches from the rear platform of the observation car "Ferdinand Magellan". This "whistlestop" tactic came to represent the entire campaign with huge crowds along the way. A full million people turned out for a New York City ticker-tape parade. The large, mostly spontaneous gatherings at Truman's depot stops, represented an important change in momentum in the campaign. While the National Press Corp. continued reporting Republican Thomas Dewey's apparent impending victory as a certainty.

In the end, Truman held his Midwestern base of progressives and won most of the Southern states despite his civil rights plank He achieved victories in a few critical "battleground" states. The final tally showed that the president had garnered 303 electoral votes, Dewey 189, and the third party candidate Strum Thurmond only 39.

Truman's inauguration was the first ever televised nationally. His second would be grueling because of foreign policy challenges; he had to come to terms with the end of the American Nuclear monopoly. The Soviet Union's atomic bomb project progressed much faster than expected and they exploded their first bomb on August 29, 1949. On January 7, 1953, Truman announced the detonation of the first U.S. hydrogen bomb.

Truman was a strong supporter of the North Atlantic Treaty Organization (NATO), he successfully steered the treaty through the Senate in 1949, and appointed Dwight D. Eisenhower as the first commander.

On December 21, 1949, Chiang Kai-shek and his Revolutionary Army, left Mainland China fleeing to Taiwan after attacks by Mao Zedong's Communist Army during the Chinese Civil War. In June 1950, Truman ordered the U.S. Navy's Seventh Fleet into the Tiawan Strait to prevent further conflict, he also asked the Republic of China (ROC), to refrain from any further attacks on the mainland.

On February 9, 1950, Republican Senator Joseph McCarthy accused the State Department of having communists on the payroll and whether Truman had all the subversive agents that had entered the government during the Roosevelt years. McCarthy's claim was short of proof, but Truman was facing frightening new realities, the Soviet Union's nuclear explosion, the loss of U.S. atom bomb secrets, the fall of China to Communism, and new revelations of Soviet intelligence penetration of other U.S. agencies, including the Treasury Department.

On June 25, 1950, the North Korean People's Army, under the command of Kim Il-Sung invaded South Korea, precipitating the outbreak of the Korean War. Truman called for a naval blockade of Korea without sufficient ships to carry it out. He then asked the U.N. to intervene; it did, authorizing armed defense for the first time in its history. In the first four weeks of the conflict, The American infantry forces hastily deployed to Korea proved too few and were under-equipped. Responding to criticism over readiness, Truman fired his much-criticized Secretary of Defense, Louis A. Johnson, replacing him with retired General George Marshall. UN forces led by General Douglas MacArthur, led the counterattack, scoring a stunning surprise victory with an amphibious landing at the Battle of Inchon that nearly trapped the invaders. As the UN forces marched north toward the Yalu River boundary with China, the Chinese surprised them with a large scale-invasion in November. The UN forces were forced back below the 38th parallel and then recovered. By early 1951, the war became a fierce stalemate at about the 38th parallel where it began with the U.S. and the UN suffering heavy casualties.

Truman rejected MacArthur's request to attack Chinese supply bases north of the Yalu River, but MacArthur promoted his plan to Republican House Leader Joseph Martin, who leaked it to the press. On April 11, 1951, Truman fired MacArthur from all his commands in Korea and Japan.

The dismissal of General MacArthur was among the least politically popular decisions in presidential history. Truman's approval ratings plummeted and he faced calls for his impeachment. Fierce criticism from virtually all quarters accused Truman of refusing to shoulder the blame for a war gone sour and blaming his generals instead. "I fired him, (MacArthur), because he wouldn't respect the authority of the President...I didn't fire him because he was a dumb son-of-a-bitch, although he was, but that's not against the law for generals. If it was, half to three-quarters of them would be in jail." Harry S. Truman quoted in Time Magazine.

The war remained a frustrating stalemate for two tears, with 30,000 Americans killed, until a peace agreement restored borders and ended the conflict.

The Truman administration presented a ten-point agenda for civil rights reform in February 1948; this provoked a firestorm of criticism from the Southern Democrats. Truman referred to compromise by saying "my forebears was confederate, but my very stomach turned over when I had learned that Negro soldiers, just back from overseas were being dumped out of army trucks in Mississippi and beaten.

In 1951, the U.S. ratified the 22nd Amendment making a president ineligible to be elected for a second time after having served more than two year's of a previous president's term. However, a Grandfather clause explicitly excluded the current president from this provision. Truman decided not to run for re-election.

After a fall in his home in late 1964, his physical condition declined. In 1965, President Lyndon B. Johnson signed the medicare bill at the Truman Library and gave the first two medicare cards to Truman and his wife Bess to honor his fight for government health care as president. On December 5, 1972, he was admitted to Kansas City's Research Hospital and Medical Center with lung congestion from pneumonia, he developed multiple organ failure and died at

7:50 am on December 26. He was 88 years old. The man whose slogan "The Buck Stops here", was gone.

Dwight D. Eisenhower, Number 34, 1953-1961

Republican, 63 years old from Denison, Texas. Wife Mamie Doud Eisenhower. They had two children. Eisenhower was a decorated soldier. During World War II, he served as Supreme Commander of the Allied Forces in Europe, with responsibility for planning and supervising the successful invasion of France and Germany in 1944-45, from the Western Front. In 1951, he became the first supreme commander of NATO.

After the Japanese surprise attack on Pearl Harbor, Eisenhower was assign to the General Staff in Washington with responsibility for creating the major war plans to defeat Japan and Germany. On December 20, 1944, he was promoted to General of the Army, equivalent to the rank of Field Marshall in most European armies. In this position, he was charged with planning and carring out the Allied assault on the coast of Normandy in June 1944, under the code name Operation Overlord, the liberation of Western Europe and the invasion of Germany. A month after the Normandy D-Day landings on June 6, 1944, the invasion of Southern France took place; the war in Europe ended on May 8, 1945, with Germany's unconditional surrender.

Shortly after his return in 1952, a "Draft Eisenhower" movement in the Republican Party persuaded him to declare his candidacy in the 1952 presidential election. His campaign slogan was simply "I Like Ike". During his campaign, he promised to go to Korea and end the war there.

Eisenhower had a relatively quiet presidency; the country was not in a shooting war. Throughout his presidency, Eisenhower preached a doctrine of Dynamic Conservatism. He continued all the major "New Deal" programs still in operation, especially Social Security. He expanded its programs and rolled them into a new Cabinet-Level agency, the Department of Health, Education and Welfare, while extending benefits to an additional ten million workers.

One of Eisenhower's resounding achievements was the signing of the Federal Aid Highway Act of 1956. He justified the bill by saying it is essential to American security during the Cold War. It was believed that large cities would be targets in a possible future war and the highways were designed to evacuate them and allow the military to move in. He knew the advantages of the German Autobahns in moving logistics to supply its war machine. He believed an Interstate Highway System in the U.S. would not only be beneficial for military operations, but also be the building block for continued economic growth.

The Eisenhower Administration declared racial discrimination a national security issue. He knew that the Communist around the world was using America's position on racial discrimination as a point of propaganda attack. Following the Supreme Courts decision on Brown vs. The Board of Education, in which segregated "separate but equal" schools were ruled to be unconstitutional, Eisenhower told District of Columbia officials to make Washington a model for the rest of the country in integrating black and white public school children. He proposed to Congress the Civil Rights Acts of 1957, and 1960, signing those acts into law. The 1957 Act for the first time established a permanent civil rights office inside the Justice Department. These acts constituted the first significant civil rights acts since the Civil Rights Act of 1875, signed by President Ulysses S. Grant.

The "Little Rock Nine" incident of 1957, involved the refusal by Arkansas to honor a Federal court order to integrate the schools. Under Executive Order 10730, Eisenhower placed the Arkansas National Guard under Federal control and sent Army troops to escort nine black students into Little Rock Central High School, an all-white public school. The integration did not occur without violence. Eisenhower and Arkansas governor Orval Faubus, engaged in tense arguments over this injustice.

In the 1960 election, Eisenhower chose his own Vice-President Richard Nixon to run against Democrat John F. Kennedy, Eisenhower had served two terms and in accordance with the new 22nd Amendment, he was barred from another run for the office of the presidency. On January 17, 1961, Eisenhower gave his final televised address to the nation from the Oval Office. In his farewell speech, Eisenhower raised the issue of the Cold War and the role of the U.S. Armed Forces.

Eisenhower retired to the place where he and Mamie had spent much of their post-war time, a working farm adjacent to the battlefield at Gettysburg, Pennsylvania. Eisenhower died of congestive heart failure on March 28, 1969, at Walter Reed Army Hospital in Washington D.C., he was 78 years old.

He would be appalled at the terrible conditions of one of America's most important hospitals. It has become America's disgrace.

John Fitzgerald "Jack" Kennedy, Number 35, 1961-1963
Assassinated in Dallas, Texas

Democrat, 43 years old from Brookline, Massachusetts. Wife Jacqueline Lee Bouvier, they had 4 children.

Kennedy was a decorated war hero. During his term of service in the U.S. Navy, Kennedy was the Commander of the Motor Torpedo Boats PT-109 and Pt-59, in the South Pacific. His heroic efforts in saving members of his crew and retrieving vital supplies from his damaged craft, was an act worthy of heroism.

On January 2, 1960, Kennedy launched his campaign for President in the Democratic primary election. At the Democratic Convention, he gave his well-known "New Frontier" speech, saying: "For the problems are not all solved and the battles are not all won--- and we stand today on the edge of a New Frontier ... But the New Frontier of which I speak is not a set of promises, it is a set of challenges. It sums up not what I intend to offer the American people, but what I intend to ask of them.

On July 13, the Democratic convention nominated Kennedy as its candidate. Kennedy asked Lyndon B. Johnson to be his Vice Presidential candidate. He needed Johnson's strength in the South to win what was considered likely to be the closest election since 1916.

Kennedy became a pioneer in television as well, in September and October, Kennedy, along with his Republican opponent Richard Nixon, appeared in the first televised U.S. presidential debates in U.S. history. On Tuesday, November 8, Kennedy defeated Nixon in one on the closest presidential elections of the twentieth century. He was the youngest man elected president, succeeding Eisenhower, who was the oldest.

Kennedy was sworn in as the 35th President at noon on January 20, 1961. In his inaugural address he famously said, "Ask not what your country can do for you; ask what you can do for your country." He also asked the nations of the world to join together to fight what he called the "common enemies of man: tyranny, poverty, disease and war itself."

The Cold War era would be dominated by confrontations between the U.S. and the Soviet's. On June 4, 1961, Kennedy met with Khrushchev in Vienna and to his regret, he felt as though the

Premier had just bullied him. Khruschev believed Kennedy to be an intelligent president, but thought that he was weak. The critical issue between these two leaders was a proposed treaty regarding Moscow and East Berlin. Kennedy made it clear that any such treaty, which interfered with U.S. access rights in West Berlin, would be regarded as an act of war. In weeks immediately after the Vienna summit, more than 20 thousand people fled from East Berlin to the western sector in reaction to statements from the U.S.S.R. Kennedy began extensive meetings on the Berlin Issue.

With the possibility of a confrontation with the Soviet Union looming on the horizon in July 1961, Kennedy announced his decision to add $3.25 billion to the defense budget, along with over 200 thousand additional troops for the military, saying an attack on West Berlin would be taken as an attack on the United States. The speech received an 85% approval rating. The following month, the U.S.S.R. and East Berlin officials began blocking passage of East Berliners into West Berlin, erecting barbed wire fences and the Berlin Wall.

Prior to Kennedy's election, President Eisenhower had devised a plan to overthrow the Fidel Castro regime in Cuba. The action would be lead by the CIA with help from the U.S. Military, but with no covert help from the U.S.. This was a counter-revolutionary insurgency manned by anti-Castro Cuban exiles trained by the U.S. and led by CIA paramilitary officers who were to invade and instigate an uprising among the Cuban people. The operation was called the "Bay of Pigs Invasion." On April 19, 1961, Kennedy ordered the invasion to proceed. By April 19, 1961, the Cuban government had captured or killed the invading exiles, and Kennedy was forced to negotiate for the release of the 1,189 survivors. After 20 months of negotiations, Cuba released the exiles for $53 million worth of food and medicine.

On October 14, 1962, CIA U-2 spy planes photographed intermediate-range ballistic missile sites under construction by the Soviets in Cuba. When Soviet shipments to Cuba began, the National Security Council began debate as to whether the intended use of the weapons was offensive or defensive. They determined that they were offensive. Kennedy had a difficult decision to make. If he attacked the sites, it could lead to nuclear war with the U.S.S.R., but to do nothing would leave us open to threat from 90 miles from our borders. Kennedy needed a show of strength in reaction to Khrushchev at the Vienna summit. Kennedy decided on a naval quarantine and on October 22, dispatched a message of this to Khrushchev and announced it on T.V. to the American people. A cooling off period was suggested; Khrushchev said yes but Kennedy said no. Kennedy threatened to sink any Soviet ship that breached his blockade. After a Soviet ship was stopped and boarded, on October 28, Khrushchev agreed to dismantle the missile sites subject to U.N. inspection. This crisis improved the image of American willpower and Kennedy's ratings soared to 77% approval.

As one of his first presidential acts, Kennedy asked Congress to create the Peace Corp. Through this program; Americans volunteer to help underdeveloped nations in areas such as education, farming, health care and construction. Since 1961, over 200,000 Americans have joined the Peace Corp, serving in 139 countries.

In 1963, a South Vietnamese coup arrested and assassinated their leader Ngo Dinh Diem. Washington would no longer tolerate Nhu's actions so Lodge asked Diem and his brother to step down and out of the country; they refused. Eisenhower considered Laos the "Cork in the bottle" in regards to the regional threat in Southeast Asia. Kennedy voiced a change in policy from supporting a free Laos to indicating that Vietnam should be deemed America's tripwire for communism's spread in the area. Kennedy initially followed Eisenhower's lead, by using limited military action against the Communist forces led by Ho Chi Minh. Late in 1961, the Viet Cong began assuming a predominant presence when they seized the provincial capital of Phuoc Vinh. Kennedy increased the number of helicopters, military advisors and undeclared U.S. Special Forces in the area. In the fall of 1962, Secretary of State Dean Rusk voiced strong support for U.S. involvement, saying neutralism in South Vietnam is tantamount to surrender. "Operation Ranch Hand", a broad scale aerial defoliation effort began on the roadsides in South Vietnam. By 1963, Kennedy faced a crisis in Vietnam; despite increased U.S. support, the South Vietnam military was only marginally effective against pro-Communist Viet Cong forces. However, after the coup that executed Diem and his brother, there were renewed confidence in America and in South Vietnam, that now the war might truly be won.

On his domestic policy, Kennedy called his program the "New Frontier". It promised federal funding for education, medical care for the elderly, economic aid to rural regions, and government intervention to stop the recession. Kennedy also promised an end to racial discrimination. Few of Kennedy's major programs passed Congress during his lifetime, although, under his successor Johnson, Congress did vote them through in 1964-65.

Putting an end to state-sanction discrimination was high on the agenda of domestic issues. The United States Supreme Court had ruled in 1954 in "Brown vs. Board of Education that racial segregation in public schools was unconstitutional. Many school sytems especially in the Southern States disregarded this decision. Segregation was prohibited in other public facilities such as buses, restaurants, theaters, courtrooms, bathrooms and beaches, but many states defied the court order. Kennedy spoke out in favor of integration and civil rights. During his campaign for president, he spoke with Coretta Scott King, the wife of Dr. Martin Luther King Jr., who was in jail for demonstrating for equal rights for African Americans. Kennedy was able to have him released. This drew black support to his candidacy.

There was a group called the "Freedom Riders" that organized an integrated public transportation effort in the south, but were repeatedly met with violence from whites, including law enforcement, both federal and state. Kennedy assigned federal marshalls to protect the Freedom Riders.

In September 1962, James Meredith enrolled at the University of Mississippi, but was prevented from entering. Attorney General Robert Kennedy responded by sending 400 U.S. Marshall's, while President Kennedy reluctantly federalized and sent 3,000 troops after the situation on campus turned violent. Campus riots left two dead and dozens injured, but Meredith did finally enroll in class.

Women were suffering from discrimination as well as blacks. The Presidential Commission on the status of Women in 1961, revealed that women were also experiencing discrimination, their final report was issued in 1963. On June 10, 1963, Kennedy signed the Equal Pay Act, a federal law amending the Fair Labor Standards Act, aimed at abolishing wage disparity based on sex.

Over 100,000 concerned citizens of all races and creeds gathered in Washington for the civil rights march on Washington for jobs and freedom on August 28, 1963. Dr. King gave his famous "I Have a Dream" speech. Kennedy was fearful of negative effects on the prospects for the civil rights bills in Congress, so he declined an invitation to speak. Thousands of police were placed on standby and not one arrest relating to the demonstration occurred.

The U.S. space program was behind the Russians, the satellite Sputnik had been launched and was orbiting the earth. Kennedy was eager for the U.S. to take the lead in the space race for strategic reasons. Kennedy first announced the goal for landing a man on the Moon in the speech to a Joint Session of Congress on May 25,

1961, saying, "First, I believe that this nation should commit itself to achieving the goal, before this decade is out, of landing a man on the Moon, and returning him safely to earth. No single space project in this period will be more impressive to mankind, or more important for the long-range exploration of space; and none will be so difficult, or expensive to accomplish". Kennedy believed that we should know all about space, but he thought the expense was too great. He believed we should accomplish this feat by the end of the decade.

President Kennedy would take a trip to Dallas, Texas to smooth over factions in the Democratic Party. Governor Connally and his wife would accompany him in his car. As his motorcade passed the Texas School Book Depository, shots rang out striking the president in the upper back; a second shot struck him in the head. Lee Harvey Oswald, an employee of the Texas School Book Depository from which the shots were fired, supposedly ran from the building and was confronted by an Officer Tipton, whom he shot and killed; he was subsequently charged with the assassination of President Kennedy. Governor Connally was struck in the wrist by a bullet as well, according to the Warren Commission, the same bullet that struck Kennedy. Oswald denied shooting anyone and that he was a patsy. On November 24, Jack Ruby entered the underground passageway as Oswald was being moved through the tunnel and shot him to death in front of the Dallas police. Ruby would successfully appeal his conviction and death sentence but would die of cancer on January 3, 1967, while waiting for a date for retrial. Did Oswald really kill Kennedy, did he act alone, did he fire all three shots in such a short window of opportunity and time and how could a shot from the back knock his head backwards, rather than forward? According to the Warren report, it could.

Vice President Johnson would be sworn in as president on Airforce One in route to Washington. He was the youngest President to die in office to date. He was 46 years old.

Lyndon Baines Johnson, Number 36, 1963-1969

Democrat, 55 years old from Stonewall, Texas, wife, Linda Bird Johnson; they had two children.

Lyndon B. Johnson was one of only four people who served in all four elected Federal offices of the United States. He served as Representative, Senator, Vice President and President. Johnson succeeded to the presidency following the assassination of John F. Kennedy. He is the only president ever to be sworn in outside of Washington D C. He went on to complete Kennedy's term, and was elected president in his own right in 1964. As president, he was responsible for designing the "Great Society" legislation that included laws that upheld Civil Rights, Public Broadcasting, Medicare, Medicaid, Environmental Protection, Aid to Education and his "War on Poverty". He also escalated direct American involvement in the Vietnam War, this escalation would continue from 1964 to 1968.

Johnson played a roll in a historic episode during the early 1960s, known as the "Chicken War." France and West Germany had placed tariffs on imports of U.S. chicken. When diplomacy failed to work, on December 4, 1963, two weeks after taking office, President Johnson imposed a 25 percent tax, (almost 10 times the average U.S. tariff), on potato starch, dextrin, brandy, and light trucks. Officially, the tax targeted items imported from Europe as approximating the value of lost American chicken sales in Europe. Soon after, Volkswagen cargo vans and pickup trucks, the intended targets, practically disappeared from the U.S. market.

The plight of Black Americans in their struggle to gain parity with white Americans continued; the civil rights marches led By Dr Martin Luther King Jr. was widespread on the American landscape. Dr King had sought relief in Washington from President Kennedy who originally proposed the civil rights bill in June 1963. However, after Kennedy's death, it was Johnson who broke a filibuster by Southern Democrats that began in March, 1964, and pushed the bill through the Senate. Johnson signed the revised and stronger bill into law on July 2, 1964, with Dr. Martin Luther King Jr. standing behind him as a guest. It has been said that as Johnson put down his pen, he told and aide, "We have lost the South for a generation", anticipating a backlash from Southern whites against his Democratic Party.

In 1965, Johnson signed into law a second civil rights bill, the Voting Rights Act, which outlawed discrimination in voting, thus, allowing millions of southern Black Americans to vote for the first time. "Seven of the eleven southern states of the former confederacy" --Alabama, South Carolina, North Carolina, Georgia, Louisiana, Mississippi and Virginia,---were subjected to the procedure of pre-clearance in 1965, while Texas, home to the majority of the African American population at the time, followed in 1975.

After the murder of civil rights worker Viola Liuzzo, Johnson went on television to announce the arrest of four Ku Klux Klansmen implicated in her death. He angrily denounced the Klan as a "hooded society of bigots," and warned them to "return to a decent society before it's too late." Johnson was the first President to arrest and prosecute members of the Klan since Ulysses S. Grant about 93 years earlier. He turned the themes of Christian redemption to push for civil rights, thereby mobilizing support from churches, north and South.

President Johnson did more to improve the living standards for the American people with his "Great Society" than any President in American history. The Great Society program, with its name coined from one of Johnson's speeches, became Johnson's agenda for Congress in January 1965; aid to education, attack on disease, Medicare, Medicaid, urban renewal, beautification, conservation, development of depressed regions, a wide-scale fight against poverty, control and prevention of crime and removal of obstacles to the right to vote. Congress, at times augmenting or amending, enacted many of Johnson's recommendations.

In 1964, Johnson encouraged the Congress to pass the Revenue Act of 1964, and the Economic Opportunity Act, which was associated with the war on poverty. Johnson set in motion bills and acts, creating programs such as Head Start, food stamps, Work Study, Medicare and Medicaid, which still exist today. The Medicare was established on July 30, 1965, to offer cheaper medical services to the elderly, today, covering tens of millions of Americans. Johnson gave the first two Medicare cards to former President Harry S. Truman and his wife Bess after signing the Medicare bill at the Truman Library. Lower income groups receive government-sponsored medical coverage through the Medicaid program.

Johnson recognized that guns were too readily available to radicals, criminals and those that would do great bodily harm to American citizens. The death of John Kennedy, Martin Luther King Jr. and Robert Kennedy, was evidence of that fact. Therefore, on October 22, 1968, Lyndon Johnson signed the Gun Control Act of 1968, one of the largest and most far reaching federal gun control laws in American history. This act represented a dramatic increase in federal power.

Johnson's problems began to increase in 1966. By the end of the year, public opinion began to turn against Johnson. Frustration over Vietnam, too much federal spending, taxation, and less support for his Great Society programs, and public disenchantment with the civil rights programs, had eroded his standings. In two weeks in May,

1968 alone, American deaths numbered 1,800 with total casualties at 18,000. Johnson said "If we allow Vietnam to fall, tomorrow we'll be fighting in Hawaii and next week in San Francisco".

The casualties continued to mount and the American people began to protest the war and Johnson's presidency. There were student protest on college campuses, draft cards were being burned and citizens were chanting, "Hey, hey LBJ, how many kids did you kill today?" Along with the unpopular war effort, there was unrest taking place in most major cities. Blacks were complaining of police brutality, and other abuses perpetrated on poor citizens across the nation. There were riots in Detroit, Michigan, Los Angeles, California, Philadelphia, Pennsylvania, and over 100 cities across America. Many citizens died because of it. The United States Army was deployed to quell the civil unrest, and turned their guns on American citizens to gain control of the uprisings.

Protesters marched on the Democratic National Convention in Chicago. There were hundreds of thousands of Hippies, Yuppies, Black Panthers and many others voicing their displeasure with the Vietnam War and the conditions of America's ghettoes. The Chicago seven was prosecuted for their roll in the protest and unrest surrounding this convention. Among all of the anger and dismay surrounding the Vietnam War, support for Johnson's position began to shrink. Johnson's view of his involvement in the Vietnam War as president was "I knew from the start that I was bound to be crucified either way I moved. "If I left the woman I really loved... The Great Society - in order to get involved in that bitch of a war on the other side of the world, then I lose everything at home. all my programs, But if I left that war and let the Communists take over South Vietnam, then I would be seen as a coward and my nation would be seen as an appeaser and we would both find it impossible to accomplish anything for anybody anywhere on the entire globe."

The struggles of the office of the presidency, the unpopular war in Vietnam and the death of more than 50,000 American service men, had taken a toll on Johnson. At the end of his term in 1969, Johnson made the announcement that, "I will not seek, nor will I accept, the nomination of my party for another term as your President".

Johnson died of a heart attack on January 22, 1973 at his ranch in Stonewall, Texas; he was 64 years old.

Richard Milhous Nixon, Number 37, 1969-1974,

Republican, 55 years old from Lorba Linda, California. Wife, Thelma Catherine "Pat" Ryan. They had two children. He was the only President to resign the office, as well as, the only person to be elected twice to both the Presidency, and the Vice Presidency.

During World War II, Nixon served in the United States Navy and rose to the rank of Lieutenant Commander. As a politician, Nixon held many public offices including Vice President to Dwight D. Eisenhower. Nixon was a determined politician with the presidency of the United States a sought after goal that he fought diligently to gain.

During his campaign for president, he portrayed himself as a figure of stability in a period, and country, filled with unrest and social upheaval. He called his conservative followers the "Silent Majority," his running mate was Spiro Agnew, the governor of Maryland.

Nixon's campaign was aided by turmoil within the Democratic Party, coupled with the decission of President Johnson that he would not seek re-election. The Vietnam War weighed heavily on President Johnson, and he sought relief by leaving office. Nixon promised to end the Vietnam War, and win the peace in the Pacific.

Hubert Humphery would win the nomination for the Democratic Party and would enter a three-way race for the office of the president of the United States. The Independent candidate George Wallace, would be the third party candidate. Nixon defeated them both to become the 37th President of the United States on November 5, 1968. Nixon was inaugurated on January 20, 1969.

Nixon set out with a very aggressive agenda, he wanted to reconstruct the Western Alliance, develop a relationship with China, pursue arms control agreements with the Soviet Union, activate a peace process in the Middle East, restrain inflation, implement anti-crime measures, accelerate desegregation and reform welfare. The Vietnam War gained priority.

Nixon approved a secret bombing mission of North Vietnamese positions in Cambodia in March 1969, code named "Operation Menu". In June 1969, in a campaign promise, Nixon reduced troops in Vietnam by 25,000 soldiers. From 1969 to 1972, troop reduction in Vietnam was estimated to be 405,000 soldiers. In July 1969, Nixon visited South Vietnam and soon inacted phased troop withdrawals, but authorized incursions into Laos to interrupt the Ho Chi Minh trail that passed through Laos and Cambodia.

Nixon formed the Gates Commission to look into ending the military service draft, implemented under President Johnson. The commission issued its report in February 1970, describing how adequate military strength could be maintained without conscription. The draft was extended to June 1973 and then ended.

Under President Nixon, American involvement in the war steadily declined from a troop strength of 543,000 to zero in 1973. Once American support was diminished, in 1975, North Vietnam was able to conquer South Vietnam and form one country.

In 1970, the Democratic Congress passed the Economic Stabilization Act, giving Nixon power to set wages and prices. A payboard set wage controls limiting increases to 5.5% per year and the Price Commission set a 2.5% annual limit on price increases. The limits did help control wages but not inflation. The public felt they were being rescued from price-gougers. Nixon was worried about the effects of increasing inflation and accelerated unemployment, so he indexed Social Security for inflation and created Supplemental Security Income (SSI). In 1969, he had presented the only balanced budget between 1961 and 1998.

Another large part of Nixon's plan was the detachment of the dollar from the gold standard. Nixon completely eradicated the gold standard, preventing other countries from being able to claim gold in exchange for their dollar reserves. In a speech Nixon said, "The American dollar must never again be a hostage in the hands of international speculators... Government... does not hold the key to the success of a people. The key is in your hands."

Nixon's plan also included the predisposition of a 10% investment tax credit, assistance to the automobile industry in the form of removal of excise taxes, (provided the savings were passed directly to the consumer), an end to fixed exchange rates, devaluation of the dollar on the free market and a 10% tax on all imports into the U.S.

Nixon initiated the environmental decade by signing the National Environmental Policy Act, the Clean Air Act of 1970, and the Federal Water Pollution Control Act amendments of 1972, as well as establishing many government agencies. They include the Environmental Protection Agency (EPA), the Occupational Safety and Health Administration (OSHA), and the Council on Evironmental Quality. The Clean Air Act was noted as one of the most significant pieces of environmental legislation ever signed.

On June 17, 1971, Nixon formally declared the U.S. War on Drugs. On October 30, 1972, Nixon signed into law the Social

Security Amendments of 1972, which included the creation of the Supplemental Security Income Program, a Federal Welfare Program still in existence today.

The Nixon years witnessed the first large-scale integration of public schools in the South. He was determined to implement exactly what the courts had ordered, desegregation, but did not favor busing children. Nixon, a Quaker, felt that racism was the greatest moral failure of the United States. He concentrated on the principle that the law must be color-blind. He said, "I am convinced that while legal segregation is totally wrong, forced integration of housing, or education, is just as wrong." Nixon tied desegregation to improving the quality of education and enforced the law after the Supreme Court, in Alexander vs. Holmes County Board of Education, (1969). He also prohibited further delays. By the fall of 1970, two million southern black children had enrolled in newly created unitary fully integrated school districts; only 18% of southern black children were still attending all-black schools, a decrease from 70% when Nixon came into office.

Nixon also implemented the Philadelphia Plan, the first significant federal affirmative action program in 1970. He also indorsed the Equal Rights Amendment after it passed both houses of Congress in 1972, and went to the states for ratification as a Constitutional Amendment. Nixon signed the landmark laws Title IX in 1972, prohibiting gender discrimination in all federally funded schools, and the Equal Employment Opportunity Act. In 1970, Nixon had vetoed the Comprehensive Child Development Act, denouncing the universal child-care bill, but signed into law Title X, which was a step forward for family planning and contraceptives. It was during the Nixon Presidency that the Supreme Court issued its Roe vs. Wade ruling, legalizing abortion.

In 1969, Nixon's first year in office, the United States sent three manned missions to the moon, becoming the only nation in the world to do so. On July 20, Nixon addressed Neil Armstrong and Buzz Aldrin, two of the Astronauts, live over radio during their historic Apollo 11 moonwalk. Nixon also placed a telephone call to Armstrong on the moon, the longest distance phone call ever made. On January 5, 1972, Nixon approved the development of NASA's Space Shuttle program. Also in 1972, Nixon became the first American President to visit China. Over 100-television journalist accompanied the president. Nixon despised the print journalist. The visit ushered in a new era of Sino-American relations. Fearing the possibility of a Sino-American alliance, the Soviet Union yielded to American pressure for détente. Détente is a permanent relaxation in international affairs during the Cold War, basically between the United States and the Soviet Union.

In Nixon's bid for a second term as President, he was ahead in most polls for the intire election cycle. He defeated his Democratic opponent George McGovern in one of the largest landslide election victories in U.S. political history. However, on Octobner 10, 1973, Vice President Spiro Agnew resigned amid charges of bribery, tax evasion, and money laundering from his tenure as Maryland's governor. Nixon chose Gerald Ford as his new running mate.

In Nixon's 1974 State of the Union address, Nixon called for comprehensive health insurance. On February 6, 1974, he introduced the Comprehensive Health Insurance Act. Nixon's plan would have mandated employers to purchase health insurance for their employees, and in addition, provide a federal health plan similar to Medicaid, that any American could join by paying on a sliding scale based on income. It failed.

The Watergate Scandal: Nixon's downfall

The Democratic Party's offices were housed in the Watergate complex in Washington D C.; five men were caught as a result of the break-in into those offices. A security guard named Wills noticed that there was tape on the door locks; he thought nothing of it so he removed the tape and continued his route. On his return, he noticed that the tape had been replaced. He notified authorities and the break in was exposed. This became one of a series of scandalous acts involving the Committee to Re-Elect the President. Nixon downplayed the scandal as mere politics. As the FBI eventually confirmed that Nixon aides had attempted to sabotage the Democrats, many began resigning and senior aides faced prosecution.

Nixon's alleged roll in ordering a cover-up was exposed following the testimony of John Dean. When Nixon's white house tapes were subpoenaed, they featured an unexplained eighteen and a half minute gap. It was attributed to the president's personal secretary Rose Mary Woods, as human error. Nixon insisted that he had made mistakes, but had no prior knowledge of the break-in or the burglary. On November 17, 1973, during a televised question and answer session with the press, Nixon said, "People have got to know whether or not their President is a crook. Well, I am not a crook. I've earned everything I've got." The house Judiciary Committee, controlled by

Democrats, opened impeachment hearings against the President on May 9, 1974. These hearings resulted in bi-partisan votes for Articles of Impeachment, the first vote being 27-11 in favor on July 27, 1974 on obstruction of justice. The Smoking Gun tape released on August 5, 1974, revealed that Nixon knew of the cover-up from its inception, and had suggested to administration officials that they try to stop The FBI's investigation. Nixon resigned the office of the presidency on August 9, 1974, after addressing the nation on TV the previous evening. Nixon died on April 22, 1994, in New York City, New York; he was 81 years old.

Gerald Rudolph Ford Jr., Number 38, 1974-1977

Republican, 61 years old, from Omaha, Nebraska. Wife, Elizabeth B Warren (Betty Ford). They had 4 children, 3 boys and 1 girl. Ford's birth name was Leslie Lynch King, Jr. His father was abusive so his mother left him and remarried and he was given his stepfather's name Gerald Rudolph Ford Sr.. Ford was never formally adopted, and did not legally change his name until December 3, 1935.

Ford was a veteran of World War II, and served in the United States Navy as Lieutenant Commander. Ford was the first person appointed to the Vice Presidency under the terms of the 25th Amendment, (after the resignation of Spiro Agnew). When he became President upon Richard Nixon's resignation on August 9, 1974, he became the only President of the United States who was never elected President, or Vice-President.

The economy was faltering when Ford took office, so one of his first acts to deal with this problem was to create the Economic Policy Board by Executive Order on September 30, 1974. Ford went before the American public in October 1974, and asked them to "Whip Inflation Now." He also urged Americans to wear the "WIN" buttons. As unemployment began to soar, Ford believed that inflation was the primary threat to the economy. He believed by controlling inflation, the problem of unemployment would be curtailed. Ford asked Americans to reduce their spending and consumption in an attempt to mesh service and sacrifice. He also introduced a one year 5 % income tax increase on corporations and wealthy individuals. This would take $4.4 billion out of the budget bringing federal spending below $300 billion. Inflation was 7%.

Ford was an outspoken supporter of the Equal Rights Amendment, and issued Presidential Proclamation 4383 to that effect. It said that in this "Land of the Free," it is right, and by nature, it ought to be that all men and all women are equal before the law. He then proclaimed August 26, 1975, as Women's Equality Day.

Ford signed the Education for All Handicapped Children Act of 1975, which established special education throughout the United States. Unemployment hit 7.2 percent in December 1974, as the country sank into a mild recession. In January 1975, Ford proposed a 1-year tax reduction of $16 billion to stimulate economic growth, along with spending cuts to avoid inflation. Congress increased the proposed amount of tax cuts to $22.8 billion with no spending cuts. In March, 1975, Congress passed, and Ford signed into law, these income tax rebates as part of the Tax Reduction Act of 1975, this resulted in a federal deficit of around $53 billion for the 1975 fiscal year, and $73.7 billion for 1976.

Ford continued the détente policy with both the Soviet Union and China, easing the tensions of the Cold War. Still in place from the Nixon Administration was the Strategic Arms Limitation treaty (SALT). The thawing relationship that was brought about by Nixon's visit to the communist country.

Ford faced two assassination attempts during his presidency occurring within three weeks of each other. While in Sacramento, California on September 5, 1975, Lynette Squeaky Fromme, a follower of Charles Manson, pointed a Colt .45-caliber handgun at Ford; as Fromme pulled the trigger, Larry Buendorf, a Secret Service agent, grabbed the gun and managed to insert the webbing of his thumb under the hammer, preventing the gun from firing. It was later found that, although the semi-automatic pistol had four cartridges in the magazine, the slide had not been pulled to place a round in the firing chamber, making it impossible for the gun to fire. Fromme was later convicted of attempted assassination of the president and was sentenced to life in prison, but was paroled on August 14, 2009. Seventeen days later, while leaving the St. Francis Hotel in downtown San Francisco, Sara Jane Moore, standing in a crowd of onlookers across the street, pointed her .38-caliber revolver at him; Just before she fired, former Marine Oliver Sipple grabbed at the gun and deflected her shot. The bullet struck a wall about six inches above and to the right of Ford's head, then ricocheted and hit a taxi driver, who was marginally wounded. Moore was later sentenced to life in prison. She was paroled from prison on December 31, 2007, having served 32 years.

Ford reluctantly agreed to run for office in 1976, and had to counter a challenge for the Republican Party nomination. Then former Governor of California Ronald Reagan faulted Ford for failing to do more in South Vietnam, and for signing the Helsinki Accords. Reagan launched his campaign for president, but withdrew from the race at the Republican Convention in Kansas City, Missouri.

Democratic nominee and former Georgia Governor Jimmy Carter, campaigned as an outsider and reformer, gaining support from voters dismayed by the Watergate scandal and Nixon pardon. In the end, Carter won the election Gerald Ford would remain active within the Republican Party for many years. He died December 26, 2006, from cerebrovascular disease; he was 93 years 165 days old, making Ford the longest-lived United States President.

James Earl "Jimmy" Carter, Jr., Number 39, 1977-1981

Democrat, 53 years old from Plains, Georgia. Wife Rosalynn Smith Carter, they had 4 children, 3 boys and 1 girl. Carter was a Lieutenant in the United States Navy, but never served in combat. He was also a former State Senator before he became Govenor of Georgia in 1971.

When Carter entered the race for President of the United States, his name recognition was at 2%. Carter was considered to have little or no chance to win against nationally known politicians. However, the Watergate scandal was still fresh in the minds of the voters. Carter, considered a Washington outsider, became more attractive to the voters. His centerpiece for his campaign was government reorganization.

Carter became the front-runner early on by winning the Iowa caucuses and the New Hampshire primary. In the South, where George Wallace appeared to be most likely to win, Carter ran as a moderate favorite son and swept the region. Carter chose Senator Walter F. Mondale as his running mate. Carter was elected over Gerald Ford in the fall of 1976, and was sworn in as President in January 1977.

Carter's tenure was one of continuing recession and inflation. He attempted to calm various conflicts around the world. His efforts to gain piece in the Middle East lead to the signing of the Camp David Accords. He also gave back the Panama Canal to Panama, and signed the SALT II nuclear arms reduction treaty with Soviet leader Leonid Brezhnev. But the final year of his administration was marred by the

Iran hostage crisis, where 52 Americans were taken hostage and were not released until Carter left office and President Ronald Reagan took office.

In 1978, Carter declared a federal emergency in the neighborhood of Love Canal in the city of Niagara Falls, New York. More than 800 families were evacuated from the neighborhood, which was built on top of a toxic waste landfill. The Superfund Law was created in response to this situation. Federal money was appropriated to demolish the approximate 500 houses and the schools, which were built on top of the dump.

Carter was opposed to abortion but would support legalized abortions in accordance with the Roe vs. Wade decision. He also opposed the dealth penalty, and any form of segregation.

In 1980, Carter signed into law H.R. 5860 aka Public Law 96-185 known as "The Chrysler Corporation Loan Guarantee Act of 1979." Chrysler Corp., and the United Auto Workers Union, lobbied for this loan guarantee to save an American company and its 125,000 workers and the 600,000 workers that would have been impacted by a loss of employment had Chrysler failed and went into bankruptcy. Carter had lost the election to Ronald Reagan who made it clear that he would not sign the Act into law. The Act was signed just weeks before Carter left office.

One of Carter's most bitterly controversial decisions was his boycott of the 1980 Summer Olympics in Moscow in response to the 1979 Soviet invasion of Afghanistan. This was the only time the U.S. failed to participate. The Soviets returned the favor in the 1984 Summer Olympics in Los Angeles, and did not withdraw troops from Afghanistan until 1989, eight years after Carter had left office.

In 1980, Ronald Reagan defeated Carter. He continued to help Americans and America in his post presidential works. He was also the first President to win the Nobel Peace Prize.

Jimmy Carter and Walter Mondale are the longest-living post presidential team in American history. On December 11, 2010, they had been out of office for 30 years and 325 days, surpassing the former record set by President John Adams and Vice President Thomas Jefferson, who both died on July 4, 1826.

Carter still works to improve the lives of America's greatest asset, its citizens.

Ronald Wilson Reagan, Number 40, 1981-1989

Republican, 69 years old from Tampico, Illinois. Wives, Jane Wyman, 1940-1948, Nancy Davis, 1952 till his death in 2004. They had 5 kids, 2 boys and 3 girls. At age 69, Reagan is the oldest man elected to the office of the presidency.

Reagan was defeated in his run for the Republican presidential nomination in 1968, and again in 1976, but was successful in both the nomination and the election of 1980, as he defeated Democratic incumbent Jimmy Carter for the Presidency of the United States. Reagan ran on a platform of lower taxes to stimulate the economy, less government, states rights, and a strong national defense.

Reagan selected George Herbert Walker Bush as his running mate. During his Presidency, Reagan pursued policies that reflected his personal belief in individual freedom, brought changes domestically, expanded the military, and contributed to the end of the Cold War.

In his inaugural address, he spoke of this country's economic malaise saying: "In this present crisis, government is not the solution to our problems; government is the problem."

The Reagan Presidency began in a dramatic manner; as Reagan was giving his inaugural address, the 52 U.S. hostages held by Iran for 444 days, were set free.

On March 30, 1981, only 69 days into the new administration, would be assassin John Hinckly Jr. waited outside the Washington Hilton Hotel and opened fire on President Reagan and his party as they were leaving. Reagan was shot and immediately ushered into his car by secret service agents who covered his body with their own. His press secretary James Brady was shot in the head, Washington police officer Thomas Delahanty, and Secret Service agent Timothy McCarthy, were struck by gunfire as well. Reagan was reported to be close to death during surgery, but survived. He is the only serving U.S. President to survive being shot in an assasination attempt. All wounded individuals survived and Hinckly is still in prison today.

Early into the Reagan administration, the Professional Air Traffic Controllers Organization Union (PATCO), would launch a nationwide strike, violating a regulation prohibiting government unions from striking under the terms of the Taft Hartley Act of 1947. Reagan considered this an emergency situation and issued an order where he stated that if the air traffic controllers "do not report for work within 48 hours, they have forfeited their jobs and will be terminated." They defied the order and Reagan fired 11,345 air traffic controllers. Reagan was once the President of the Screen Actor's Guild, and also supported the Polish Labor Union Solidarity in its fight against Soviet domination. Even so, he did not hesitate to bust this union.

Reagan entered office with inflation averaging 12.5%, with unemployment hitting annual highs of 9.7% in 1982, and 9.6% in 1983. To correct the failing economy, Reagan implemented policies based on supply-side economics, later called "Reaganomics." He proposed tax cuts that were to stimulate the economy enough to expand the tax base. As a result, his critics pointed to large increases in the federal budget deficits, and the national debt. He instituted a record peacetime defense buildup including a 40% real increase in defense spending between 1981 and 1985. The signing of the Economic Recovery Tax Act of 1981, where the top marginal tax bracket was lowered from 70% to 50%, and the lowest bracket from 14% to 11%. In 1982, the Job Training Partnership Act, was signed into law. The Tax Reform Act of 1986, reduced the top rate further to 28% while raising the bottom bracket from 11% to 15%, and reducing the number of brackets to 4. Congress passed and Reagan signed into law, tax increases of some nature in every year from 1981 to 1987, to continue funding government initiatives such as TEFRA, Social Security, and the Deficit Reduction Act of 1984, despite the fact that TEFRA was the "largest peacetime tax increase in American history. Reagan also revised the tax code with the bipartisan Tax Reform Act of 1986.

Critics labeled his economic policies as trickle-down economics. The belief that tax policies that benefit the wealthy will create a "trickle-down" effect to the poor. He also cut programs including Medicaid, food stamps, Federal education programs, and the EPA. Even though he protected Social Security and Medicare, he attempted to purge many people with disabilities from Social Security rolls.

Some of Reagan's critic's beleave that his policies may have influenced the stock market crash of 1987. In order to cover his new budget deficits, Reagan borrowed heavily both domestically and abroad, raising the national debt from $997 billion to $2.85 trillion. He said it was the greatest disapointment of his presidency.

On October 23, 1983, an American peacekeeping force in Beirut, Lebanon, was attacked in the bombing of the Beirut barracks, killing 241 American servicemen and wounding 60 others. A suicide truck bomber attacked the barracks. Reagan called the attack "despicable", and pledged to target the Sheik Abdullah barracks in Baalbek,

Lebanon, the training ground for Hezbollah fighters, but the mission was later aborted.

On October 25, 1983, just two days later, Reagan ordered U.S. forces to invade Grenada, code named "Operation Urgent fury," where a 1979 coup established an independent non-aligned Marxist-Leninist government. Reagan also cited an allegedly regional threat posed by a Soviet-Cuban military build-up in the Caribbean, and concern for the safety of several hundred American medical students at St. George's University as an adequate reason to invade. Reagan did not allow complete media coverage. There were no pictures of this action, and this tiny nation was defeated in a few days. After a new government was appointed by the Governor General, U.S. forces withdrew.

Reagan escalated the Cold War with the Soviet invasion of Afghanistan, and ordered a massive buildup of the United States Armed Forces. As the Cold War heated up, Reagan called the Soviet Union "an evil empire". After Soviet fighters shot down Korean Air Lines Flight 007, on September 1, 1983, with 269 passengers with Georgia Congressman Larry McDonald aboard. Reagan labeled the act a "massacre," and declared the Soviets had turned against the world.

Reagan's new policy would become known as the Reagan Doctrine. Reagan provided overt and covert aid to anti-communist resistance movements in an effort to "rollback" Soviet backed communist governments in Africa, Asia, and Latin America. Reagan then provided assistance to the Mujaheddin forces against the Soviet Red Army.

In 1984, Reagan won re-election against his opponent Democrat Walter Mondale, by the widest margin in history. Reagan won 49 out of 50 states and a record 525 electoral votes. Mondale only won his home state, and the District of Columbia.

Midway into his second term, Reagan increased his efforts in the war on drugs. In 1986, he signed a drug inforcement bill that budgeted $1.7 billion to fund the war with a mandatory minimum penalty for drug offenses. The bill created significant racial disparities in the prison population, with a great financial burden for America. Nancy Reagan took up the fight with "just say no".

In 1986, the Iran-Contra scandal would shake the Reagan administration to its core. The Act of Congress forbids the use of monies from covert arms sales to Iran to fund the Contras in Nicaragua. This became the largest political scandal in the U.S.

during the 1980s. The International Court of Justice ruled that the U.S. had violated international law in Nicaragua, due to its obligations not to intervene in the affairs of other states. A Congressional report concluded, "If the president didn't know what his national security advisers were doing, he should have." Reagan's popularity declined from 67 percent to 46 percent in less than a week, the greatest and quickest decline ever for a president. The scandal resulted in fourteen indictments within Reagan's staff, and eleven convictions.

In his effort to end the Cold War, Reagan held four summits with Soviet General Secretary Gorbachev. Reagan believed that if he could persuade the Soviets to allow more democracy and free speech, this would lead to reform and the end of Communism. In a speech at the Berlin Wall on June 12, 1987, Reagan challenged Gorbachev by saying "General Secretary Gorbachev, if you seek peace, if you seek prosperity for the Soviet Union and Eastern Europe, if you seek liberalization, come here to this gate! Mr. Gorbachev, tear down this wall"!

He and Reagan would sign the Intermediate-Range Nuclear Forces (INF) Treaty at the White House, which eliminated an entire class of nuclear weapons. This laid the framework for the Strategic Arms Reduction Treaty, or "START- I".

When Reagan visited Moscow for the 1988 summit, he was viewed as a celebrity by the Soviets. The Berlin Wall was torn down beginning in 1989, and two years later, the Soviet Union collapsed. Reagan's prediction had come true.

Reagan finished his term and left the White House January 20, 1989. He bought a home in Bel Aire, Los Angeles, in addition to the Reagan Ranch in Santa Barbara, and occasionally made appearances on behalf of the Republican Party.

In August 1994, at the age of 83, Reagan was diagnosed with alzheimers disease, an incurable neurological disorder that destroys brain cells and ultimately causes death. Americans began to question when did he began to suffer from the mental degeneration? As his retirement years progressed, he began to lose his mental capacity. On February 6, 2001, Reagan reached the age of ninety, becoming the third former president to do so. John Adams and Herbert Hoover were the others. Gerald Ford would later reach 90. Reagan died in his home in Bel Aire, California on June 5, 2004. He was 93 years old.

George Herbert Walker Bush, Number 41, 1989-1993

Republican, 65 years old from Milton, Massachusetts. Wife, Barbara Pierce Bush. They had 6 children, 4 boys and 2 girls.

Following the attacks on Pearl Harbor in 1941, Bush put college aside and became the youngest aviator in the U.S. Navy, at the time; he was 18 years old. He was assigned to torpedo squadron (UT-51). His task force was victorious in one of the largest air battles of WWII: the battle of the Philippine Sea. In his attack on the Japanese installation on Chichijima, his aircraft was hit by flak and though burning, he continued to drop bombs on the target before going into the sea several miles away from the action. He was able to bailout with one of the other two-crew members, but only he survived to be picked up by the rescue helicopter.

In 1988, Bush launched a successful campaign to succeed Reagan as president, defeating Democratic opponent Michael Dukakis. Bush had served as Reagan's Vice-President, and was indorsed by Reagan to run.

Bush was inaugurated on January 20, 1989, succeeding Ronald Reagan. He entered office at a time period of change in the world; the fall of the Berlin Wall, and the collapse of the Soviet Union. The left over deficits from the Reagan years posed a problem that he had to deal with. At $220 billion in 1990, the deficit had grown to three times its size since 1980. He found it necessary to have the Democratic Congress act on the budget. The democrats wanted to raise taxes, the republicans wanted to cut spending. Bush was forced by the democratic majority to raise taxes. Bush had promised "no new taxes" during his campaign. He would later say that he wished he had never signed the bill.

The Panamanian leader Manuel Noriega, a U.S. ally, was accused of spying for Fidel Castro, and trafficking drugs into the United States. Ronald Reagan sent two thousand troops into Panamanian territory in preparation to remove Noriega from power. Economic sanctions were imposed including freezing $56 million in Panamanian funds in U.S. banks. The U.S. also prohibited American companies and the government from making payments to Panama.

In May of 1989, Guillermo Endara was elected president in a democratic election. Noriega annulled the election results. Bush removed the American Embassy, and dispatched additional troops in preparation for an invasion. After Panamanian forces shot a U.S. serviceman in December 1989, Bush ordered 24,000 troops into the country with an objective of removing Noriega from power. Bush dubbed the action "Operation Just Cause".

The mission created controversy, but American forces gained control of Panama, and placed Endara in power. Noriega was returned to the U.S. to face trial for racketeering and drug trafficking charges in April 1992.

President Bush's first term seem to be filled with one conflict after another. On August 1, 1990, Iraq, led by Saddam Hussien, invaded Kuwait; Bush condemned the invasion and began seeking support from the European, Asian, and Middle Eastern allies. When King Fahd of Saudi Arabia requested U.S. military aid, fearing a possible invasion of his country, President Bush met that request with Air Force fighter jets. Iraq saught to negotiate a deal that would allow Saddam Hussein to take over half of Kuwait. Bush rejected this proposal and insisted on complete withdrawal of Iraqi forces.

Bush spoke to a joint session of Congress seeking authorization of air and land attacks with his stated objectives. Iraq must withdraw without conditions, Kuwait's government be restored, the security and stability of the Persian Gulf be assured, and American citizens abroad, be protected.

On the morning of January 17, 1991, operation "Desert Storm" began when allied forces launched the first attack, which included more than 4,000 bombing runs by coalition aircraft. A ground invasion was launched on February 24th. The allied forces penetrated Iraqi lines, and after 100 hours of fighting, and intercepting the retreating Iraqi Army, Bush stopped the offensive. Critics say he should have continued to Baghdad, but he said that could cost many American lives, and we would have to occupy Baghdad, and in effect, rule Iraq. Bush's approval ratings skyrocketed after the successful offensive.

Bush's administration, along with the Progressive Conservative Canadian Prime Minister Brian Mulroney, spearheaded the negotiations of the North American Free Trade Agreement (NAFTA). This would eliminate the majority of tariffs on products traded among the United States, Canada, and Mexico, to encourage trade amongst these countries. The treaty also restricts patents, copyrights, and trademarks, and outlines the removal of investment restrictions among the three countries.

The agreement came under heavy scrutiny amongst mainly Democrats, who charged that NAFTA resulted in a loss of U.S. jobs. John J. Sweeney of the Boston Globe argued that "the U.S. trade deficit with Canada and Mexico ballooned to 12 times its pre-NAFTA size, reaching $111 billion in 2004.

During his re-election bid in 1992, Bush faced Bill Clinton as his Democratic challenger, but a third party candidate, Ross Perot would win 19% of the vote. Bill Clinton would defeat Bush in a 43% to 38% popular vote margin. Bush received 168 electoral votes to Clinton's 370. One of the primary factor's in Bush's defeat was his violation of his campaign promise of 1989, "Read my lips; no new taxes", but in 1990, he agreed to raise taxes. The voters turned against him.

Bush would retire with his wife Barbara to their home in the exclusive neighborhood of Tanglewood in Houston, Texas.

In 1993, Bush was awarded an honorary Knighthood (GCB) by Queen Elizabeth II. He was the third American President to receive the honor; the others were Dwight D. Eisenhower, and Ronald Reagan. He is still somewhat active today.

William Jefferson Clinton, Number 42, 1993-2001

Democrat, 46 years old, from Hope, Arkansas. Wife, Hillary Rodham Clinton. They had one child, a girl, Chelsea Clinton. Bill Clinton was born William Jefferson Blythe III, but would later take the last name of his stepfather. At 46, Clinton was the third-youngest president, and was the first baby boomer president. He has been described as a New Democrat. Some of his policies, such as the North America Free Trade Agreement (NAFTA) and welfare reform, have been attributed to a centrist third way philosophy of governance.

Clinton was inaugurated on January 20, 1993, and in his speech he said "Our democracy must be not only the envy of the world, but the engine of our own renewal. There is nothing wrong with America that cannot be cured by what is right with America."

Clinton's economic plan focused on deficit reduction rather than middle-class tax cuts, even though his campaign rhetoric was contrary to this move. One of his early acts was to sign into law the Family and Medical Leave Act of 1993, which required large employers to allow workers to take unpaid leave for pregnancy or a serious medical condition. Clinton was instrumental in inacting the "Don't ask, don't Tell" policy, as long as homosexuals keep their sexuality secret, they may serve in the military. Many American's, especially the Gay Rights advocates, felt Clinton should have integrated the military by executive order, following the lead of President Harry Truman who used it to desegregate the U.S. Armed Forces.

President Bill Clinton and Vice President Al Gore were responsible for pressing almost all federal agencies, the U.S. court system, and the U.S. military, onto the Internet. Also, in 1993, Clinton supported ratification of the North American Free Trade Agreement (NAFTA), by the U.S. Senate. The treaty was ratified by the Senate and signed into law by the President on January 1, 1994, in the face of objections by many Americans who were fearful of massive job loses across the border to Mexico and Canada. On November 30, 1993, Clinton signed into law the Brady Bill; this bill imposed a five-day waiting period on the purchase of handguns. To aid the low-income workers of America, Clinton expanded the Earned Income Tax Credit. He used the Community Reinvestment Act to encourage banks to increase their lending in low-income communities, and pushed Fannie May and Freddie Mack to do the same.

One of Bill Clinton's most prominent items on his legislative agenda was national health care. The First Lady Hillary Clinton was involved in this effort. Even though the Democratic Party held a majority in Congress, the measure died. In 1994, the democrats lost control of Congress in the mid-term elections for the first time in forty years.

In 1993, Clinton signed the Omnibus Budget Reconciliation Act; it passed the congress without a Republican vote. It cut taxes for fifteen million low-income families, and made tax cuts available to 90% of small businesses, and raised taxes 1.2% on the wealthiest taxpayers, while mandating that the budget be balanced over a number of years.

Senators Ted Kennedy, a Democrat, and Senator Orin Hatch, a Republican, teamed up with Hillary Clinton and succeeded in passing the Children's Health Insurance Program, the largest health care reform in the years of the Clinton Presidency. He also signed the Illegal Immigration Reform, and Immigration Responsibility Act (IIRIRA). This act called for reducing legal immigration to about 550,000 a year. He also expanded the federal death penalty to include crimes not resulting in death, such as, running a large-scale drug enterprise, murderers of federal law enforcement officers, and nearly 60 additional categories of violent felons. He also avoided an assassination attempt in the Philippines by terrorist working for Osama bin Laden.

In the 1996 presidential election, Clinton defeated his republican opponent Bob Dole by 49.2% of the popular vote to his 40.7%, with the Reform candidate Ross Perot receiving 8.4% of the popular vote.

Clinton became the first Democratic incumbent since Lyndon Baines Johnson to be elected to a second term, and the first Democrat since Franklin Roosevelt to be elected President more than once.

During his second term, Clinton would face many problems, domestic, foreign, and personal. Following the 1998-midterm elections, the House voted to impeach Clinton by charging him with lying to a Grand Jury during the Paula Jones lawsuit. When asked under oath about a sexual relation with Monica Lewinsky, a 22-year-old White House intern, Clinton said he never had sex with that woman. The house voted to impeach Clinton based on allegations that Clinton lied about his relationship with Lewinski, and obstruction of justice. The Senate later voted to aquit Clinton on both charges.

There were several military events to occur during Clinton's presidency. The battle of Mogadishu occurred in Somalia in 1993. During the operation, two U.S. Black Hawk helicopters were shot down, trapping American soldiers behind enemy lines. An urban battle ensued that killed 18 American soldiers, and wounded 73 others, with one taken prisoner. The Somalians dragged American bodies through the streets with this tragic sight being seen on television news programs around the world. U.S. forces were soon withdrawn from Somalia.

In 1995, U.S and NATO aircraft attacked Bosnian Serb targets to halt attacks on the U.N. safe Zones, and to pressure them into a peace accord. Clinton deployed U.S. peacekeepers to Bosnia in late 1995, to uphold the Dayton Agreement.

In response to the 1998 Al-Qaeda bombings of U.S. Embassies in East Africa that killed a dozen Americans, and hundreds of Africans, Clinton ordered cruise missile strikes on terrorist targets in Afghanistan and Sudan. Clinton received criticism because a pharmaceutical plant in Sudan was destroyed.

One of Clinton's objectives was to improve race relations in America. The Black community embraced him and supported his every effort to make America a better nation. When Bill Clinton left office in 2001, he left the nation with a balanced budget and a $256 billion surplus. The nation had enjoyed a 22 million-job increase under his watch.

He continues to involve himself in the causes of freedom, and he works with past and present presidents to improve this country and to bring the feeling of brotherhood to less than a perfect union.

George Walker Bush, Number 43, 2001-2008

Republican, 46 years old from New Haven, Connecticut. Wife Laura Welch; they had two girls. Bush is the eldest son of former President George H.W. Bush, the 41st President of the United States. In June 1999, Bush entered the Republican primary with no incumbent running; the race was wide open. In the end, Bush gained the nomination using what was called the dirtiest tactics in recent memory.

On July 25, 2000, Bush asked Dick Cheney to be his running mate; the Republican Party at the 2000 Republican National Convention would nominate him. Bush was sworn in as president on January 20, 2001. His run for president against Clinton's Vice President Al Gore, was a close and controversial one. Florida would become the pivotal state where the final results would determine the presidency. A recount of the ballots were called for, and a dispute arose over the counting of ballots that were not clearly marked due to hanging chads. The courts determined the final results with George Bush being the president elect.

Early on in his presidency, terrorist from Afghanistan attacked America. Under the dictates and direction of Osama bin Laden, the World Trade Center twin towers were attacked on September 11, 2001, and brought down killing over 3,000 American citizens. The terrorist high-jacked 4 passenger aircraft from nearby airports and flew one into each of the towers, one into the Pentagon, and another was over taken by the passengers and crashed into a field in Pennsylvannia.

With the approval of Congress, Bush would launch his War on Terrorism, and along with an international coalition, order an attack and the invasion of Afghanistan. The standing order as it always is in a military confrontation, is to close with, kill or capture the enemy. Al-Qaeda was the perpetrators, but was allowed to train in Afghanistan by the Taliban. The war effort was designed to kill Al-Qaeda and drive the Taliban out of power. The war still rages on today as America's longest war.

In 2003, Bush went before the American people and announced his intent to invade Iraq. He told America that Saddam Hussein had weapons of mass destruction, and that it was imperative that we launch an attack against Iraq, or face the possibility of a mushroom cloud. The coalition forces never found any weapons of mass destruction. Saddam Hussein was hung and his sons were killed. George Bush and Dick Cheney lied about weapons of mass destruction and they knew it was a lie. As a result of this lie, we fought for 8 years with 4,500 American soldiers killed, 35,000 were wounded before finely leaving Iraq under President Barack Obama. There are more than 100,000 Iraqis citizens dead. George Bush was spending billions of dollars per month on this war effort that America didn't have. He borrowed it from the Chinese and drove America into trillion dollar deficits.

At a time when this country was facing trillion dollar deficits from a poor economy, President Bush sought public support for his plan for a $1.35 trillion tax cut, one of the largest in U.S. history. Bush argued that unspent government funds should be returned to the taxpayers. The surplus is the people's money. Bush argued that a tax cut such as this would stimulate the economy and create jobs. Every conceivable increase in the Bush proposal had a negative effect on the country. When he entered office, the real GDP grew at an average annual rate of 2.5%, considerably below the average for business cycles from 1949 to 2000. The DOW average was 10,587, when he left office it was 7,949, one of the lowest levels for his presidency. The poverty rate rose from 11.3% to 12.3%. Median household income dropped by $1,175 between 2000 and 2007, and the national debt had risen to $11.3 trillion. By the end of Bush's presidency, unemployment climbed to 7.2%

In December 2007, the United States entered the longest post-World War II recession, which included a housing market correction, a subprime mortage crisis, soaring oil prices, and a declining dollar value. In February 2007, 63,000 jobs were lost, a five-year record. To aid in the situation, Bush signed a $170 billion economic stimulus package, which was intended to improve the economy. Many economists determined that the situation became the worst financial crisis since the Great Depression.

In November 2008, over 500,000 jobs were lost, which marked the largest loss of jobs in the United States in 34 years. The Bureau of Labor Statistics reported that in the last four months of 2008, 1.9 million jobs were lost. By the end of 2008, the U.S. had lost a total of 2.6 million jobs.

One of the administration's early major initiatives was the No Child Left Behind Act, which was designed to close the gap between rich and poor student performance, but critics argued that the Act was underfunded and left the burden on the states.

During his second term, Bush signed into law an un-funded Medicare Drug Benefit Program that according to Jan Crawford

Greenburg, resulted in "the greatest expansion in America's welfare state in forty years;" the bill's cost approached $7 trillion. In addition to this, he sought to privitize Social Security, but his efforts failed.

In 2006, Bush urged Congress to allow more than 12 million illegal immigrants to work in the United States with the creation of a "temporary guest-worker program", Bush did not support amnesty for illegal immigrants. He also urged congress to provide additional funds for border security and committed to deploying 6,000 National Guard troups to the Mexico-United States border. In June 2007, Bush strongly supported the Comprehensive Immigration Reform Act of 2007; the bill envisioned a legalization program for undocumented immigrants; with an eventual path to citizenship, and many other measures. The bill was eventually defeated in the Senate on June 28, 2007.

Hurricane Katrina was one of the worst natural disasters in U.S. history. Katrina struck the north-central Gulf Coast of the United States and devastated New Orleans. Flooding the 9th Ward, and other areas leaving hundreds dead and thousands homeless in its wake. Bush declared a state of emergency in Louisiana on August 27, 2005, and in Mississippi and Alabama the following day. He authorized the Department of Homeland Security (DHS) and Federal Emergency Management Agency (FEMA), to manage the disaster, but his announcement failed to spur these agencies to action.

The eye of the hurricane made landfall on August 29, and New Orleans began to flood due to levee breaches; later that day, Bush declared that a major disaster existed in Louisiana. He officially authorized FEMA to start using federal funding to assist in the recovery effort. On August 30, DHS Secretary Michael Chertoff declared it "an incident of national significance", triggering the first use of the newly created National Response Plan. Three days later, on September 2, National Guard troops first entered the city of New Orleans. The same day, Bush toured parts of Louisiana, Mississippi, and Alabama, declaring that the success of the recovery effort up to that point was "enough".

As the disaster in New Orleans intensified, critics charged that Bush was misrepresenting his administration's role in what they saw as a flawed response. Leaders attacked Bush for having appointed apparently incompetent leaders to positions of power at FEMA, notably Michael Brown, whom he praised during his tour of the area by saying "you done one hell of a job Brownie", he would later fire

Michael Brown. It has been argued that with Hurricane Katrina, Bush passed a political tipping point from which he would not recover.

During Bush's second term, the controversy continued to mount. Seven United States attorneys from the Justice department were dismissed during midterm. The White House maintained that the U.S. attorneys were fired for poor performance. Attorney General Alberto Gonzales would later resign over the issue, along with other senior members of the justice Department. Many citizens believed that the dismissals were due to a disagreement on some of Bush's policies, and whether they were in accordance with the law and Constitutional interpretation.

The House Judiciary Committee issued subpoenas for advisers, Harriet Miers, and Josh Bolten, to testify regarding this matter, but Bush directed them not to comply with those subpoenas, invoking his right of executive privilege. The Justice Department has determined that the President's order was legal. On March 10, 2008, the Congress filed a federal lawsuit to enforce their issued subpoenas. On July 31, 2008, a United States district court judge ruled that Bush's top advisers were not immune from Congressional subpoenas.

In August 2009, Karl Rove and Harriet Miers testified before the House judiciary Committee. A Justice Department inquiry into the firing of U.S. attorneys concluded that political considerations played a part in as many as four of the dismissals. No charges were filed. According to the prosecutors, evidence did not demonstrate that any prosecutable criminal offense was committed with the removal of David Iglesias.

In the months following September 11, bush issued an executive order authorizing the President's Surveillance Program, which included allowing the (NSA), National Security Agancy, to monitor communications between suspected terrorist outside the U.S. and parties within the U.S., without obtaining a warrant as required by the Foreign Intelligence Surveillance Act. When questioned whether FISA could be applied legally in times of war, the program was re-authorized by the President on the basis that the warrant requirements of FISA were superseded by the subsequent passage of the Authorization for Use of Military Force Against Terrorists. This decision, and the program, became controversial. On January 17, 2007, Attorney General Alberto Gonzales informed U.S. Senate leaders that the program would not be reauthorized by the President, but would be subjected to judicial oversight.

Controversy followed the president when he authorized the CIA to use waterboarding as one of several enhanced interrogation techniques. The CIA considered waterboarding legal based on secret Justice Department Legal Opinion, arguing that terror detainees were not protected by the Geneva Conventions ban on torture. The procedure was used over 180 times on K. Sheikh MuHammed. If it took that many attempts to gain information, the procedure must not be effective.

During the last few months of his term, the economy went into the ditch with layoffs and job loses as high as 700,000 a month. The President continued to say that the "fundamentals of the economy was strong". As the stock market crashed and Americans began to withdraw their money from the banks, Bush signed into law the TARP Act of 2008, to save the banking industry as business after business began to fail. President Obama would bare the brunt of that legislation when Republicans attacked him for it.

Barack Hussein Obama was elected to the presidency in November 2008, and would be sworn-in in January 2009. President Bush would leave the presidency and retire to his home in Crawford Texas.

Barack Hussein Obama, Number 44, 2008-12 incumbent

Democrat, 47 years old, from Honolulu, Hawaii, Wife Michelle Robinson Obama, they have two girls. Barack Obama is the first Black President of the United States. He previously served as a United States Senator from Illinois, from January 2005 until he resigned after his election to the presidency in November 2008.

On February 10, 2007, obama announced his candidacy for the office of president of the United States. A large number of candidates entered the Democratic Party Presidential Primaries. The field narrowed to a duel between Obama and Hillary Rodham Clinton. Clinton finally ended her campaign, and endorsed Obama on June 7, 2008. He selected Delaware Senator Joe Biden as his Vice Presidential running mate. Obama defeated the Republican Presidential Candidate John McCain and his Vice Presidential running mate Sarah Palin, the Governor from the State of Alaska.

The inauguration of Barack Obama as the 44th President, and Senator Joe Biden as his Vice President, took place on January 20, 2009. One of his first orders was to direct the U.S.military to develop plans to withdraw American troops from Iraq. He also ordered the closing of the Guantonamo Bay detention camp as soon as practicable, and no later than January 2010. This did not happen.

The first bill signed into law by President Obama was the Lilly Ledbetter Fair Play Act of 2009, relaxing the statute of limitations for equal-pay lawsuits. Later he would sign the reauthorization of the State Children's Health Insurance Program (SCHIP), to cover an additional 4 million children currently uninsured. He also signed economic stimulus legislation in the form of the American Recovery and Reinvestment Act in February 2009, and the Tax Relief, Unemployment Insurance Reauthorization, and Job Creation Act of 2010. Other domestic policy initiatives includes the Patient Protection and Affordable Care Act, (Obama Care), the Dodd-Frank Wall Street Reform and Consumer Protection Act, and the Don't Ask, Don't Tell Repeal Act of 2010.

Obama intervened in the troubled automobile industry in March 2009, renewing loans for General Motors and Chrysler Corp. to continue operating while reorganizing, with the government owning 60%, and Canada owning 12% stakes in the companies. Both companies would recover and flourished. The loans were repaid, and thousands of new jobs created. The Presidents opponent Mitt Romney had declared that the companies should be allowed to fail, or merge because the loans would not work. He, as usual, was wrong.

He signed the health care bill, The Affordable Care Act, into law on March 23, 2010. A bill sought after by previous presidents going back 75 years. The Republicans, the party of no, would not support the bill, or anything Obama proposed. They have made every effort to repeal this legislation rather than making changes to improve it. Those efforts consisted of 57 different votes in the Senate to repeal the law, but to no avail. One of the laws biggest opponents, Senator Ted Cruze, promised to repeal "every word of the act," if elected President in the 2016 national election; if he is the Republican nominee. The hypocrites wife quit her job to help him campaign for the nominee of the Republican Party, and he signed up for the Affordable Care Act. I hope he is blasted for it by his own party. Their policy was to defeat Obama at all cost. The Senate Minority Leader, Mitch McConnell, a Republican from Kentucky, announced this fact. After the Democrats lost the Senate in the 2012 elections, he became the majority leader.

Obama would increase troop strength in Afghanistan to 145,000 and assign General David Petraeus as commander in June 2010, after relieving Lt General Stanley A. McChrystal in May 2009. General Petraeus would later fall to a sex scandal.

The President would order a covert operation to enter Pakistan and shoot the world's most notorious terrorist, Ben Laden, dead, and bring his body out of the country. Finally, the United States had justice for the more than 3,000 American deaths in the twin towers in New York City, that was brought down by planes that was flown into them by the same terrorist group. The third plane was flown into the Pentagon, and the fourth, crashed into a field in Pennsylvania. This tragic event took place during the George W. Bush Administration

Obama has received more death threats than any president in history. He has been disrespected, ridiculed, misidentified, and swamped with racial slures. His birthplace has been questioned, his religion trounced upon. When he ran for President, he was criticized for belonging to a Baptist church with the Reverend Jeremiah Wright as pastor. He was a Christian then, now they call him a Muslim. Republican Mike Huckabee called him a Mau Mau from Kenya, Rush Limbaugh, a radio personality, called him Barack the magic Negro. Glenn Beck of the Fox News Network, said he hates white people. Another called him a tar baby. All Republicans, trying to bring down a man that has shown greater character than representatives of the entire Republican Party. The hate for this man because of his color, is appalling. **"This is truly, the Raping America".**

About the Author

The author, with this publication, delves into his second adventure into the world of literature and the written word. Here are the thoughts of an individual that came from a background of caution and inquiry. A man that's trained to pay attention to details. As a UAW international representative with the experience of collective bargaining with multinational corporations, I believe I have the knowledge to speak to these issues. Read, be enlightened, and enjoy.

In May 1992, I made a presentation before the commerce department in the US Department of Labor. I was invited to appear before the Sixth National Labor-Management Conference. I have worked closely with senators and congressmen in the performance of my duties. I believe I have something to say.

Printed in the United States
By Bookmasters